A LIFE IN PERSPECTIVE

Reflection on a Life and Purpose

William R Armstrong

Published in March 2023 by Catherine Armstrong, Cambridge, England

Copyright William Ritchie Armstrong 2023

The right of William Ritchie Armstrong (wrarmstrong@hotmail.co.uk) to be identified as the author of this work has been asserted by the author in accordance with the Copyright, Design and Patents Act 1988

All rights reserved. No part of this publication may be reproduced, stored in or Introduced into a retrieval system, or transmitted in any form, or by any means (electronic, mechanical, photocopying, recording or otherwise) without the prior written permission of the publisher.
Any person who does any unauthorised act in relation to this publication may be liable to criminal prosecution and civil claims for damages.

The author hereby expresses his gratitude to Dave Hartley for permission to reproduce his mill town picture on the back cover of this publication.

Interior formatting & ebook conversion by team at ebookpbook.com

Every effort has been made to trace copyright holders and to obtain their permission for the use of copyright material. The publisher apologises for any omission and would be grateful if notified of any corrections that should be incorporated in future reprints of this book.

ISBN 978-0-9934010-3-9
eISBN 978-0-9934010-4-6

A CIP catalogue record for this book is available from The British Library

Dedicated to Family and Fellow Pilgrims

Contents

Introduction		vii
Part 1	**Roots**	**1**
Chapter 1	Early Years	5
Chapter 2	Dark Peak, Satanic Mills	17
Chapter 3	Woven Threads	27
Chapter 4	Growing Up in the 1960s	42
Chapter 5	Armstrong Clan	63
Chapter 6	Scottish Seams	74
Part 2	**Formative Years**	**95**
Chapter 1	Leaving School, Finding Direction	99
Chapter 2	College, Career and Marriage	130
Part 3	**The Spicers Story**	**165**
Chapter 1	Foundation and Growth	169
Chapter 2	Apprenticeship	177
Chapter 3	Leadership	196
Chapter 4	The Final Years	240

Part 4	**Reflections**	279
Chapter 1	Conversation with Thoth	283
Chapter 2	Proverbs of Perspective	358
Chapter 3	Conversation with Eleos	364
Chapter 4	Poems on Purpose	386
Chapter 5	Life a Pilgrimage	397

Books of Possible Interest	401
Acknowledgements	403

Introduction

This book is the result of my good fortune in having been able to retire from work relatively early and consequently having had the time to research and reflect on the life I have lived. It has been many years in the writing and is the product of a reflective disposition as well as one that has been reluctant to dispose of printed material that, at various points in life, seemed important. A nature also that meticulously recorded thoughts and feelings in diaries and letters during a troubled, but not necessarily untypical, adolescence.

The book is set out in a roughly chronological sequence although certain subjects have broken out of that general discipline to give a perspective within the topic. It is an attempt to understand my own life better, in part viewed from the standpoint of old age before memory begins to fade. It is not, consciously at least, an exercise in self-justification. It is intended for publication as I approach death and in the hope that it may be of some interest to family and others. I make no claim to this life being especially noteworthy, it is above all significant primarily to me. Hopefully I have learned lessons from my experience and I am happy to share that which I think I have learned. Each person's story is different and of value, not only to themselves but to those they have interacted with. All are worthy of respect. This is the story of one life, as seen by the person who lived that life, and is shared in as much as it may be of interest to others treading the path we all must tread; the pilgrimage that is life.

The book begins with the environment into which I was born, that a mix of community, at a particular place and time, and family. That family was rooted in industrial working class northern England and lowland Scotland. It explores a landscape shaped by the Industrial Revolution and the once mighty cotton industry of the north-west. An industry at its height in the 19th century and in almost terminal decline by the 1950s of my childhood. The 1960s brought relative prosperity for many of working class origin and it appeared for a time as if the UK was on a path to meritocracy and egalitarianism. That resulted in my political engagement and an eventual return to full-time education, having left school at fifteen. It also brought the angst of adolescence with its crises of confidence and torment in relation to the opposite sex. My graphic diaries of the day lay bare in some detail those formative years.

Marriage brought stability, as did my joining the company of Spicers. Spicers was originally a manufacturer of paper but evolved to become a stationery manufacturer and then wholesale distributor of office products. With that company I was to spend 34 years of my life starting as an accountancy trainee in a UK based business and ending as chief executive of a European wide business. That 200 year old company no longer exists; its death was in part the result of 'vulture capitalism' and the financial engineering that came to the fore in post industrial Britain. This book chronicles my time with Spicers but also provides a perspective on the company's history and its subsequent demise following my departure.

Marriage and later two children provided an anchor for the

sometimes turbulent waters of career. That gave not only stability but happiness for many years. Like others I struggled with finding a balance between career and home.

The conscientiousness that produced regular promotion at work also involved a growing time commitment to fulfil ever greater responsibilities. Work in reality became the priority at the expense of my family and that eventually led to separation and divorce. What followed was a difficult time, bringing back some of the anguish of my youth, but on the whole the demands of work kept those feelings in check. Fortunately I made a conscious decision on separation to maintain a good relationship with my ex-wife and to develop the bonds with my children. Later a new relationship, born out of work, resulted in a second marriage and another child. My work orientation did not fundamentally change until retirement came, but my second partner was more tolerant of the demands of my job and of my psychological make-up.

With retirement came freedom from at times demanding responsibility but also from the things that responsibility entailed that never came naturally. I was born an introvert; I will die an introvert. Introverts draw energy from within and from solitary reflection. Generally they are not comfortable in larger gatherings. Leading a business requires constant communication with others to direct, motivate and encourage and that requires regular presentations to customers, employees and suppliers, as well as social engagement. It is a skill that can be learned, but whereas an extrovert will engage naturally and may revel in the attention of such gatherings, its effect on the introvert is draining.

Introverts have significant qualities that many extroverts lack and some very successful businesses have been built upon complementary partnerships between these contrasting personality types. Spicers was one such business. Escaping the responsibilities I had grown used to was for me real freedom and provided space to pursue long sidelined interests. It also gave me an opportunity to return the support I had received from my wife, in pursuit of her interests.

My search for meaning has been a recurring need since adolescence, sometimes crowded out by the demands of work and family, but always returned to when time permitted. Retirement provided that time in abundance. Time to read, time to research, time to reflect, time to write. The quest has taken many turns. The cold mechanical universe of today's scientific orthodoxy can provide no answers to ultimate questions; how can something be created from nothing; how can animate life emerge from inanimate matter; where did the laws, and consequent order inherent in the reality we perceive, come from; what is the purpose of life and what follows mortal death?

These fundamental questions, that have puzzled humanity since consciousness awoke (another mystery), are the questions that philosophers, religious leaders and others have tried to answer throughout history. As far as the human condition is concerned, and the idea of purpose, many different belief systems have developed. For those that choose to look, common themes may be found across many of these beliefs, even if they are sometimes cloaked in metaphor. Doctrinal constructs can also serve to obscure underlying truths. The final part of *A Life in Perspective* is my attempt to find an accord between my life experience and the revelations and reflections of others. Belief and meaning are ultimately personal to the individual and can never be subject to objective proof. Indeed there can be no objective truth. Truth is ultimately as perceived from an individual, subjective, standpoint. That perception may be shared by others but that does not make it an objective truth, only a commonly held perception. History is littered with commonly held perceptions that were later displaced.

Introduction

In this book I have drawn some lessons from my personal experiences. Those lessons have at times been hard won. We all make mistakes and I have made my fair share. Mistakes can be beneficial if we choose to learn from them. I have no expectation of reaching death in some perfected state, I am and will remain work-in-progress. This book gives my perspective on a life lived with some environmental backdrop to provide context. In as much as it may in part correspond with your experience or encourage you to consider your life and the idea of its purpose, then it will have value beyond that which I have obtained in writing *A Life in Perspective*.

Part 1
Roots

Chapter 1   Early Years
Chapter 2   Dark Peak, Satanic Mills
Chapter 3   Woven Threads
Chapter 4   Growing up in the 1960s
Chapter 5   Armstrong Clan
Chapter 6   Scottish Seams

We are all in part the product of our environment. That environment does not need to be the key determinant of who we grow to become but that is not to deny its influence on how we see the world and respond to it. We are not always in control of that which befalls us but as conscious and responsible beings, we are ultimately in control of how we choose to respond. Maturity is, in one sense, willing acceptance of that 'respond' responsibility.

This part of *A Life in Perspective* looks at the environment into which I was born setting out in some detail major influences; familial, cultural and economic. Immediate family has perhaps the greatest impact in our early years. All is normal for the child until awareness grows of a wider world. Parents begin as all powerful beings and are only later seen to be human and fallible, just as fallible as ourselves. For most they are the major source of care and encouragement as we set out on life's journey. They play a vital role in nurturing and guiding us just as the wider family provides us with a sense of security and belonging. The family has been a key building block of community across most societies throughout history. As that block weakens, in this era in our culture, new challenges emerge not only for society at large but also for the individual and their deep seated psychological needs.

One of the first projects I undertook on retirement was to research my family tree. By then my parents were dead but I had in my possession material, some inherited, that gave me a better insight into their lives. I was fortunate in the parents I had and the family environment into which I was born. Both parents came from large families, one based in the industrial north west of England

and the other the coalfields of southern Scotland. The economic and cultural landscape in which families function is forever changing. The opening part of A Life in Perspective tries to provide a picture of the landscape of my childhood and how it had come to pass. It would be a mistake to only see the hardships of times past. There were downsides but also positive aspects just as the environment of today contains a different mixture of opportunities and difficulties. We all must navigate the sometimes turbulent waters of our own time, however, the essential human challenges and consequent choices we face, are perennial in their nature.

Chapter 1
Early Years

I was born in August 1948 at Partington Maternity Home Glossop, Derbyshire, the first born of Phyllis aged 20 and William Armstrong aged 27. I was given the forenames of William Ritchie exactly those of my father, William a recurring name in my Scottish family tree and Ritchie the maiden name of my father's mother. My parents then lived at 31 Bankbottom, Hadfield in a four roomed terraced house with separate outside toilet; rented from their employer, the owner of nearby Waterside textile mill. They had married in Hadfield Methodist church on Bank Street, a few hundred yards from their house, on 27th December 1947. Both were described as 'silk weavers' on the marriage certificate. Waterside mill was originally predominantly a cotton mill, spinning and weaving, but between the world wars new synthetic fibres were developed, one of which, rayon, was called artificial silk. Production of this in the second world war was expanded to produce barrage balloon and parachute fabrics.

Less than a year after my birth their second child arrived, Alan Ramsay, on 27th July 1949, Philip John followed on the 14th February 1951. My mother related that on her departure from the maternity home, aged 22 with Philip, the nurses' farewell included a "*see you next year Mrs Armstrong*". That brought to mind her own mother's eight pregnancies and resulted in an immediate conversation with her husband about the future use of contraception. Philip was to be their last child. On the positive side, three small children in cramped accommodation qualified my parents for a council flat in nearby Glossop.

Whitfield

The Whitfield council estate was newly built and relatively small in scale, it consisted of a mixture of two floor dwellings; flats and houses. It was built opposite a war-time development of prefabricated, corrugated asbestos, single floor buildings, known locally as the 'pre-fabs'. Although these were meant to only have a life of 10 years, they survived for several decades. On the other side of the council estate lay Whitfield House surrounded by extensive grounds. In 1951 it was an old people's home but had originally been built as a Wood family residence. The Wood family was one of the Victorian dynasties that helped make Glossop and Hadfield into major 'cotton' towns. By the middle of the twentieth century that era was over but both towns were shaped by the legacy of wealth created from the spinning and weaving of cotton.

Number 13 Whitfield Avenue was to be the family home for the next 13 years. It was a first floor flat consisting of a utility room at the stair top, living room with outside small balcony, kitchen and pantry, bathroom with toilet and two bedrooms. Additionally, there was a downstairs 'coal hole' to store fuel for the living room fireplace, the only fixed source of heating in the flat. Coal was delivered to that hole, with its own separate outside access door, in one hundredweight (just over 50 kilos) hessian sacks by a coalman, who lugged the sack on his back from the flatbed delivery lorry.

At about the same time Phyllis's elder sister, Doris, also moved into a similar flat a few doors away with her husband John Hyde and their two children, Ronnie and Miriam. A little later another sister, Ruth, moved from Hadfield into a terraced house on Hague Street at the top of Whitfield Avenue, with her husband Eric Oldfield and their only son, Eric. The estate and surrounding area housed a large number of young children of similar age; part of the post-war 'baby boom'. Lawns between housing blocks were soon appropriated as football pitches and newly planted trees, justifying the 'avenue' name, doubled as goal posts. One forbidden playground, nevertheless regularly visited, involved scaling the 'plantation' wall adjacent to the housing estate and gaining access to the grounds of Whitfield House. Here we could climb trees, make dens and explore while trying to avoid the occasionally vigilant grounds' staff. Cousins Miriam, Eric and I were born only a few months apart and consequently were regular playmates during childhood. We were to be reunited later in life for a shared 70th birthday trip to the Isle of Man, the surviving offspring of the three sisters who had moved from Hadfield to Whitfield in the early 1950s.

School

My father continued to work at Waterside mill, catching the bus to Hadfield from Glossop town centre, but mother gave up her mill employment with the arrival of children. As we reached nursery and infant school age, she took up part time employment at Glossop Central Kitchen on Pikes Lane. This supplied children's meals to several local schools. One of my earliest memories is of walking my youngest brother Philip half a mile to his nursery school before doubling back to my own infant school, Whitfield Church of England school on Ashton Street, adjacent to the parish church. The school had been founded in 1848 by the Wood family, to educate the children of their mill workers, and the school buildings I attended between 1953 and 1959 were constructed in 1913 (and were demolished in 1981).

As the eldest child I was given, and willingly accepted, early responsibility. My mother would depart from the house before 7.30am for her part time job, as would my father for his commute to Hadfield. That left me in charge of my brothers, having to ensure they were ready for and delivered to school on time. Before leaving home there were also chores to be done; making beds, washing up the breakfast things and making up the coal fire for the evening. I was the chief organiser, not always a role appreciated by my brothers Alan and Philip. Physical redress for failure to co-operate was just an accepted way of dealing with disagreements. It was applied by our mother to us, and subsequently by me to my brothers. My father's role in physically chastising us as children was rare but not unknown. The not so affectionate nickname given to me by my brothers of 'bighead' describes how they felt about the early morning regime. For me the motive was to assist my mother rather than bully my brothers. I obviously took things too far and at some point my mother sided with my brothers against me. That had a profound effect and I felt it to be a serious breach of trust between us. It was one of the few times my mother really hurt me; her physical chastisement often delivered in anger never had that effect. My desire to be supportive continued but in a slightly more guarded way.

If provoked I could be quite aggressive as a child and that aggression would manifest in regular fighting with other boys. Mrs Arnfield, my form teacher in the final two years at Whitfield, decided to apply some positive psychology to the situation and managed to turn me from a potential troublemaker to peace keeper. She did this by recruiting me and my friend John Bouchier to 'police' the school yard. It proved an effective strategy. Corporal punishment at Whitfield was the norm and accepted as unremarkable. The headteacher, Mr Plant (nickname Polly Plant), used the cane. Other teachers had their weapons of choice, some the plimsoll, some the strap. All were frequently used but generally in a restrained manner to maintain order. We had a cooked lunch at school supplied by the kitchens where my mother worked. Following the meal I was occasionally selected to deliver to Mr Plant the cup of tea he liked to end his meal with. My challenge was to carry the tea to his office without spillage from cup to saucer. A challenge not always met.

I had several crushes on girls during my time at Whitfield school. One was on Mary who lived at the top of Whitfield Avenue, she played the piano and was occasionally called upon to give recitals at school assemblies. My infatuation never got beyond long-distance stares, the idea of talking to her was just too much to contemplate. The only real male friendship I made at school was with John Bouchier. That friendship had its ups and downs with periodic physical fights between us punctuating the relationship into our teenage years.

My school reports show moderate progress over my time at Whitfield from C and D grades to C and B. At the end of my time there I faced the 'eleven-plus' examination and passed. My two brothers, Alan and Philip, both failed that same examination and consequently I went to grammar school aged eleven and they attended West End secondary modern school. Philip's grades at Whitfield school, as shown in his yearly reports, were consistently better than mine, but his fate to some extent, was sealed by one examination at eleven years old. My father, a grammar school boy himself, was unhappy when Alan failed the examination, so much so that he paid for him to be privately educated at Birch Hall school near Oldham until he was thirteen. He then took a thirteen-plus examination, for delayed grammar school entry, only to fail again. Philip's failure brought forth only resigned acceptance on the part of my father.

At this time there were shops on almost every corner in Glossop, visits had to be on foot as very few people owned cars. Within a short walk of home there were at least a dozen shops, some specialist like green grocers and butchers, others general stores with limited ranges. Shopping for my mother was one of my regular jobs.

As small children we would often accompany our parents on walks into the surrounding picturesque countryside. Regular destinations included; the Gnat Hole, a small valley containing buildings once used, long before, as a woollen mill; Derbyshire Level close to the estate of another Wood family residence, Moorfield House; and Whiteley Nab the nearby hill overlooking Glossop from which there were extensive views of the whole town and the valley in which it sat. Sometimes our walks would venture further afield with one favourite destination being Mossy Lea, close to Old Glossop, for picnics and river damming to create a pool for paddling and swimming.

Sunday School

Attendance at Sunday school was a requirement of we three brothers by our parents throughout early childhood, perhaps as much to give them respite on a Sunday as to improve our religious education. Initially this was accommodated at 'top chapel' on Hague Street at the top of Whitfield Avenue, and then at Littlemoor chapel on Victoria Street in Glossop.

Whitfield Wesleyan Methodist chapel opened in 1813 and its most treasured possession was a pulpit gifted by Methodists in nearby New Mills. What made the pulpit special was that it had once been used by John Wesley to preach sermons. The Methodist movement resulted from a break with the Church of England and one of its most important early leaders was John Wesley. He and others developed a belief system, or 'method', which took it away from the established Protestant Church. Its teachings stressed the importance of the scriptures and Christ's prime commandment 'to first love God and then to love thy neighbour as thyself'.

It believed the personal conversion experience was all important and thus that all were potentially saved not a select chosen few. That belief drove an evangelical mission to seek those important personal conversions with preachers stressing that in the eyes of God the working class were equal to the upper classes. The church also began to play an important part in providing a basic education for workers' children. Consequently Methodism grew rapidly, particularly in northern mill towns. Society membership expanded nationally from 56,000 in 1791 to 1,463,000 in 1851. As well as encouraging plain dress, for members and preachers alike, it discouraged what it saw to be frivolous or harmful activities, such as alcohol consumption, gambling and dancing. It also created powerful hymns that reinforced its core beliefs and which played an important part in its services. John Wesley's brother Charles composed hymns including *'Love divine, all loves excelling'*, *'Jesu lover of my soul'* and *'Hark the herald angels sing'* amongst many others; over six thousand in all.

A Sunday school was established at Whitfield in 1832. Sunday schools were originally set up in the 18th century to provide a basic education for working class children. That role changed following the Education Act of 1870 when the state took on responsibility for universal elementary education. Sunday schools still thrived but focus slanted towards religious education. Whitfield chapel continued to develop with investments in new buildings in the 1880s and 1930s. It closed as a chapel in 1968 and the building now houses a masonic lodge.

Although we brothers attended a Church of England designated school, my parents never joined C of E services or encouraged us to go to Sunday school there. The church was seen to be the church of the establishment, or as my father called it 'the Conservative Party at prayer'.

For a time, absent a parental edict, I attended services of my own volition at Littlemoor chapel. It was an Independent Methodist chapel that opened in 1811 funded by local well-to-do families. A school was added in 1840. It continued to expand and thrive until the second world war after which began a long slow decline. In 1976 13000 bodies in its graveyard were exhumed and reinterred in Glossop cemetery. The chapel building is now a fitness centre.

Whit Walks occurred each year in Glossop. The Christian Church's Festival of Pentecost falls on the seventh Sunday after Easter. It commemorates the descent of the Holy Spirit upon the apostles of Jesus. It is traditionally known as Whitsun, or White Sunday, and was followed by a week of festivities called Whitsuntide. As the population moved from countryside to town during the Industrial Revolution the celebrations became less important in many regions. However in some of the manufacturing towns of north west England the celebration was seen as a welcome break from work in the mills. Whit Walks were part of that tradition and made up of church members, Sunday school pupils, local dignitaries, scouts, girl guides, brass bands and others parading through the closed-off streets of Glossop. I qualified on two counts; as a Sunday school attendee and as a member of the junior scout movement, under eleven's being called 'cubs'.

As we grew a little older our parents found another way of

getting some Sunday rest from their often squabbling offspring. We were delivered to my mother's other sister, Aunty Margaret, in Hadfield for two or three hours. She lived at 20 Bank Street, the same street of my parents' marriage vows and a stone's throw from their first home on Bankbottom. Margaret lived there with her husband George, a Manxman (originally from the Isle of Man), and they had no children. On one visit there I recall the arrival of my aunt and mother's eldest brother Ives. He too lived in Hadfield at that time and his visit was to solemnly announce the death of his son, Noel, who had died in his twenties. He was the cousin who occasionally visited us at Whitfield and had given my parents an audio recording of *High Society*, the film musical.

Holidays and Grandparents

Annual holidays from an early age were invariably taken in Scotland with my father's family. I had been introduced to my Scottish family early in life. I was baptised as a baby in my grandparents' home in Carmuir, Forth alongside my cousin, John Armstrong. Then, with my mother's confinement, pending the birth of my brother Alan, when I was around 10 months old, I was left with my Scottish grandparents.

For our annual holiday excursion to Scotland my mother and father and three small children would catch the train from Glossop to Manchester, change stations and then travel on to Carstairs in Lanarkshire. Here we were met by my Uncle Ramsay in a large taxi and transported to Carmuir. My granny and grandad lived in an upstairs council flat at number 64. They had three bedrooms and lived there with their two adult sons, John a coal miner and Ramsay. For one or two weeks every summer they also accommodated a third son, my father, and his family, which meant that nine of us were housed in a relatively small flat. It all worked out reasonably well, with sofa beds and other makeshift arrangements, without too much upheaval or friction as I recall. My grandmother, Margaret, died in 1958 when I was 10 years old and that stands out in my memory as being one of the few times that I saw my father's tears, as he digested the news contained in a telegram.

Trips to Scotland were never complete without visiting my father's only sister Aunt Mary, and her husband Uncle Tam, at number 7 Averton in Forth. Most of their children, namely Margaret, Mary, Ramsay and Robin, had married and left home by the time of my childhood visits. Margaret and Mary had married two brothers, Alec and John Kerr.

Ramsay had married Cathy and Robin, Margaret. Initially all still lived in Forth, adding to the sense of large family and strong community. Youngest son Tom was the last to marry and was still at home with his parents when I used to visit. Growing up we were much more oriented towards our geographically remote father's family in Scotland, with its Carmuir and Averton hubs, than to our mother's Hadfield based wider family.

My mother's mother Elizabeth Smith died a few months before I was born in 1948. She was then living with her daughter Margaret, the one who later entertained us brothers on Sunday afternoons. Elizabeth was, in her final years, separated from her husband.

The tale related by my mother was that her father, Fred, was partial to alcohol. His wife had given birth to ten children since marrying him in 1907, all survived with the exception of triplets who died in 1917 shortly after their birth. Fred had the outlook of many working-class fathers of his day, he left his wife to bring up their large family while he brought home a wage. Regular visits to the pub were seen as a right. On return from the inn he expected his meal on the table. If it were not, he might easily lose his temper and, no doubt fuelled by alcohol, lash out. My mother had always been something of a tomboy as a child and quite physically strong. She was the youngest child and still at home with the next eldest sibling, her sister Doris, when on one fateful occasion their father returned home and started to hit their mother. Whether by prior agreement or spontaneously, Doris and Phyllis intervened and in turn set about their father with any available weapon. That resulted in all three of them, Doris, Phyllis and their mother leaving the family home for good and taking refuge with elder brothers and sisters who lived nearby. It took many years for my mother to achieve a reconciliation with her father. As a child, I can recall meeting Grandad Smith on only one occasion.

Pocket Money

From an early age I was intent on earning pocket money. This was largely obtained by delivering newspapers for the local newsagent, more about which later. Additionally, when I reached my teens, on Saturdays in the shooting season, I would spend the day 'beating' on the heather clad moors that surrounded Glossop. That involved, along with others, being picked up in an old army truck early in the morning and transported to the site of a grouse shoot. There we would be marshalled into a line and walk, making as much noise as we could muster, towards the line of guns waiting for the birds to be driven from the heather towards them and their fate.

Grouse shooting was a pursuit of the wealthy. On one occasion, I recall, the shoot was joined by Basil de Ferranti. He was the grandson of Sebastian de Ferranti who was an electrical engineer and although of Italian descent was born in Liverpool. With others, he founded what was to become Ferranti Limited, a major player in the design and commissioning of electrical power plants from the late 19th century. His grandson, educated at Eton and Cambridge University, joined the family firm and in his later years was involved in Conservative Party politics. His visit to the shoot on this occasion was by helicopter, unfortunately his pilot chose to land in a field full of cows which determined that the helicopter posed a threat and decided to stampede, demolishing the fence that had until then penned them in. It provided some welcome entertainment for the assembled audience of beaters.

The grouse shoot was on moorland adjacent to Moorfield House, one of those large houses built by the Wood family. The Woods were one of three families that came to dominate cotton product manufacturing in Glossop and Hadfield, as the Industrial Revolution took hold in the north west of England. Their power would eventually eclipse that of the aristocratic dynasties that had acquired the Manor of Glossopdale following the Norman Conquest.

Chapter 2
Dark Peak, Satanic Mills

The north west corner of Derbyshire is sandwiched between Greater Manchester, previously part of Lancashire and Cheshire, and Yorkshire. Historically Hadfield lay in Cheshire but it is now part of Derbyshire along with Glossop. They nestle at the western edge of Bleaklow, part of the Dark Peak, not so much the mountain suggested as inhospitable moorland sitting on gritstone stretching across the Pennine ridge to Sheffield and industrial Yorkshire. The White Peak in contrast lies further south in Derbyshire. Its rolling hills, limestone outcrops and pretty villages is what most people associate with the Peak District. However, both peaks are contained within the national park. The Dark Peak better fits Glossop and Hadfield which are more an extension of the urban landscape stretching to Manchester than part of Derbyshire's rural idyll.

Glossopdale and Longdendale valleys, the latter containing Hadfield and Padfield, are two adjacent valleys long devoted to industry rather than farming, their rivers fed from Bleaklow's moorland.

Glossop's History

The name Glossop is thought to be Anglo Saxon in origin coming during the Angles settlement of the 7th century and derived from Glott's Hop, hop meaning valley. Prior to its obtaining that name the valley housed, during the Roman occupation, an important auxiliary fort named in Victorian times Melandra Castle. It was built around 80 CE by soldiers recruited from the northern coastal area of what is today Germany and the Netherlands. It was occupied by a large contingent of soldiers until about the year 150. After the Roman withdrawal came the Anglo-Saxon settlement and then domination of England. Germanic tribes made up of Angles, Saxons and Jutes migrated to different parts of the country eventually to be united in a single kingdom. That kingdom was conquered by the Normans in 1066.

The Normans were of Scandinavian or Viking origin but had colonised the north of what is today France. From their expanding base in Normandy they eventually turned their attention to England. It was to be a systematic conquest. The resulting Domesday Book survey referred to Glossop as a small hamlet but its name was given to a manor granted amongst other land holdings by William the Conqueror to William Peveril, one of his military leaders and thought also to be his illegitimate son. This manor the Peveril family forfeited in 1157 when it alienated Henry II and ownership was transferred to Basingwerk Abbey, a Cistercian order. The Abbot then effectively became the new Lord of the Manor of Glossopdale that incorporated a number of local villages including (Old) Glossop, Hadfield, Padfield and Whitfield. The manufacture of woollen products in the manor dates back to the 12th century when Cistercian management of their estate involved the rearing of sheep and development of a trade in wool. Glossop's poor soil on the edge of the moors was better suited to grazing livestock than cultivating crops. In 1433 the Abbot decided to lease the whole of Glossopdale to the Talbot family in exchange for an annual rent.

A century or so later, with the dissolution of the monasteries by Henry VIII, the Talbot family, headed by the Earl of Shrewsbury, received full title to the Manor. Ownership passed in 1606 to the Howard family as part of Anthea Talbot's dowry on her marriage to Thomas Howard, 14th Earl of Arundel. The Catholic Howard family's fortunes had been restored by James the first in 1603 following a long period of persecution resulting from their doubted loyalty to the Protestant monarchy. Thomas Howard's own father Philip Howard had died at the hands of Queen Elizabeth in London Tower in 1595. Philip is now designated a martyr and saint by the Catholic church and a Glossop Catholic secondary school is named after him. Many Talbot and Howard family names and titles appear in the town's street names, buildings and parks.

By the 1700s Glossopdale was established as a textile manufacturing region. At this time production was largely carried out in the home. Some households might focus on spinning the wool, others would possess rudimentary looms to weave cloth. They were supplied with raw materials by agents who would then take their production, usually paying per piece of work completed. This type of production method was known then as 'putting out'. As well as locally sourced wool, merchants in Lancashire began to source cotton and flax as raw material for an expanding local textile industry.

The humidity in the area, abundant water supply, proximity to the major port of Liverpool and improving transport infrastructure, such as canals and later railways, facilitated this growing industry. In 1760 800 tons of cotton were imported into Britain but by 1800 this had grown to 25,000 tons. A triangular trade developed; ships would leave Liverpool with manufactured products in the form of printed fabrics and sail to west Africa, there the textiles would be exchanged for a human cargo of slaves and these were then shipped to the southern United States where slaves would be traded for raw cotton, before making the return journey to Liverpool.

As the industry expanded new inventions were developed to improve production efficiency and capacity. In 1764 James Hargreaves developed the spinning jenny and a few years later, Richard Arkwright the water powered spinning frame. Power driven looms followed in the 1770s. All these inventions created an imperative to concentrate production in factories or as they were known locally 'mills'. Here expensive equipment could be better utilised and rivers channelled to drive water wheels to power the new spinning machines and looms.

The first cotton mill to be built in Longdendale valley in 1775 is attributed to Samuel Oldknow at Vale House, Tintwistle, close to Hadfield – a location now submerged beneath a reservoir. Vale House grew to become a village of 100 cottages with a population of 600. The mill eventually comprised 2 carding rooms where the raw cotton was prepared, 9 spinning rooms and 3 weaving rooms.

By 1831 there were 112 cotton mills in Derbyshire and by 1846 some 60 in the parish of Glossop alone. In 1859 an analysis of the workforce in one mill employing 500 people showed 50% to be adult women, 24% girls, 19% adult men and 7% boys. In 1851 within the villages of Glossop, Padfield, Hadfield, Whitfield, Chunal, Dinting, Simmondley and Charlesworth, a survey showed that of the 3,562 children between the ages of 5 and 14 years, 931 were working in cotton mills.

Aristocracy

The Howard family are at the top of the British aristocratic tree, immediately below the monarchy itself. The family head, the

Duke of Norfolk is Earl Marshall, Premier Peer and this title has been held since 1483, except for periods when the Catholic family came into conflict with the Protestant monarchy. The family's manor in Glossop became an important source of revenue as manufacturing overtook farming as the principal use of land. The family's local land agents, the Ellisons, capitalised on industrial development on behalf of the Lord of the Manor and they themselves invested directly in building mills on land leased from the Howards. Annual income from the Manor of Glossop rose from £3,495 in 1777 to £11,192 by 1822 and was second in importance only to Arundel. The Howard family invested heavily in local infrastructure creating turnpike roads, reservoirs and railways as industry and its associated population mushroomed. In 1801 Glossop's population was 2,759, increasing to 9,631 in 1831, 19,587 in 1851 and reached 22,416 by 1891. The Industrial Revolution had fuelled an almost ten fold increase in the town's population in just 90 years.

In 1853 Glossop Hall was built by Edward Howard on the site of the family's earlier 1729 Royle Hall. Edward, who later became the 1st Baron Howard of Glossop, was the first member of the Howard family to actually live in the town. Family occupation ended in 1924 when the 3rd Lord Howard of Glossop decided to bring to a close the 300 year history of family association with the area. He auctioned off 7400 acres of land covering 27 farms and countless buildings. Glossop Hall and surrounding estate sold for £15,500 and Kingsmoor public school took over the Hall itself. Part of the grounds opened to the public as Manor Park in 1927. The school moved out in 1956 and the Hall was finally demolished a couple of years later. As the fortunes of the cotton industry declined in the twentieth century, so did Glossop's population. It fell to 17,500 by 1961.

Cottonocracy

The Ellisons, land agents for the Howard family, bridged the gap between aristocratic control of Glossop and control by a 'cottonocracy', that is an oligarchy of mill owners. Matthew Ellison had come to the town in 1797 at the behest of his employer. By 1815 he had built, on his own family's behalf, Wren Nest mill alongside Glossop Brook. His daughter Barbara married Robert Sumner and their son Francis was to play a leading part in the development of Glossop as both mill town and borough. On reaching twenty-one he inherited Wren Nest mill. In 1829 he installed its first steam engine and rapidly expanded the business to become one of three dominant cotton mills in the area along with Howard Town and Waterside mills. The Lord of the Manor and local mill owners did not always see eye to eye. There were disputes about water and issues around the infrastructure necessary to facilitate a rapidly growing industry and its attendant workforce. In 1865 a petition was sent to the Queen to establish Glossop as a 'borough', a political and administrative entity subject to local democratic control.

Francis Sumner was chief proponent of borough status and saw it granted a year later. Elections were then called to elect 24 councillors. The franchise was limited, 832 voters in total, and weighted toward the mill owners' interests resulting in them gaining 11 of the 24 seats. The new council adopted the Howard family lion emblem on its official seal and the motto *Virtus, Veritas, Libertas*. Francis Sumner became Glossop's first mayor. On his death in 1884 Wren Nest mill had 2700 weaving looms fed by a spinning capacity of 120,000 spindles and it employed 1300 workers. As well as being a prominent mill owner he also found time to fulfil other community roles; Glossop Mayor and Justice of the Peace, High Sheriff of Derbyshire and local leader of the Catholic church. A bequest from his will built St Mary's Catholic church in

Glossop. He, like the Ellisons and Howards, was a Roman Catholic religiously and Whig politically. The two parties then dominating British politics were the Liberals (Whigs) and Conservatives (Tories). The new borough status added political control to the mill owners', already considerable, power.

Democratic influence was some time off for the many thousands of mill workers employed locally. In 1838 a People's Charter was created that sought by democratic means to widen the right to vote to working people. It proposed; a vote for every man aged 21 or over, electoral parliamentary constituencies of similar population size, payment of MPs and annual elections to place a check on corruption. Petitions were drawn up with millions of signatures and presented to Parliament in 1839, 1842 and 1848. A number of Reform Acts were passed during the 1800s and the later ones were influenced by the Chartist movement and, later still, the female Suffragette campaign. In 1832 men meeting a property qualification were enfranchised. In 1867 all male householders or lodgers paying a rent in excess of £10 per annum in boroughs were enfranchised, and the property qualification threshold in country districts was lowered. A third Reform Act in 1884 re-drew constituency boundaries to make them more equal in size. However, it would take the first world war to really widen the franchise. In 1918 all men over 21 years old and all women over 30 were given the vote. Women eventually gained the vote at 21 ten years later.

John Wood came to the area in 1815 and leased two small empty cotton mills. He and his three sons successfully expanded their business and then developed a new mill complex at the crossroads of the two most important turnpike roads in the area. This development, adjacent to Glossop Brook, they named Howard Town mill. It became so large that it literally changed the location of 'Glossop' to where it is today, Howard Town becoming

Glossop and the original settlement was renamed Old Glossop. In 1896 Howard Town mill covered 14 acres and had 3,400 looms, 221,000 spindles and employed over 2,500 people. Some of those buildings still survive close to Glossop's Victorian Town Hall. The Travelodge hotel, along with other commercial businesses, are housed in part of the original mill. The Wood family intermarried with the Sidebottom family, principal Hadfield mill owners, and like them were religiously Anglican and politically Tory. They became great local benefactors. The twelve acre Howard Park which housed public baths, swimming pool and Wood's Hospital was a family gift to Glossop in 1887 to commemorate the 50th anniversary of Queen Victoria's coronation.

It was a short walk from another of the family's homes in Glossop, Talbot House on Talbot Road, a substantial property built by Lord Howard and opposite the ultimate site of Glossop Grammar School. As well as being involved in the construction of Whitfield parish church, and the adjacent infant school that I attended as a child, the Wood family were also responsible for building some of the large country houses familiar to me in childhood, such as Whitfield House adjacent to Whitfield Avenue and Moorfield House, close to the moors used for grouse shooting. A Wood family monument can be found in the graveyard of Whitfield's C of E Church. Here the remains of John Wood and his son Samuel are interred and his grandson (Baronet) Samuel Hill Wood is remembered.

As the mills grew so did the need for housing for the rapidly growing workforce. Many of the existing terraced rows in Glossop were built to accommodate workers at Howard Town mill (later called Wood's mill) and Wren Nest mill (later Sumner's mill). When steam power replaced waterpower for the mills, it was Lord Howard who invested £10,000 in 1845 to build a branch line connecting Glossop with Dinting and thus the main Manchester to Sheffield railway line. This enabled coal to be easily transported to power the large cotton mills of Glossopdale. Coal smoke filled the air, quickly blackening the new buildings as mill chimneys sprouted in the valley. A forest of industry giving birth in turn to thousands of domestic chimney pots.

The other great family making up the local 'cottonocracy' was the Sidebottom dynasty whose empire centred on Waterside in Hadfield. Between Tintwistle and Hadfield, on the southern bank of the River Etherow, in Longdendale valley, this site had begun life as a fulling mill, a finishing process for woven wool. Messrs Turner and Thornley in 1777 built a mill here for the spinning and weaving of cotton. It was originally known as Brookside mill. In 1828 the site was sold to the Sidebottom family. John Sidebottom was from Mottram in Longdendale, a surveyor and architect as well as yeoman. He was determined to get his sons involved in the mushrooming textile industry. His second son James acquired Waterside mill and employed his own sons in the expansion of the business. By 1850 Waterside was a village in its own right, with houses and infrastructure built to accommodate the growing workforce.

In 1887 Waterside and Bridge mill, which had been built on the other side of the river Etherow by Willam Sidebottom, contained 4,700 looms, 293,000 spindles and employed over 3,000 workers. They specialised in producing printed calico fabric for the Far East. This market began to shrink in the 1890s as local Asian production grew. A final blow came when a fire destroyed much of Bridge mill. The Sidebottoms put the Waterside business into liquidation, selling off all the textile equipment. In 1899 John Garside of Ashton-under-Lyne, Lancashire, founder members of the Calico Printers Association (CPA) acquired the buildings. They invested heavily in new equipment and began to utilise new manmade fibres, in addition to cotton. Automatic looms were acquired from the USA and later France, an indication of how the UK textile industry, the crucible of the first ever Industrial Revolution, was losing the initiative to foreign invention and equipment. The new custodians of Waterside, the CPA, continued to provide good local employment for the next 80 years, not on the scale of the Sidebottom era but still substantial. On leaving school in 1942 my mother got a job at the mill and in 1947, after being demobbed from the RAF, my father too found work there.

Chapter 3
Woven Threads

My parents met through their employment at Waterside mill in Hadfield and their first home was owned by their employer. My mother, Phyllis Smith, was born on 1st of May 1928 and then lived in nearby Padfield. She attended Castle School on Hadfield Road, leaving at the age of fourteen. Castle School had been founded as a Wesleyan day and Sunday school in 1808. It was taken over by the state in 1906 and then had around 300 pupils. My mother's mother was Elizabeth Smith nee Fish and she had been born in Hadfield in 1886. By 1901 she was working at the mill and living with her parents at 40 Bankbottom along with five siblings, the same street Phyllis would live when she first married in 1947. This row of houses had been built between 1830 and 1860 to accommodate the growing workforce employed in Waterside mill.

Satanic Mill Life
A typical day for a mill worker around 1900 would involve being woken at 5am by a 'knocker up'. The latter's role was, using a long pole, to knock on upstairs bedroom windows all along the street. Within half an hour the sound of wooden clogs would be heard

on the cobbled streets as workers made their way to the mill for a 6am start. A 12-hour shift lay ahead for men, less for women and children. Work in the mill was hard physically and hot. The noise was terrific and workers soon learned to lipread because of the din from the machines. Accidents were not uncommon. Mill owners laid down strict rules and expectations of their employees with fines for disobedience.

The lot of the average worker had changed a great deal over the previous century and a half. The 1700s had seen a move from agricultural work to home based textile work, first using wool, later cotton. Local agents supplied raw material and rudimentary spinning and weaving machines were housed in the home. Cloth was returned to the same agent who paid per completed piece of work. As water powered machines were developed in the second half of the 18th century so the imperative to focus production in mills grew. As production grew so the economics of mill manufactured fabrics undermined prices and home based production fell away, just as demand for mill labour expanded. Now the machines dictated the pace of work. James Kay wrote in 1832 *"the animal machine...is chained fast to the iron machine, which knows no suffering, no weakness"*.

The loss of independent action on the part of the worker was perhaps the biggest psychological change, together with the realisation that the workers' time was now the mill owners' time for long parts of the day. That work regime became increasingly demanding, best illustrated by the contents of one poster of 1836 displaying *"Rules to be observed in the power loom mill"*. Fifteen rules were set out, the first of which laid down fines for late arrival at work. Up to 5 minutes late, fine 3 pence, over 5 minutes 12 pence. This at a time when a typical wage may have been 10 shillings a week or 120 pence. Rules and fines covered; tidiness, adherence to work processes, quarrelling, fighting and leaving the place of work without permission. As production grew so the need to find additional labour grew, the local community could no longer meet that demand. Child labour was sought from far and wide. Parishes responsible for the upkeep of orphans and illegitimate children were glad to relinquish that burden by transferring children to be apprenticed, or indentured, to mill owners, who kept them in return for long hours of unskilled work in the mill. In 1802 The Health and Morals of Apprenticeship Act limited hours of children to twelve a day. Mill owners were often reluctant to add to their costs by restricting hours of work or by introducing safer working practices. William Blake in his 1804 poem *Milton* coined the phrase *"dark satanic mills"*. This poem was used as the basis for composer Hubert Parry's hymn *Jerusalem* in which *satanic mills* are contrasted with *England's green and pleasant land.*

The Combination Act of 1800 banned workers from forming unions to place demands on mill owners. When trade deteriorated mill owners often resorted to reducing workers' wages, causing both hardship and resentment. This contributed to the Luddite rebellion in the 1810s. Following mill owners' rejection of representations from weavers, a wave of unrest resulted in factories being burned and machines smashed. Glossop's Hurst Mill brought charges against some of its mill hands for illegal activities and rioting.

In 1818 the first organised strike occurred amongst Lancashire spinners and a year later a large peaceful demonstration at St Peter's Field, Manchester was addressed by those seeking reform. Local magistrates declared the gathering illegal and called out the military. As the crowds swelled to 80,000 or more the cavalry were ordered to charge. Eleven people died and four hundred were injured and it became known as the Peterloo Massacre.

Following the rejection by Parliament of a second Chartist

petition in 1842 and the imposition of wage cuts in many local mills a meeting was held on Mottram Moor, between Mottram and Hadfield, that called for textile workers to withdraw their labour. That strike quickly spread, eventually half a million workers were involved in mills and mines across the country, it was the first national strike. Some workers went further, resulting in the Plug Plot riots. A plan was hatched by workers in Darwen Street Blackburn, to remove the plugs from steam engines, then being installed in local mills. A number of mill engines were attacked and this resulted in the army being called out and six workers killed. In the 1830s and 1840s foot soldiers and cavalry were regularly dispatched to Glossop in support of mill owners faced with worker unrest.

Frances Trollope's novel of 1840 *The Life and Adventures of Michael Armstrong, Factory Boy* brought the plight of children employed in mills to a wider audience. Reform gradually came, partly as a result of violent revolts but also because of enlightened mill owners, such as Robert Owen, who introduced more humane workplace regimes. The development of trade unions, following the repeal of the Combination Act in 1824, also furthered change. It is estimated that there were 100,000 trade unionists by 1850 and over a million by 1874.

A series of Factory Acts were passed at intervals throughout the 1800s. The 1819 Act had banned children under nine from working in cotton mills and restricted hours to a maximum of twelve per day for children aged between nine and sixteen. Reforms followed every few years with another milestone in 1844 when working hours for nine to thirteen year olds were restricted to nine hours a day and those thirteen to eighteen and all women were limited to a maximum of twelve hours a day. Some machine guarding also became obligatory. Notices were required to be displayed in mills setting out Factory Act provisions and Factory Inspectors appointed to enforce legislation, but mill owners were rarely held to account. The 1878 Act defined children not to be employed, as those under ten and created a maximum working week of fifty six and a half hours for women and young persons, fourteen to eighteen years old. Children between ten and fourteen were now required to spend half their time in education to learn the 'three Rs'; reading, writing and (a)rithmetic.

In 1861 the American Civil War interrupted the supply of cotton to the north west of England. 90% of Glossop's mill workers were put on short-time employment or lost their jobs. People became dependent on charity for survival. Soup kitchens were set up by the local relief committee. In return for relief payments, men were required to do public works, such as excavating reservoirs in Padfield. Youths and unmarried mothers had to attend school for five hours a day or they lost relief support. Many tenants were evicted for non-payment of rents and some families chose to migrate to other parts of the country or further afield to America, Australia and the colonies. The proportion of the population in distress and receiving relief benefits in Glossop was 40%. The only real relief came with the end of the Civil War when cotton once again flowed across the Atlantic and the local textile industry resumed its growth.

Roots: Mother's Mother
Elizabeth Fish, Phyllis's mother, was born on 26th June 1886 in Hadfield. She grew up in the shadow of Waterside mill, the biggest cotton mill in Hadfield, although by the time she worked there in 1901 (aged 14) Waterside was past its peak both as a producer and employer. Cotton was in her blood. Her grandfather's family on her father's side, had come from Darwen in Lancashire,

another 'cotton town', no doubt drawn to Hadfield by the boom in mill employment. William Fish had been born in Darwen in 1815, but by the time of the 1851 census, he was a cotton spinner living in Hadfield with his wife Elizabeth (nee Raynes) and their four children. Walter Fish, their fifth child and my grandmother's father, was born on 19th April 1862. At the time of the 1881 census, Walter's mother had died and he was living with his father and some of his siblings in Padfield Lane, his employment was listed as 'cotton labourer'.

Work in the cotton mill was hot, humid and noisy. In the carding rooms where raw cotton was processed, to facilitate spinning, the air was full of fibres. Those fibres were inevitably breathed in by those working there. This gave rise to 'brown lung disease' or 'byssinosis'. In the spinning rooms male mule spinners were prone to cancer of the groin from continual contact with the lubricated moving parts of the mule. Textile mills stank from the animal fat used as a lubricant and temperatures were kept high and humid to aid the handling of cotton. Long working hours combined with poor working conditions could easily result in a lapse of concentration, resulting in injury or death from drive belts or unguarded machine working parts.

In 1882 Walter Fish married my grandmother's mother, Ruth (nee Worsley). They wed on 25th September in Hyde (then in Cheshire). Ruth had been born in Stockport on 3rd May 1865. Her father was a 'card grinder' in a local cotton mill at the time of her birth. By 1881, she was living with her uncle and aunt in Brosscroft, Padfield and working in the cotton mill. In 1882, aged 16, she married Walter who was 20 years old. Both were mill employees at the time, he as a 'grinder' and she as a 'card room hand' both jobs located where raw cotton fibres were prepared for spinning into thread. By 1891, they were living on Bradshaw Street in Hadfield and both Ruth and Walter were still employed in the carding room of the mill. They now had two children, William aged seven and Elizabeth aged four, the latter my mother's mother. By 1901, they lived on Bankbottom, four more children had arrived by then and the two eldest were now employed in the mill. Walter had moved on to become an excavator at the waterworks, possibly employed as a labourer, helping to construct the chain of nearby reservoirs. Mill ponds and reservoirs had originally been built to meet the power needs of mills and water needs of the local population. From the 1850s a new imperative had arisen; to create much larger reservoirs in the Longdendale valley to meet the growing water consumption needs of, what is today, Greater Manchester.

The house that my parents occupied on Bankbottom had four rooms, two downstairs and two up, with an outside 'privy' or toilet. In 1950 this was deemed as potentially overcrowded for a family of five, however a generation before that the same space had to accommodate much larger families. My maternal grandparents had seven children that survived childbirth, my great grandparents had six children, both were typical of their times. Cooking was on a range built around the coal fire. Typical fare might include home grown vegetables and inexpensive meat, such as shin beef, or cow heel pie. Tripe was a local favourite, cow's stomach, often served up raw with salt and vinegar. Bath night was usually once a week and involved bringing the zinc washing tub in from the yard and placing it in front of the fire. A succession of bathers would then utilise the same heated water.

The upside of large families was the close proximity of many uncles, aunts and cousins, all usually within walking distance. When new mill based communities first started some mill owners would seek to capture a large share of their employees' wages, not only in rent for accommodation but also by setting up shops to supply their necessities. Various Truck Acts tried to restrict employers' exploitation of their workers. The development of *Co-op* stores grew following the adoption of key principles in 1844 by the Lancashire Rochdale Co-operative Society. These principles included; open common ownership or membership, democratic control, an ethos of serving the community and an undertaking that any financial surplus generated would be returned to shopper members as a dividend, in proportion to their purchases from the store. These principles resulted in Co-op stores spreading across the north of England and well beyond.

In 1901 Elizabeth Fish was employed in the mill at the age of fourteen, just as her mother had been at a similar age and her daughter Phyllis would be. On 10th February 1907 Elizabeth married Fred Smith at St Andrew's Church in Hadfield; they were both twenty years old. His address was given as Cumberworth in Yorkshire and hers was Main Road in Padfield. The marriage certificate described him as a labourer and her as a weaver. Five months after their marriage their first child was born on 19th July 1907 and named Ives after Fred's father. Twenty-one years later, their last child Phyllis was born in Partington Maternity Home, Glossop. Including the first and last born, there were 10 children in all. The five elder children were named Ives, Walter, William, Margaret and Ruth. In 1917 triplets Alice, Harold and Fred were born but did not survive. Then in 1924 Doris was born and finally Phyllis in 1928.

Roots: Mother's Father

Fred Smith was born on 25th July 1886 in Cumberworth, Yorkshire, just over the Pennines from Hadfield, between Denby Dale and Holmfirth, the area that later became famous as the setting for TV series *Last of the Summer Wine*. His parents, Ives Smith and Ellen Riding, had married in December 1877. Ives was a wool weaver who had been born in Wooldale in 1853. Ellen had been born in Cumberworth in 1856 and at the time of the 1871 census, she was employed as a 'wool feeder'. In 1876, she had an illegitimate child Harriet Ann Riding and a year later she married Ives in Cumberworth. Harriet was brought up as part of their family. Nine children followed and Fred was their fifth. By the time of the 1901 census, Ives's job was described as 'gardener's labourer domestic'. On his son Fred's marriage certificate in 1907, his father's occupation was described as 'game keeper'.

Ives's own father, William Smith, was also a wool weaver, although his wedding certificate described him as 'a clothier', possibly meaning agent. Ives was the seventh of twelve children. The Smith family line, together with their wives' families all centred on the Yorkshire area covering Cumberworth, New Mill, Wooldale and Kirkburton. The wives' family names were: Riding, Ives, Senior, Bray, Lockwood and Ibberson.

Fred Smith appears to have been a labourer much of his working life. At 14 years of age he was a 'brickyard labourer' and on his death certificate it states he was a 'retired grave digger'. We do not know what brought Fred to Hadfield where he met Elizabeth Fish and then married her. After the birth of their first born, Ives, Fred took his family to Yorkshire where the next eight children were born, returning to Hadfield for the birth of Phyllis, their last child, in 1928. Later he was to return to Yorkshire and his death certificate in 1960 indicated that he was then living with his son, Ives, at Thorn Cottage, Farnley Tyas, Kirkburton, not far from his birthplace.

My mother had spent much of her adult life estranged from her father, as did some of her siblings. As well as witnessing his assaults on her mother, she had seen his bullying of her elder brother, Walter, which she believed had contributed to his fragile mental health. At the time of her death in 1948 her mother was living with her eldest daughter Margaret in Salisbury Street, Hadfield. Elizabeth was then afraid to leave her daughter's house in case she met her estranged husband. She died a few months after seeing her youngest daughter, Phyllis, married; according to my mother then 'content that all her children were now settled'. My maternal grandmother died a few months before I was born so I never knew her. My mother remained close to her sisters Doris, Ruth and Margaret and brothers Ives and Walter, less so to brother William who moved to Hyde.

Mother's Brother and Sister

Walter, born in 1908 was eccentric, perhaps because of his father's bullying. Early in his life he was inclined to become a priest and attended Cliff (theological) College in Calver Derbyshire but failed to graduate. He then spent much of his life in and around Hadfield, dressed usually in an eccentric manner. At some point he met Lois who became his lifelong female partner although they never married. They lived for many years on Woodhead Road in a partially derelict house, without utility services. It sat on the hillside overlooking Valehouse reservoir, the site of Longdendale's first cotton mill in 1775. The house was filled with junk that Walter collected. He used to walk the streets of Padfield, Hadfield and Glossop pushing an old pram in which he collected items given to him. Some of these he was able to sell to provide the basic necessities for himself and Lois. As teenagers, whenever we saw Walter on the street, we would do our best to avoid him and the embarrassment of being seen to know him. That was despite having visited his tumble down house with our mother when we were younger, where he would invariably seek out toys for us from his accumulated jumble. He was harmless and kind and our embarrassment did us little credit.

The sibling of my mother that we had the most contact with as children was Aunty Doris. She was four years older than my mother and they had forged a bond at home, no doubt cemented by the action that removed their mother from her abusive husband. Doris had married John Hyde circa 1945, he was an 'overlooker' (production supervisor) at Waterside mill. They had two children, Ronnie and Miriam. The Armstrong and Hyde children all grew up in close proximity, having moved from Hadfield to Whitfield at the same time, and played together a great deal as small children. Later when we acquired a larger council house at the top of Whitfield Avenue, the Hydes did likewise.

Sometime in 1963 Doris unashamedly took a lover Bill who lived in Glossop and was a married man. He regularly called at her home, with her husband present, and took her out, presumably with her husband's acquiescence. Doris, aged 41, gave birth to a late child in 1965 some 17 years after the birth of her previous child, Miriam. At about the same time that Doris gave birth, Bill's wife also gave birth to a daughter. He and his wife had previously adopted two boys believing they could not have children of their own. At some point Bill's wife visited Doris to confront her and Bill subsequently disappeared from the Hyde household. John and Doris's marriage remained intact into old age. They eventually returned to Hadfield and their roots, as did my mother's other sister Ruth Oldfield.

Mill Rest

Glossop Cemetery is in fact situated in the parish of Padfield, on a ridge overlooking Glossop and Old Glossop on one side and Hadfield and Padfield on the other. The two ancient valleys of Glossopdale and Longdendale are separated by that ridge. The cemetery holds many generations of my mother's family. Her sister Ruth Oldfield is buried here along with her husband Eric. In the grave adjacent lies Ruth and my mother's brother Walter, the uncle we avoided as teenagers, he died in 1981. On Walter's gravestone is remembered his mother Elizabeth but her remains are in fact interred in the plot behind his sister Ruth's grave. Elizabeth Smith nee Fish is buried with her parents Walter and Ruth. Their grave was unmarked but now contains a headstone naming parents and daughter as well as remembering my own parents and brother Philip. It is the plot where my own remains will eventually rest.

Mill Heritage

A flavour of mill life in the 1800s can be had by visiting National Trust's Quarry Bank Mill in Cheshire. The Trust has not only preserved the cotton mill founded by Samuel Greg in 1784 but has installed many working nineteenth and twentieth century textile machines. Originally it was a water driven spinning mill but later added weaving and became steam powered. It operated much as Waterside in Hadfield did, with workers drawn from the local community and further afield.

The Apprentice House has been preserved where indentured child labour, taken from workhouses and parishes, was accommodated. The Greg family home on the same site can also be visited. Samuel and his wife Hannah were leading Unitarians. Unitarian beliefs originated in Eastern Europe and theology deviated significantly from well established Christian doctrine. Whereas most conformist churches held that God manifested as a trinity; Father, Son and Holy Ghost, the Unitarians believed that God was One and that Jesus was not God, but a prophet. Elizabeth Gaskell, another Unitarian, was a regular visitor to the Greg house. One of her most famous novels is *North and South* in which mill owner and worker perspectives are given of industrial life in the middle of the nineteenth century.

Hadfield Fame

Hilary Mantel, author of acclaimed historical novels such as *Wolf Hall*, spent the early years of her life living on the Brosscroft road between Padfield and Hadfield. Her memoir *Giving up the Ghost* describes how, as a child, she would regularly visit her grandparents who lived on the adjoining Bankbottom road.

On the other side of the River Etherow from Waterside mill lies the village of Tintwistle where fashion designer Vivienne Westwood was brought up. She was born in Glossop's Partington maternity home and attended its grammar school.

The town of Hadfield gained widespread fame in the 1990s when it was used as a film set to represent *Royston Vasey*, the home of *The League of Gentlemen*, a surreal and dark comedy series produced by the BBC.

Fish and Smith Family Trees

The immediate forebears of Elizabeth Fish and Fred Smith follow.

A Life in Perspective

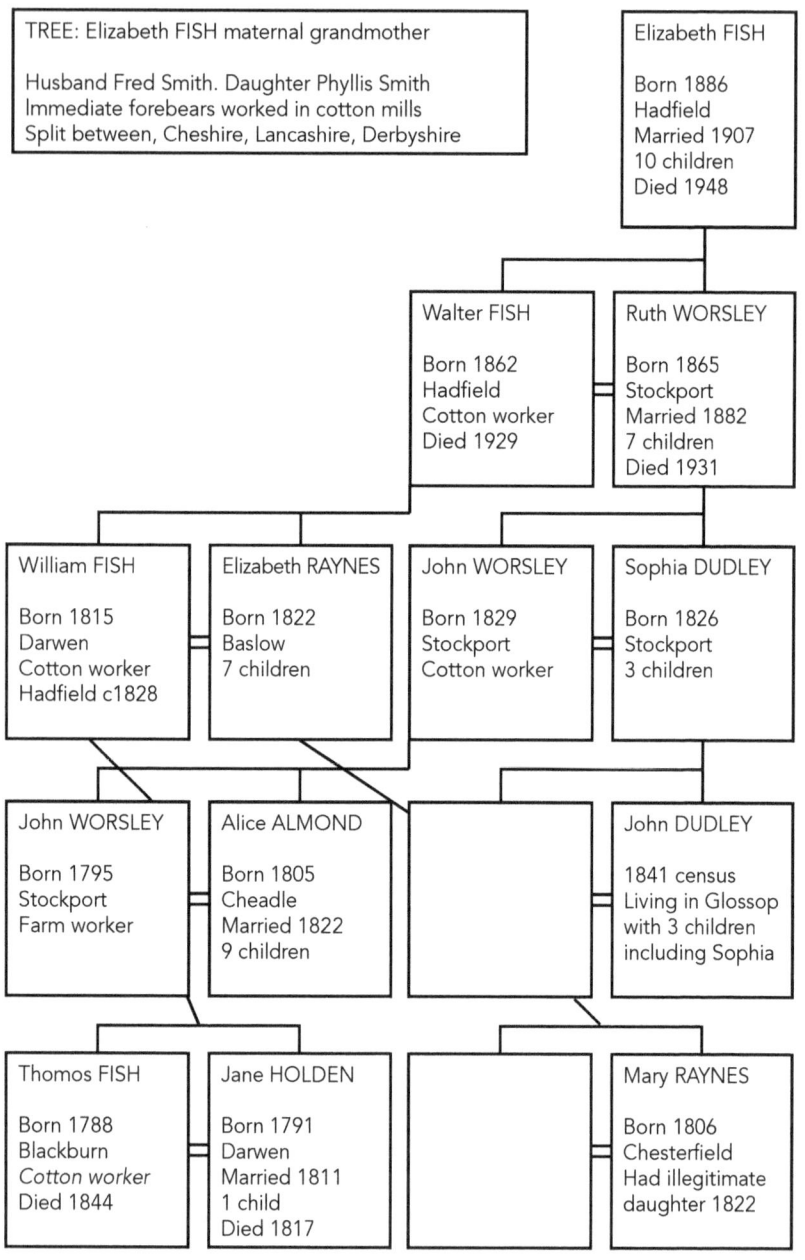

Roots

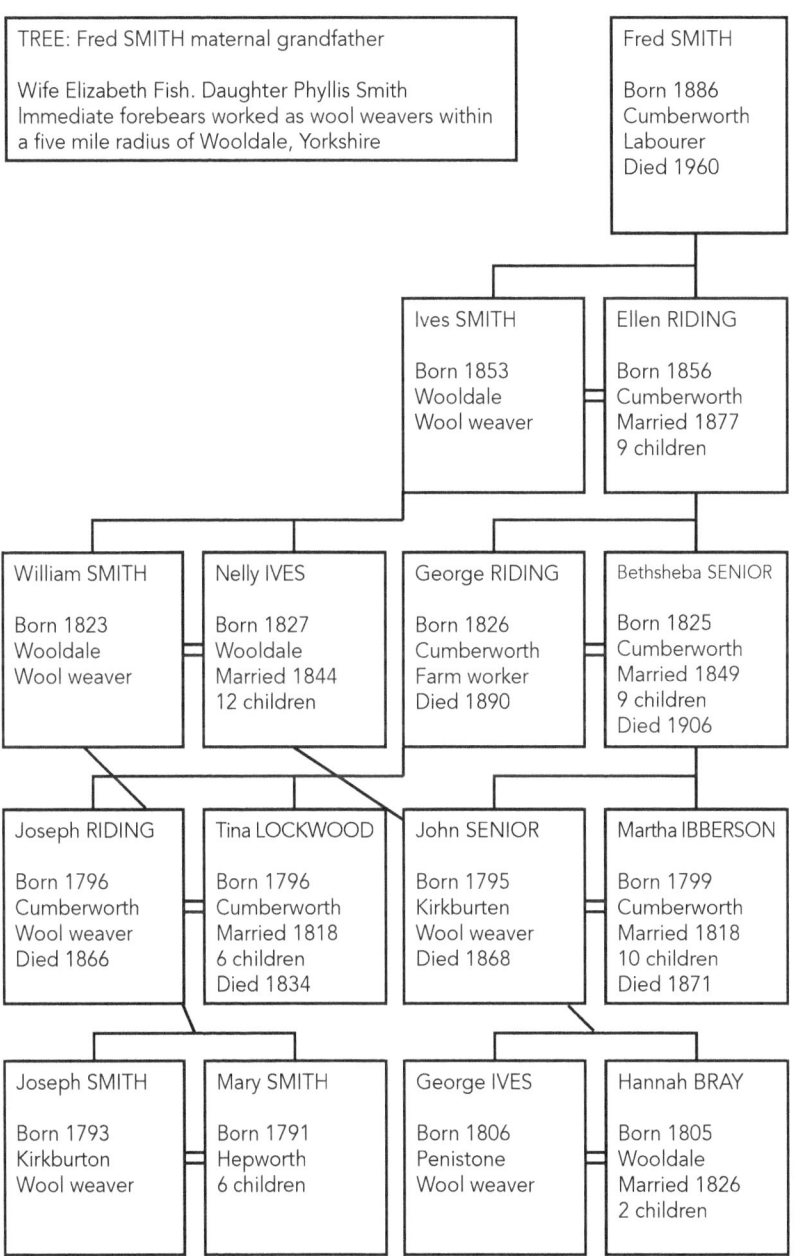

Chapter 4
Growing Up in the 1960s

In September 1959 I took my place at Glossop Grammar School. The school's motto, embroidered on my school cap badge, was that of the borough *Virtus Veritas Libertas*, Virtue Truth Liberty. The Latin words once also conveyed subtler inferences; *virtus* had connotations of courage, character and worth, *veritas* encompassed kindness and beauty as well as truth and *libertas* suggested independence as well freedom. All were worthy qualities encouraged by school and town.

My arrival coincided with a change of location, the school having previously been housed in a solid Victorian building on Talbot Street. That building had been constructed by the 2nd Lord Howard of Glossop for use as a technical school and opened in 1901 to teach cotton spinning and weaving as well as masonry and brickwork. A year later the requirements of the Balfour Education Act resulted in it becoming a general education secondary school. In 1916 this transmuted into a grammar school with the opening of West End school in Glossop and Castle school in Hadfield. Both were new secondary (modern) schools that had evolved from previous chapel schools, West End from Littlemoor and Castle from Hadfield Wesleyan. Grammar school fees were abolished by the

1944 Education Act and the eleven plus examination became the sole criterion for entry. Cecil Lord had become headmaster in 1937 and saw through both a change in the selection process for admittance and the move to a new purpose built school on Talbot Road in 1959. This consisted of three adjacent modern blocks of differing heights accommodating classrooms, science laboratories and wood/metal working facilities, all a short walk from extensive sports playing fields and tennis courts. By 2021 the 'new' school had been completely demolished whereas the original Victorian school building was in use as a Community Centre and looked capable of standing for another century.

Lowry

In 1959 the new school main entrance, adjacent to the school's large assembly hall, housed a proud possession given to the school on its opening – an original L.S.Lowry painting *Mill Scene*. It hung in the school for many years before being loaned to Salford City Art Gallery and eventually sold.

Laurence Stephen Lowry was born in Stretford, Manchester in 1887. From early childhood he developed a passion for drawing and painting and on leaving school he enrolled in evening classes at the Municipal School of Art. In his early twenties he became a rent collector for Pall Mall Property Company and there he stayed until retirement at age 65. His mundane job provided the income for him to pursue his passion, painting. One of his favourite subjects was the urban industrialised landscape, in particular cotton mills, that he saw every day as he collected rents for his employer. Recognition of his work began in the 1930s when Manchester City Art Gallery bought one of his paintings and four years later when he was elected to the Manchester Academy of Fine Arts. He never married and lived with his mother, caring for her during a long period of ill health until her death in 1939. In August 1948, the month of my birth, he moved from Manchester to Mottram in Longdendale. There he was to stay until his own death in 1976 in Wood's Hospital, Howard Park in Glossop, three miles from his Mottram home.

School Report

Cecil Lord was headmaster during my first year at grammar school. I had only one personal contact with him and that was a slap around the head, a kind of Lord's anointment. This was the consequence of dropping my school bag as I descended a flight of stairs and in so doing releasing a bottle of ink that smashed on the new school floor. Unfortunately this coincided with Mr Lord's intended ascent of that same staircase. John Climo replaced him as headmaster in 1960 giving me an opportunity to un-blot my copybook. Mr Climo stayed in the position until 1971 and he oversaw the school's next transition to comprehensive school in 1965, a year after my own departure.

I spent five years at the school. My three term reports for the first year showed me to be below class average in attainment. My second year showed progress to be above average, likewise my third year. At the 1961 Speech Day ceremony I received my one and only public commendation for 'progress and industry' and was presented with a copy of Charles Dickens's *Old Curiosity Shop*. By my fourth year, I had returned to below average performance. My final year produced five GCE 'O' Levels, Maths (2), English Language (5), Chemistry (3), Physics (4) and Geography (5). Of the four subjects I failed I retook two in the autumn, having officially left school in the summer, and gained a further two 'O' Levels in History (5) and Art (6). The numbers in brackets indicate the grades, the lower the number the higher the grade.

In 1964, on completion of my time at the school, John Climo wrote on my final report: *'a pleasant and capable boy who will do well in any situation involving personal integrity'*. I took that as encouragement as I wondered what to do next in life. In my year at Whitfield school, from a class of 35 pupils, 21 passed their eleven plus examinations; 9 boys and 12 girls. Of the 9 boys who passed only one stayed on into sixth form at grammar school, an indication of the times or of the working class catchment area for Whitfield. The possibility of staying on at school beyond age 16 never entered my head.

Diary Days

Coincidental with my move to secondary school I kept diaries, initially these took the form of small pocket diaries that my father had brought home from work. A sample of entries for the first seven days of 1961: 'went to Uncle Walt's house', 'dad came home' (presumably from a Hogmanay visit to Scotland), 'went to Manchester and got a new suit', 'joined the Co-op' and 'did shopping for Mum and played the rest day'. Other entries included 'went to see *Dentist in the Chair* at the pictures', 'played football' – noting that we had won 15-13, also a more poignant entry; 'buried Freddie', cousin Ronnie's tortoise. That year I made two trips to Scotland, one on my own at the end of May for a two week stay with Uncle Ramsay, and then again with my parents in August, involving a week at Carmuir and a further week in Dunbar on the Scottish east coast, staying at the Lothian Hotel, family plus Ramsay. It was our first family hotel holiday.

Delivering Papers

During the same year I began my first paper round. This entailed selling football results papers on a Saturday evening, *Football*

Pinks as they were called. It was an era when most people had radios but not necessarily television sets. It was effectively a selling job; I would collect a bag of papers from the newsagent and wander the streets shouting 'football pink' loud enough to bring out customers, predominantly men, from their houses. On occasion if I strayed onto the sales territory of a rival seller, or what they felt constituted 'their' territory as these were undefined, I might be told to leave 'or else'. 'Or else' was simply the threat of physical retribution. My income for the evening would depend on sales. A more stable income followed with a regular daily paper round that involved simply posting evening papers through the letterboxes of the newsagent's regular customers, who paid at the shop on a weekly basis.

In 1962 I also recorded daily diary entries. In February that year I bought on hire-purchase, funded by my paper round, a new BSA Gold Crest bike in yellow and black with drop handlebars, a prestigious acquisition. It was used to commute to school, which lay on the other side of Glossop, and for long bike rides, occasionally with my mother.

One trip we made together was up the Longdendale valley into Yorkshire where we visited Aunty Annie in Upper Cumberworth. It was the first and last time I was to meet her. She was my grandfather's elder sister and would have then been about 79 years old. The yellow bike resulted in my once being interviewed at school, by headmaster John Climo and a policeman, as I arrived one morning and deposited my bike in the racks provided. I found out later that they were investigating the molestation of a girl in Manor Park by a boy with red hair on a yellow bike. At the time of the offence I was on a school trip to watch a performance of *Iolanthe* and so, fortunately, was not questioned further. Policemen in those days were more visible on the street, or 'on the beat' as it was called, and not confined to police stations or police cars. I even have a certificate of 1962 signed by police constable Marshall confirming that my bicycle was in good roadworthy condition (not the constable who interviewed me with John Climo).

The Fire Service too was very much part of the community. A neighbour of ours was a volunteer fireman. In an era before telephones were commonplace he, along with other volunteers, would be summoned to the station, in the centre of Glossop, by the wail of a siren which could be heard throughout the town. That would result in him mounting his bicycle and pedalling hard for the town centre. Glossop fire station today is located close to Whitfield House, now housing association owned sheltered accommodation, in the grounds we played in as children, now described as Whitfield Park.

Throughout the course of 1962 and beyond I delivered newspapers to earn pocket money to fund not only payments on my bike but other luxuries such as; a Timex watch, fur lined gloves and my first flight in an aeroplane. The latter was on a day trip to Southport where ten shillings (50 pence) bought a five minute passenger flight in a Tiger Moth aeroplane that used the resort's extensive sandy beach as an airstrip. My paper delivery job was for Dale's Newsagents on Victoria Street owned and run by two brothers, John and George. I migrated from football papers to evening papers, then on reaching age 15 was allowed to obtain a more lucrative morning paper round. This involved getting up at 6.30am to deliver daily papers on my bike before going to school. My regular route involved passing close to Turnlee (and Dover) paper mill, not far from Whitfield.

Making Paper

Turnlee mill, originally built in 1832, was acquired by Olive and Partington in 1873 and they expanded the business installing improved paper making machines and processes. Edward Partington, later Lord Doverdale, was another of Glossop's great industrial benefactors. He built Glossop's Liberal Club, now home to theatre group *The Partington Players*, and was religiously a non-conformist. Following a short illness he donated £30,000 to the borough to build a nurses and convalescent home for the benefit of local residents. It opened in 1908 on North Road and also became a maternity home in 1920. That was where both I and my mother were born and helps to explain why my birth certificate states that I was born in a 'convalescent home'. My paper round involved walking over a footbridge across a river that passed through Turnlee paper mill and went on to feed Glossop Brook, then the river Etherow. The colour of water in that river would vary by the day depending on the production process waste being deposited. The river was known locally as the 'Chemic' brook. The paper mill's main raw material was wood and that involved large quantities of logs being delivered daily by train into Glossop.

Those logs would then be hauled from Glossop town centre up Victoria Street across Charlestown Road to their Turnlee destination. Initially this was achieved by horse and cart, then by steam powered traction engines. The *Tiger Tractors* were still in use when I was a child and I would often see them on my way to Whitfield infant school which lay just off Charlestown Road. Their use ended in 1960. Turnlee was sold to Inveresk Paper company in the 1920s and closed in 1963 with the loss of 600 jobs.

Wakes Week

During 'Wakes Week' paper rounds were suspended. This was a week when most local businesses closed in Glossop and their employees took their annual holiday en masse. It was a tradition in many mill towns with different towns choosing different 'wakes' weeks. Dale's shop closed for the duration and a temporary paper stall was erected on the street to sell daily papers to those not away on holiday. As it coincided with school holidays I often helped man the stall. The term 'wake' had its origin with the church. A wake was a vigil or night of prayer, preceding the sabbath, sometimes celebrating the local church's consecration. During the industrial revolution the tradition of wake was adapted to become a regular summer holiday, particularly in mill towns. Each town would nominate its week leading to a mass local holiday exodus, often on charabancs to Blackpool, Southport or New Brighton on the Lancashire coast. As manufacturing fell into decline and motor cars became more prevalent the wake practice died out.

Fighting
Physical altercations punctuated the year, mainly involving my mother and brother and were duly noted in my diary; 'beat Alan up' 'fought with Alan' 'had scrap with William McKinley' 'mother mad with us, Alan and I belted'. My mother's physical assaults eventually came to an end in my teenage years when I, by then taller than she, prevented her lashing out by pinning her arms to her side.

One diary entry describes at length an almost ritualised last fight with my friend John Bouchier, also then at grammar school. Early evening there came a knock at the door of 13 Whitfield Avenue. It was a friend of John issuing me with a challenge to fight him. I wasn't aware of the reason for the fight but accepted the challenge. John was waiting close by. We walked to the top of the avenue to find a suitable location and found a patch of communal lawn not overlooked. The lack of emotion or apparent cause made the occasion more surreal, obviously some irritation had been triggered at school. It was more of a boxing match than wrestle and I recall positioning John so that the street light behind was in his eyes not mine. Several punches ensued with me wondering whether his friend was around and about to join in. He wasn't. A few solid blows from me eventually resulted in John losing heart and retreating defeated. I returned home. The following day at school a number of fellow pupils approached me to ask how the fight had gone, so it had not only been pre-planned by John but he had told others of his intention. My response was simply to tell the enquirers, as to the result, 'you had better ask John'.

Recreation

One of my solitary pursuits was fishing. This involved a trip to the Longdendale reservoirs near Padfield that provided day permits for coarse fishing. With my basic rod, line and float plus a can of worms or maggots I fished for whatever would take the bait. Perch were the most frequent catch, any large enough were taken home for my mother to cook. I don't recall my catch ever providing food for the family, but my mother was happy to occasionally indulge my fisherman's pride.

Occasionally I would go with my father to watch a Glossop FC home game. Glossop's football history stretched back into the 19th century. Samuel Hill Wood, of the Wood cotton dynasty, managed to persuade the football league to include Glossop North End in an enlarged second division in 1898, having scoured the country for able footballers. His efforts were rewarded with Glossop NE achieving promotion to the prestigious first division after only one season. This triumph was short lived with a return to the second division the following year and there the club remained for the next fifteen years. My father and I enjoyed Glossop football at an even lower league level in the 1960s with modest but enthusiastic crowds. Samuel Hill Wood had greater football success when he moved, in retirement, to London and in 1929 became chairman of Arsenal FC.

Adventures took many forms, not always noble or sensible, but boy's adventures of their day nonetheless. Bonfire night (Guy Fawkes) each year was eagerly awaited with its fireworks and fire. Bangers were the fireworks of choice for boys rather than the more expensive and decorative options. Catherine wheels and rockets had some merit, but generally the noisier the outcome the better. Dropping bangers into empty milk bottles, left outside peoples houses for the milkman's next delivery, also produced lots of broken glass. Every house had a metal dustbin, its name suggesting its original primary purpose; to deposit ash or dust from the ubiquitous coal fires.

Dustbin men regularly emptied those bins into dustcarts. Empty bins acted as amplifiers for bangers deposited by boys in search of mischief. Joe Oldham was an old age pensioner who lived in the downstairs flat beneath ours. His garden lay adjacent to ours and it was uncultivated and therefore, with his agreement, perfect for a bonfire. We, the local kids, then acquired the wood we needed, some from the adjacent grounds of Whitfield House or the 'plantation' as we called it. When the stack was complete a carefully created Guy was positioned on top, having been previously carted around the area on a bogey cart and presented to passing adults with the fundraising entreaty 'penny for the Guy'. In fact it was money for fireworks. On one occasion as darkness fell and the fire was lit I decided to create my own super banger and filled an empty ketchup bottle with paraffin, tossing it on the fire.

Unfortunately it only reached the fire edge so I, very foolishly, recovered it only to find the plastic screw cap now on fire. Quickly I threw the bottle toward the fire and turned my back only to see a very bright flash on the house wall I was now facing, as the bottle exploded. Fortunately, by some miracle, no one was injured.

Diary Detail

One of my Christmas presents that year was a Five Year diary with space for lengthier entries than my previous diaries could record. I was diligent daily in year one, less so in the following years when less frequent but longer narrative entries took over.

The winter of 1962/3 was long and hard with snow on the ground for almost three months. It was the coldest winter recorded in the UK since 1740. On Christmas Day snow showers worked their way south from Scotland, then a blizzard struck on 29th December in the West Country with drifts 15 feet deep. Despite the weather the family travelled to Scotland for the Hogmanay celebration; 'seeing in' the new year was always a bigger occasion there than Christmas. On this trip I recorded that I got to bed at 3.15am. One of the things that made the visit special for me was a gift from my father. He had left at Carmuir, after the war, a brass model of a de Havilland Mosquito aircraft, and this he gave to me. The aircraft type was one of those he helped to maintain during the war. I really appreciated the gift and retain that model to this day.

Long before central heating, supplementary warmth to coal fires came from electric fires and paraffin heaters. It was not unusual upon waking to find condensation ice patterns, or ferns, on the inside of the bedroom windows. We returned to Glossop from Scotland to discover a flat full of soot. Our neighbour Joe Oldham had lit a paraffin heater in the kitchen to warm the flat for our return. Unfortunately, he had turned the wick too high and the result was soot literally everywhere. It took us a long time to clean up.

The following day I had my afternoon paper round delivering 'locals', that is the local edition newspaper *The Glossop Chronicle & Advertiser*. The origin of the paper lay in nineteenth century politics. The Liberal Party established the *Glossopdale Chronicle* in 1859. It was bought out by the Wood family in 1868 who then changed its allegiance to the Conservative Party. This prompted local Liberals to establish a rival paper *The Glossop Advertiser*. Eventually in 1937 these two papers merged and overt political allegiance was abandoned. The last edition of *The Glossop Chronicle and Advertiser* was produced on 27th July 1963. My paper round in early January that year took over two hours because it had to be completed in blizzard conditions. On the upside, snow meant fun for the kids on the Whitfield estate. The avenue was on an incline and consequently the pavements became toboggan runs as children with sledges consigned pedestrians to the road. Mother, far from preventing this takeover, became a keen participant.

That week, Alan bought Elvis Presley's single record *Return to Sender*. The pop era was underway and provided the backdrop for the next few years. British pop groups began to multiply and started to dominate music and popular culture on both sides of the Atlantic. Many groups were made up of working-class boys with a talent for music. My own early favourites were *The Hollies* from the Greater Manchester area. Their harmonic singing had been inspired by the Everly Brothers who had emerged in the 1950s from a working class coal mining area in Kentucky. The 'pop' culture served to empower a generation and helped drive the idea of social mobility, along with the rebirth of the Labour Party under Harold Wilson. 'Working class' became fashionable not only in music but in literature and drama. Works such as *Saturday Night and Sunday Morning* were popular and even more so after adaptation for the cinema screen. Film director Ken Loach was another important influence giving working class lives a voice with TV plays such as *Cathy Come Home* and films like *Kes*.

Over the course of the previous year my father had endeavoured to pass his driving test, with local school *Solly*, but failed several times to his growing frustration. In April 1963 he finally passed and then acquired his first car, a second-hand maroon Austin A40. This was a source of major excitement for the family with numerous related diary entries. A long detailed report described the first family excursion deep into Derbyshire on 12th April covering, it was noted, some 68 miles. Hayfield, Chapel-en-le-Frith, Buxton, Bakewell and Matlock were all visited. Chapel-en-le-Frith lies between Hayfield and Buxton. In Norman times it was the location of a small chapel built by the Keeper of the Royal Forest, the post originally held by William Peveril. In 1963 on road entry to Chapel the first thing seen was the Ferodo factory, the town's major employer. That business had been set up in 1897 by Herbert Frood and it was the first company to use asbestos in the manufacture of vehicle brake linings. It moved its operation to Chapel-en-le-Frith in 1902. The family's new motor car now made easier visits into Derbyshire, to not far distant places rarely seen. The orientation of Glossop's public transport infrastructure, towards Lancashire and Cheshire, had previously made them the more accessible destinations.

My own acquisition in the year was an air pistol obtained from my brother Alan. Later I managed to upgrade to an air rifle and was then better able to shoot sparrows and other birds in the garden, from an upstairs window; a not very commendable working class grouse shooting equivalent. The flat at 13 Whitfield Avenue had a long corridor off which the various rooms ran. One short lived game we brothers developed early in 1964, in our parent's absence and no doubt prompted by our addiction to cowboy films, involved the use of these airguns. Barricades were set up at either end of the corridor, Alan and Philip at one end with an air pistol, me at the other with the air rifle. Part of my brothers' barricade involved the cover from a rectangular paraffin heater which was a sheet of metal with a round hole of two inch diameter through which the flame could be viewed. On this occasion, that hole was a spy hole to survey the barricade opposite. It was also therefore a target for the rifle. The lead pellet I fired passed through the hole and hit my brother Philip in the eye socket, cutting through his eyelid and lodging underneath. Blood poured from the wound and panic ensued. Fortunately, Dr John Paranjoti, an Indian doctor and his English wife Greta, lived a few doors from our flat. Greta was a nurse and at home that day so she was able to minister to Philip's wound. His eye was thankfully intact, the slug having hit the bone beneath the eyebrow.

Consequently the wound was superficial, requiring just two stitches, nevertheless the whole experience was deeply traumatic for all concerned. My mother's response was immediate, the air pistol was confiscated and then burned. I managed to hide and save the rifle but a painful lesson had been learned. My sometimes reckless ways became a little less reckless thereafter. I still have vivid memories of the incident and mentally cringe at the thought of how close I came to blinding my brother.

Between 1962 and 1964, my form teacher at school was Cedric Clough. He was also my geography teacher and a positive influence on me. In December 1962 he commented on my report that I should 'make some effort to join in school activities'. That resulted in me joining a number of societies and eventually one that he ran *The Geography Association*. That resulted in a number of field trips, mainly into Derbyshire, to learn about geology.

Castleton, with its limestone caverns and Blue John mine, was a favourite destination. It lay not far from Chapel-en-le Frith, and was named after and adjacent to Peveril Castle, built by Glossopdale's first Lord of the Manor.

As my reading at school moved on to Dickens and Austen, at

home Ian Fleming's *James Bond* book series took centre stage, no doubt fuelled by the release of *Dr No*, the first of the *Bond* movies. The television at home offered only two channels. ITV's *The Avengers* and the BBC's *Steptoe & Son* were examples of black and white broadcasts that gained almost religious weekly family viewing.

Political Awakening

Also avidly watched, as my political awareness grew, was *That was the Week that Was* a satirical BBC TV show hosted by David Frost. I had developed a strong interest in aircraft and space exploration, the latter much in the news from the early 1960s with the Soviet Union and the USA locked in a battle for space supremacy. The USSR had taken the lead with the launch of *Sputnik* satellites but President Kennedy galvanised the US effort by proclaiming, what seemed at the time, an audacious target to land a man on the moon by the end of the decade.

1962 was the year of the Cuban missile crisis. US spy planes, the high flying U2s, had detected the building on Cuba of rocket launching sites. Cuba was an independent country a few miles off the Florida coast. In the 1950s it had undergone an armed revolution under Fidel Castro's leadership, first overthrowing an American sponsored regime and then forming an alliance with the Soviet communist block. In consequence it was deemed an enemy by the US government. They secretly planned an invasion using US based Cuban exiles; this failed and became known as the 'Bay of Pigs fiasco'.

The building of rocket sites, potentially housing nuclear missiles capable of reaching the USA, was deemed a significant threat. Kennedy set up a naval blockade of Cuba to prevent missiles being delivered. For many days it seemed that the world teetered on the brink of nuclear war. The USSR's ships eventually turned back and a military confrontation was averted. It was heralded in the West as a victory for the US, few questioned why it was in order for the US to have nuclear weapons targeting Russia on the latter's border but not the other way round. Later reports suggested that a deal had in fact been done between Kennedy and Krushchev, with the US respecting Cuba's independence and agreeing to dismantle missile sites in Turkey, in exchange for the same in Cuba. Within two years both Kennedy and Krushchev would be gone.

On 22nd November 1963 John F. Kennedy, President of the USA, was assassinated in Dallas, Texas. This event shocked the whole world and had massive TV and newspaper coverage. I have a long diary entry recording the facts as were then known. Facts subsequently brought into question as more information was uncovered, contradicting the lone gunman official explanation. Many people remember exactly where they were when they first heard news of the assassination, as do I. It was another key incident in my political awakening and helped trigger what would become a lifelong interest in politics. Krushchev was replaced as Soviet leader by Lenid Brezhnev in October 1964.

Adolescence

At a more personal level, 1964 saw the curse of blushing at school. It was the plague of my adolescence and caused me great angst. It was invariably the consequence of embarrassment, particularly involving girls, and was the subject of many anguished diary entries and would remain so for several years. I thought I would never be free of the affliction; prickly heat and a flushed face revealing to the world my inner feelings of inadequacy.

My first diary entry of 1964 related to New Year's Eve; 'went to bed at 5am, up at 7am to deliver papers – back to bed on return and slept until 2pm'. It was to be an eventful year. At school GCE examinations loomed, with despairing diary entries about my lack of preparation for what was to come. There were school trips to Snowdon and Norway, both walking expeditions with fellow pupils and selected staff members. I was also set to leave school and decide on my future in the world of work. We moved house in 1964 to a larger semi-detached council house at the top of Whitfield Avenue where I had, for the first time, my own bedroom.

Also in October that year there was a General Election and this was of great interest. George Brown, Labour's deputy leader, visited Glossop and the party narrowly won the election. Harold Wilson became Prime Minister, his party replacing a Conservative party still steeped in the perceived privilege of its aristocratic roots. Tory Prime Minister Harold MacMillan had been undermined by the Profumo Affair, when his Minister of War was found to have lied to Parliament about his affair with Christine Keeler. She happened to be also sharing her sexual favours with a Soviet naval attache, thus, it was deemed, posing a security risk. MacMillan had been replaced shortly before the election by Alec Douglas-Home, the choice of an undemocratic Tory old boy network. It proved an unfortunate choice given his aristocratic background and the cultural revolution then underway. A new era of working-class emancipation was unfolding and that tide was to make it a decade of change and opportunity for those from less privileged backgrounds. I was between states. The coming adult was increasingly interested in the world at large. The retreating child was still finding entertainment in old ways. An example of the latter follows. Shortly before moving out of 13 Whitfield Avenue, I undertook, with assistance from my brothers, a trick on our downstairs pensioner neighbour, Joe Oldham. I decided to tape record on a recently acquired reel to reel tape-recorder, largely used for recording pop music from the radio, a series of special announcements as 'news bulletins'. These centred on the Queen's health. The first bulletin explained she was ill and the second that her condition had deteriorated and finally one saying she was dead.

The tape recorder was smuggled into his house and his almost constant radio transmissions were periodically interrupted by the 'news bulletins'. He was partially sighted and so suspected nothing. The news was believed, so much so that on his regular evening trip to the Beehive Pub he told those gathered around that the Queen was dead. He was still convinced on his return home. I broke the truth to him the following day.

One of our other neighbours, the Paranjotis, left for India that year. Greta had been a close friend of my mothers and I had grown somewhat infatuated with her good looks and personality. They had a young son, John, who was a regular visitor to our flat and was to die prematurely as a young man. On their departure they discarded an LP recording of Tchaikovsky's first piano concerto which I claimed. It was to be my introduction to classical music. It prompted my joining a 'music club'; in return for a monthly subscription I received regularly by post recordings of classical works.

I was also at this time a regular visitor to the library, initially a Whitfield outpost on Freetown and then, on its closure, the main Glossop library housed in Victoria Hall, another substantial building originally funded in part by Edward Partington.

I found that year an American pen friend with whom I corresponded regularly, more on which later. 1964 was also the year my father suffered a perforated ulcer and as a consequence was admitted to Ashton General Hospital. I don't recall understanding, at the time, that this was a serious condition, potentially life threatening. He was soon out.

My father's own father had died in Scotland earlier in the year at the age of 84. Uncle Ramsay's letter to my father in February explained that 'the auld lad' had been admitted to hospital much weakened by regular blood loss in his urine. Ramsay was sceptical of the medical attention he had received prior to admission and had little faith in that likely to come in hospital. His scepticism in relation to the medical profession was reinforced twelve years later when his older coal-miner brother, John, died of the consequences of a strangulated hernia, mis-diagnosed by their local GP (doctor). There was discussion in 1964 as to whether we children should attend the funeral of our grandfather but in the end mother and father went without us.

Adventure

That year I spent four days on an outward-bound course at the Whitehall centre in Derbyshire. It involved lots of outdoor activities from canoeing in the rivers to rock climbing. In 1964 male friendships at school centred on two boys, David Merrill and David Gray, the latter the son of a minister responsible for the chapel where my parents had married in Hadfield. Neither relationship survived my leaving school in the summer of 1964 when they stayed on into sixth form. Neither did my infatuation with a girl at school. A relationship that never went much beyond distant flirting and embarrassed blushing.

David Merrill was one of many school companions who participated in a walking holiday in Norway in the summer of 1964. Technically it was after I had left school although I was briefly to return to retake two GCE papers in the autumn. The trip was organised by Cedric Clough my form teacher and had been paid for bit by bit through the year. It was my first visit abroad and warranted a newly created diary complete with my own photographs. We flew from Newcastle in a 44 seat Fokker Friendship turboprop aircraft landing near Stavanger. Spending one night at a local school we then travelled by passenger carrying cargo ship and fisherman's boat to our starting point for a five day trek across rugged Norwegian terrain. We spent four nights in two mountain huts at Sandsa and Stranddal, each with limited but adequate facilities, before descending to Kvilldal village where some of us were billeted for the night in a village house. I noted that it snowed during our walk, unusual because it was August. From Kvilldal we were on our way home. It was a most enjoyable trip, one which gave me a taste for Norway's dramatic landscape and its friendly people. I managed to buy some souvenirs; a brass and wood wall plaque with a fish motif for my parents and a knife in leather sheath for myself. The latter I took care to hide in my luggage as I passed warily through customs. It is a knife I still have in my memorabilia box. My final diary entry conveyed that we took off at 10.30 in the evening from Stavanger arriving at Newcastle airport early in the morning. 'Our coach was waiting to take us back to school in Glossop, didn't sleep much, arrived at 5am, walked from there back home, unpacked, then did my morning paper round'. Most of my fellow students on the trip were staying on into sixth form, so it was the last I was to see of them.

    The Pennine moors were a short walk from Whitfield Avenue but then stretched for many miles to the east as well as north and south. Higher Shelf Stones lay to the east and at around 620 metres was only slightly lower than nearby Bleaklow. It was a point of destination for more than one of my solitary walks because it was an aircraft crash site. In 1948 an American Air Force B29 Superfortress, used for photo reconnaissance, was on a routine flight from Lincolnshire to the USAF base at Warrington when it crashed descending through thick clouds. All thirteen crew were killed. Locating and exploring that site many years later was a great adventure.

Kinder Scout is another Pennine 'peak' a little further south and was an alternative destination for my moorland walks. It was the site of a mass trespass in 1932 by a group of politically motivated ramblers, some of whom had been turned away from Bleaklow a few months before by gamekeepers employed by the landowner. Around 400 people started out from Hayfield and as they neared Kinder Scout's plateau violent scuffles broke out with the landowner's men.

The objective of the trespass was to demand regular access to open countryside for ramblers wishing to escape Greater Manchester's industrial landscape. It was a working class struggle for a 'right to roam' and in conflict with the right of the wealthy land owner to have exclusive use of moorland for grouse shooting. That tradition stretched back to William the Conqueror with Peak Forest being reserved for the new aristocracy's hunting pleasure. The ramblers' wish would finally be realised by the post war Labour Government who passed into law the National Parks Act in 1949. The Peak District was the first such park to be created and its formation eventually led to the creation of the long distance Pennine Way footpath, from the Peak District to Kirk Yetholm in the Scottish borders. That area was the historical home of my Scottish Armstrong family ancestors, directly traceable to Kelso and surrounding villages. In turn that region lies adjacent to the territory once controlled by the powerful Armstrong Clan of old, foremost of the *border reivers*.

Chapter 5
Armstrong Clan

Rome's invasion of Britain ultimately failed to conquer the land to the north, then known as Caledonia, now Scotland. After three attempts the Roman Empire eventually retreated in 100 AD behind Hadrian's wall. Viking raids and settlement, beginning in the 9th century, were more successful in Scotland but they were limited to the far north and the western islands. Orkney and Shetland remained under Norwegian sovereignty until the 15th century.

The word Clan comes from the Gaelic for 'children' and came to mean an alliance of family, relatives and neighbours for mutual protection against rivals or threats. Clan structure evolved over time, one variant had the chief and his family holding land on behalf of all, with membership of the clan largely made up of those having a blood relationship with the founding family. This structure created a strong bond of loyalty with mutual familial obligation holding the clan together.

Gradually a more feudal notion of authority crept in. By the 6th century various kingdoms had formed including Pictland, Strathclyde and Lothian, these imposing a regional identity above clan structure. In the 11th century the clans had been largely brought under the control of national Scottish monarchs, however many regional clan chiefs still retained powerful influence. In the Scottish borders, where strong family bonds still cemented clan structure, they built an important reputation for providing warriors to support the monarch against English incursions. Over time conflicts arose between loyalty to the clan and allegiance to the Crown.

Although the origin of the name Armstrong is obscure, there is a tradition that it arose in the family of Siward Bjorn, the Earl of Northumbria. He was of Viking descent and a nephew of King Canute who was King of England and of Denmark, Norway and parts of Sweden. Siward was Earl of Northumbria in 1041 and in that role sought to control incursions by the Strathclyde Cumbrians from the west into Northumbria. He used members of his extended family to police the area. They became verderers, the judicial and administrative officials in the Royal Forest of Inglewood that stretched from Penrith to Carlisle. Siward's sister married Duncan the King of Scotland and when Macbeth murdered Duncan, usurping the Scottish throne, Siward intervened in support of Duncan's son Malcolm and his claim to the crown. At the Battle of Dunsinane in 1054 Macbeth was defeated. In that conflict, so legend has it, future King Malcolm was dislodged from his horse only to be scooped up by one of Siward's immediate family and placed onto the back of his own mount. That tradition claims that this then resulted in the grant of lands in Liddesdale and the name 'Armstrong' being bestowed in recognition of that individual's strength and bravery.

The first historical record of the name is from the middle of the 12th century when one Thomas Armstrong married Anne, the daughter of Sir John Cramlington of Northumbria. Other early records relate to Cumbria where William Armstrong married the daughter of the Bishop of Carlisle and in 1210 Adam Armstrong was appointed Verderer of the Royal Forest of Inglewood. The Verderer axe and Anglo-Danish sword feature on several Armstrong gravestones in the Borders and may serve to corroborate the oral tradition of a Viking connection with the name.

By the second half of the 13th century an Armstrong Clan was established in Liddesdale just to the north of the Scottish English border. The Clan chiefs became the Lairds of Mangerton, a location just south of today's Newcastleton. The Milnholm Cross overlooks that land and is a memorial to the second Laird of Mangerton, Alexander Armstrong, who was murdered at nearby Hermitage Castle in 1320. He is buried in the adjacent Ettleton graveyard. On the other side of Liddel Water lies the site of the old Armstrong Chief's family home, once a substantial fortified dwelling. That tower house was attacked, damaged, and rebuilt on several occasions over many years. The building is said to have carried the Siward emblem. Little remains of it today except for part of the basement and some low walls, along with a stone carved with the initials of Simon Armstrong, 9th Laird of Mangerton, who died in 1583.

The influence of England grew in the Scottish Lowlands after the Norman conquest. The Normans did not conquer Scotland but reached an accommodation with the Scottish Crown. This had the effect of pushing the Celtic traditions and Gaelic language to the north and west. Control on either side of the border with England grew to depend on a series of interlocking regional relationships. Military strength, together with the Church, played a role in determining which territory lay in England and which in Scotland. There were many disputes. The current border was largely determined by the Treaty of York in 1235 and involved a line being drawn from the river Tweed in the east to the rivers Liddel and Sark in the west.

To cope with wrongdoings across the Border a special legal

mechanism was created in 1248 known as The Laws of the Marches and was supervised by March Wardens. In essence, these laws required the return of fugitives from justice, the recovery of debt and the regular production of accused parties at ancient trysting places on the Border.

Between 1249 and 1596 the Laws of the Marches were in force. If an Englishman, for example, committed a crime in Scotland the Scot affected would complain to the Scottish authorities, they in turn would pass it to their English counterparts who carried out an investigation. If the charge was found to have substance the English authorities were bound to produce the person at a trysting place to answer the accusation. This comparatively civilised and legally based reciprocal arrangement worked, at best, intermittently.

Between 1296 and 1328 the so called Wars of Independence took place with incursions by English and Scottish military into each other's territory. This had the effect of destabilising the borderlands. The Armstrong clan in the 13th and early 14th century was powerful, generally law-abiding and respected. They were prominent in the service of the Kings of Scotland and England and had expanded beyond Liddesdale into the vales of Esk and Sark. An English record of the time claimed the Armstrong Clan could muster an army of 3000 horsemen. At the height of their power, the family presided over 80 fortified tower houses and 250 farms. The Clan motto was an indication of their then military status; *Invictus Maneo* meaning 'I remain unvanquished'.

In the latter half of the 14th Century there came a further dramatic change to the region with the impact of the plague (Black Death) between 1349 and 1420. Historians estimate that between a quarter and a third of all Scots died as a result of the pandemic. That, combined with constant disruption to settlements by marauding military forces, undermined the stability that had previously prevailed and led to a downward spiral into endemic criminality in the borders.

It was the start of reiving (robbing and plundering) with the Armstrongs playing a major part, given their local strength. Reiving involved armed groups on horseback raiding farms, often over the border, generally to steal livestock such as sheep, cattle and horses. Rape, violence and destruction often accompanied the attacks. Protection rackets were also instituted as a means of extortion and the word blackmail was first coined, mail being a contemporary word for rent. During that time, swathes of land between the rivers Esk and Sark changed hands many times between Scotland and England. The Crowns of each country exploited the turmoil and encouraged raids, until matters eventually got out of hand.

In 1528 the Armstrongs advanced from their base in Liddesdale and occupied the 'debatable lands', an area of about 40 square miles lying between Gretna Green and Canonbie. An attempt by Baron Dacre with 2,000 riders, failed to reclaim the land. Consequently James V of Scotland used Border laws relating to the debatable lands to hound the Armstrongs as well as other powerful clan families.

Johnnie (known as Black Jock) Armstrong of Gilnockie, second son of the Laird of Mangerton, was captured by guile and hanged without trial in 1530. A mass grave and memorial to Johnnie and his 36 men can be found in Carlenrig churchyard near Teviothead, to the south-west of Hawick. Things quietened down for a time but then border raids recommenced with Armstrong Clan loyalty fluctuating between English and Scottish monarchs.

Following the Union of the Crowns in 1603, when James the VI of Scotland became also James I of England, the Armstrong Clan chief was declared an outlaw. Archibald, 10th Laird of Mangerton, was in 1610 captured and hanged in Edinburgh's Grassmarket for raiding in England and stealing cattle from Penrith. Following his death all Armstrong Clan tower houses across the Borders were systematically destroyed. Archibald's young son fled into Cumbria and disappeared. Since then, to this day, the Armstrongs have had no acknowledged Clan Chief. The borders were subsequently purged and most other clan fortified houses destroyed. The debatable lands became the 'middle shires'. Many families, like the Armstrongs, were rounded up and despatched to Ulster with younger men conscripted to help fight wars in the Netherlands. Some of the Armstrongs escaped the purge and remained in the Borders as farmers or in local trades. Finally the 18th century land clearances removed most Armstrongs from their smallholdings and families were further dispersed.

The Clan's military might had finally been vanquished but the Armstrong name lived on and the clan motto, *Invictus Maneo*, took on a more personal imperative. Today an Armstrong Clan museum can be found housed in Gilnockie Tower, Hollows, a mile or so above Canonbie on the A7, just north of the border. The building is a recently restored tower house dating from 1520 and may have been the historical home of Johnnie (Black Jock) Armstrong. It sits by the river Esk in what was once the debatable lands, regularly fought over by England and Scotland. A little further up the Esk valley can now be found a large Buddhist monastery, hopefully bestowing lasting peace on a once troubled land.

Kinmont Willie

Born in around 1530, perhaps the most famous of the Border reivers, was one William Armstrong otherwise known as Kinmont Willie. Nicknames were commonplace then to differentiate extended family members who had not only the same surname but also forename, this a result of local family naming traditions. Kinmont Willie's notoriety resulted in a Border ballad devoted to some of his exploits. He is reputed to have lived in Morton Rigg Kirkyard, Tower of Sark, Dumfriesshire. He was the grandson of one of the men executed along with Johnnie Armstrong at Carlenrig in Roxburghshire.

Kinmont Willie and his offspring rode and raided on either side of the Border over many years. In August 1581 there was a typical raid into Tynedale when Armstrong, along with 400 of his men, led an attack at Haydon Bridge. Again in 1593 he, along with the Laird of Mangerton, led another raid to Tynedale and drove 3,000 animals back to Liddesdale.

The English Warden, the 10th Baron Thomas Scrope of Bolton, grew increasingly frustrated and complained that justice would never be done because Armstrong and the Scottish Warden were in cahoots.

In 1596 Kinmont Willie was captured by the forces of the English Warden of the West March and in violation of a Truce Day. On a typical Truce Day the attendees witnessing the criminal proceedings were granted safe conduct for the day, until the following day's sunrise. On this occasion, on the 17th March 1596, a Truce Day had been arranged at Kershopefoot, a trysting place in Liddesdale. Kinmont Willie was in attendance as a witness and neither the English nor Scottish Warden was present. He was riding home after the gathering and found himself pursued by 200 men under the command of Thomas Salkeld, who was Deputy Warden of the English West March and second in command to Lord Scrope. He was captured after a chase of four miles and taken to Carlisle Castle.

Walter Scott of Buccleuch on whose land the arrest had been made, protested to the English Warden. On 13th April, after Lord

Scrope had refused to release Armstrong and further diplomatic efforts failed, Buccleuch led a party of 80 men on a daring raid into England and broke Armstrong out of the castle.

Queen Elizabeth of England was furious that one of her Border fortresses had been broken into at a time when peace existed between England and Scotland. Her relationship with James VI of Scotland was tested and she demanded that Buccleuch appear at her court in person. James was caught between his desire to pander to his English benefactor, Elizabeth, and his allegiance to the Scots who were adamant that Buccleuch had done no wrong in rescuing a man who had been captured illegally. After their audience Elizabeth said: *"With ten thousand such men, our brother in Scotland might shake the firmest throne of Europe"*. This victory of outlaw over state was short-lived and marked the beginning of the end for both reiving and the power of the Armstrong Clan.

In 1600 Kinmont Willie attacked the village of Scotby with 140 riders burning property and taking prisoners and cattle. In 1602 he rode his last foray to the south of Carlisle and was believed to be still alive two years later. Legend has it that sometime between 1608 and 1611 he died, in his bed, of old age.

Baron Armstrong of Cragside

A more acceptable, to the establishment, William Armstrong arose in the nineteenth century. He was to ultimately become Baron Armstrong of Cragside and he acquired as his family seat Bamburgh Castle in Northumberland. He was born in 1810 and was educated at the Royal Grammar School in Newcastle. He became a lawyer but devoted considerable time to scientific research, so much so that he was elected to the Royal Society in 1843. Four years later he abandoned his law practice to devote himself to scientific experimentation, invention and then manufacturing. His highly successful business, based at Elswick Works, eventually employed 25,000 people in the manufacture of hydraulic cranes, ships and armaments.

He revolutionised the design and manufacture of artillery guns, in particular developing breech loading for efficiency and barrel rifling for improved accuracy. An early example of his parapet gun dating from 1862 can be seen in Elizabeth Castle, St Helier, Jersey.

Armstrong eventually gave his gun patents to the government and was rewarded with a knighthood in 1859 and peerage in 1887.

In 1894 he bought Bamburgh Castle. The site stood close to a village of that name, on an imposing volcanic rock outcrop overlooking the North Sea and in the distance the Holy Island of Lindisfarne. Its location had been chosen by Celts and then Anglo Saxons for their own fortifications. These were destroyed by the Vikings but the Norman invasion brought a more substantial edifice. Their building was the origin of Bamburgh castle.

Having fallen into disrepair it was restored in the 19th century, work developed and completed, including the magnificent King's Hall, by Baron Armstrong and his family. The castle is still the property of the Armstrong family, although open to the public, and is currently in the care of the Baron's family's fifth generation… one William Armstrong.

Many William Armstrongs

This section is devoted to following the Armstrong line of my family tree, though this is only one line of many that could be pursued in trying to understand family heritage. We each have four grandparents of different surnames, in turn their grandparents produce 16 surnames and then their grandparents, 64 names. So in just 6 generations, back to circa 1750, we are the product of 32 couples or 64 names. Go back a further four generations and you arrive at over one thousand names or forebears. The further back in time you travel, for those of common stock, the less certain you can be of definite succession because of the quality of contemporary record keeping. A UK full census began in 1841 and thereafter provided more reliable records of individuals, occupations, relationships, children, and their locations. National certification of births, marriages and deaths also began about the same time. Prior to that parish records are the main source of information. This was an era when the majority of families were rooted in a particular area. Families then tended to be much larger, but the mortality rate was greater. Naming traditions often led to repetition of forenames as well as surnames and with that tradition the possibility of error in tracing family trees grows considerably.

What follows is a summary of the family's Armstrong line as far as can be determined from available records. It starts with the parents of a William Armstrong born in Hawick in 1683, a few miles to the north of Liddesdale, and then eventually migrates to Kelso where another William Armstrong, born in 1799, decided to move to Edinburgh. He was a mason and my grandfather's grandfather.

William Armstrong was baptised in Hawick on 22nd October 1683. His parents were James Armstrong and Elizabeth (known as Bessie) Dickson. He married Abigail Hardie who had been born in Kelso and was baptised on 9th July 1682. Their first child John Armstrong was baptised in Roberton on 24th July 1709. John married Elizabeth (known as Elspeth) Leech, who had been born in Jedburgh and baptised on 21st February 1714.

They married in Eccles on the 20th of June 1728 and their son William Armstrong was baptised there on 5th September 1737. Elspeth's father, George Leech was present at the baptism. William married Janet Johnston, who had been baptised in Eccles on 4th January 1741. Their marriage was also in Eccles on the 11th of

June 1763 and their son William Armstrong was born in Greenlaw and baptised on 21st June 1773. William was their sixth of 9 children born between 1763 and 1781.

William became a mason and married Agnes Hamilton who had been born in St Boswell and baptised on 14th February 1779. They had three children the first of which, William, was born in Kelso and baptised on 5th January 1799. He too became a mason and moved to Edinburgh where he met and married Alison Ramsay. She had been born in Hedderwick near Dunbar in East Lothian. They married in Edinburgh on 14th November 1834 and by the time of the 1851 census lived in India Place, Edinburgh with their six children.

William, their eldest, was born in Edinburgh in 1838. He was, according to the 1851 census, an errand boy aged 12. At age 32 he lived in Arthur Street and was then a shop porter. On the 10th June 1872 he married Agnes Thomson in a Baptist Church, by which time he was an engineer's timekeeper. Agnes had been born in Edinburgh on 22nd September 1847 and at the time of their marriage she was an umbrella maker's shopkeeper. The 1881 census records that they lived in West Park Terrace, Edinburgh with their children William aged 7, John 5 and Ramsay 2. Ramsay Armstrong was my father's father.

Chapter 6
Scottish Seams

Ramsay Alison Armstrong was born on 20th February 1879 in Edinburgh and he was raised as a Baptist. The Baptist church is a branch of Protestantism dating back to the early 1600s. Its core beliefs were that salvation was by faith alone and that every person was accountable, and redeemable, before God. The ritual of baptism was seen to symbolise spiritual rebirth or re-generation and was therefore a matter of will and choice that only adults could make. Just as Jesus had been baptised by John the Baptist by total immersion in water, so the Baptists believed that baptism should be an adult public commitment to rebirth in Christ by total immersion.

Ramsay's childhood was spent in Edinburgh and Leith and he was one of at least five children. In 1901 he was an apprentice boilermaker. In 1906 he married Jessie Rosie and they had a child, William, both mother and child were to die before 1908. In November 1911 Ramsay married Margaret Ritchie. She had been born on 17th December 1886 in Forth, Lanarkshire and was the first born of 10 children. Her mother was a Catholic of Irish descent and all the children were brought up in that faith. At the age of four in 1891, Margaret was living in Loan street, Haywood (the street where 29 years later she would give birth to my father, William Ritchie Armstrong). At the age of fourteen she was a domestic servant in Biggar and continued to be employed in service when she moved to Edinburgh, where she met Ramsay Armstrong. The story of her parents William and Mary Ritchie (nee Travers) and their background follows.

Ritchie Family

William Ritchie was the illegitimate child of Ann Ritchie. She had been born in Lesmahagow, Lanarkshire, in 1845 to parents James Ritchie of Carmichael, who was a shoemaker, and Janet Lothian. They married on 9th August 1844 in Lesmahagow and had 12 children. Ann, the eldest, was a dairymaid when she had a relationship with George Fordyce, an agricultural labourer originally from Lamington, which produced a son, William Ritchie, on 11th July 1865 in Newbigging. George had been born in 1816 and was therefore 29 years older than Ann. She was only 20 years old when she gave birth to William. Ann later married Alexander McKenzie, a widower, and had a further three children.

Mary Travers's father Patrick Travers was born in 1836 in Ireland. By 1861, he was living in Braehead, Lanarkshire and was a coal miner. He married Margaret McGinn, who had been born in 1846 also in Ireland, in Carluke on 2nd June 1862. They had 8 children: 5 boys and 3 girls. Mary Travers was their third child, and was born in Braehead on 16th November 1867.

William Ritchie was twenty years old when he married Mary Travers aged nineteen, in St Patrick's Catholic Church in Stane, Cambusnethan, a suburb of Wishaw, on 3rd September 1886. At the time of their marriage, he was a ploughman living in Symington and she was a farm servant living in Wilsontown. Just 3 months after their marriage, their first child, my grandmother Margaret McGinn Travers Ritchie, was born in Wilsontown Terrace, Forth on 17th December 1886. At the time of the 1891 census the family were living in Loan street, Haywood and William Ritchie was then described as a coal miner. By 1901 the family were housed in Main Street, Forth, and William was listed as a 'van man'.

We know from the birth registration that a child, Margaret McGinn Ritchie or Meg, was born at Sunnybrae Cottage, Forth on 26th March 1907 to eldest daughter Margaret when she was 20 years old. Her own grandmother, Margaret Travers nee McGinn registered the birth and no father was named on the certificate. Meg was brought up by her mother Margaret's own parents, as if she were their child. In 1910, we believe Margaret Ritchie gave birth to a second illegitimate child, Mary Travers Ritchie; she was again brought up by Margaret's parents. Mary's marriage certificate of 1932, when she wed Robert Kettles, names her mother as Margaret but does not name a father.

At the time of the 1911 census, eleven members of the Ritchie family were recorded as living in a two room house in Forth, a room then being defined by the census as having one or more windows. Mary, the mother, was then 43 years old and the census indicates that she had had 10 children of which 9 were surviving. Three in the household were working: William senior aged 45 worked as a carter for a merchant, William junior aged 22 was a coal miner 'hewer', that is worked at the coalface, and John aged 14 was a coal miner 'drawer', responsible for moving coal underground. Three sons were at school Hugh aged 12, Edward 9 and James 7 and three daughters were at home; Annie 17, Mary 4 and Agnes aged one. Meg was on that census return and described as a granddaughter. Her mother Margaret was thought to be, at the time, living in service in Edinburgh. It is unclear where her second child, Mary, was then living.

Knowledge of Margaret's two illegitimate children was kept

from her second family with husband Ramsay Armstrong until well after Margaret's death. My father and his siblings only learned that some of their 'aunts' were in fact their step-sisters in late middle age.

Whether Ramsay Armstrong was aware of his wife's other children is unknown. Margaret's father William Ritchie died in March 1935 and her mother Mary in October 1941. Both are buried in Wilsontown St Paul's Cemetery.

Ramsay and Margaret Armstrong nee Ritchie were married in a Baptist Church in India Street, Edinburgh, on 4th November 1911, he then was employed as a cable splicer for a tram company. Margaret was 6 months pregnant at the time of the marriage and her Catholicism had lapsed. They had 5 children: Mary in 1912, John in 1914, Robert in 1916, William (my father) in 1920 and Ramsay in 1923. All were brought up as Protestants but not as Baptists; however my father was not baptised as a child and presumably nor were his siblings. The first three children were born in Edinburgh. The family then moved to Loan Street in Haywood, where Ramsay worked in the colliery, and their next two children were born. In 1929 the family were living on Quality Row in nearby Wilsontown. Two years later, when his eldest daughter married, Ramsay's job was described as a colliery blacksmith.

Scotland's Coal
The Glasgow area and the county of Lanarkshire were both rich in coal deposits. Early mines proliferated around the City but as the industry developed prices were pushed up by a cartel of coal mine owners. A solution required development of the local transport infrastructure and a canal was planned to the Monklands area, where good coal deposits were known to exist. The first length of canal was completed by James Watt in 1773 and as the canal network expanded the cartel was broken and Lanarkshire's large

coal industry was unlocked. Later development of railways further helped exploitation of the county's coal and iron ore deposits.

In 1910 220 of Scotland's collieries were in Lanarkshire and 45,000 men worked underground, with another 9,000 men and 1,200 women on the surface. That period was peak coal for the county and was followed by a protracted period of decline.

Following nationalisation of the coal industry, immediately after the second world war, the National Coal Board (NCB) concentrated mining development in Fife, Ayrshire and the Lothians, and many Lanarkshire workers were incentivised to move to these locations. By 1970 the county which had once dominated the Scottish coal industry was down to its last four collieries and with the closure of Cardowan in 1983 its long history of deep coal mining came to an end. Lanarkshire's coal seams had not been totally exhausted; opencast coal extraction, from the surface, can still be found today between Wilsontown and Haywood.

Haywood, now a ghost village, was where my father was born and was founded to accommodate workers at the nearby colliery. The local coal deposits were first worked by the Coltness Iron Company in 1862 and later by the Haywood Gas Coal Company. The type of coal mined was suitable for extraction of gas, the principal source of fuel for lighting in the nineteenth century and then later for heating and cooking in the first half of the 20th century. Coal heated in the absence of air gave off the (coal) gas leaving behind coke. The gas was stored in giant tanks or gasometers in many towns before being piped to homes and businesses.

In the 1891 Census, there were 23 rows (streets) in Haywood and its population stood at 1,200. By 1935, Haywood had virtually disappeared. Loan street, where my father had been born, was one of the last to be demolished. The church and manse buildings survived for a short time after the population had moved on to be close to their next source of work.

Life in Haywood

The coal face worker's lot was an 8 hour shift spent on his knees or side, depending on the height of the working chamber, at the coal seam. Tools of the hewer were simple: a shovel, pick and a mash, a double-hand hammer for breaking coal. The shift began with the men climbing into an aptly named cage. It dropped like a stone into the abyss. A drag on the rope and the cage slowed and suddenly bumped to a stop. What followed was a long walk, bent double, to the coal seam. The height of the face would typically be between 18 and 24 inches. As the face-man won the coal he threw it out onto the underground roadway where it was hand filled into a hutch, a box-like wheeled truck. Underground roads were created with tracks to suit the dimensions of the hutches, around three feet high and wide. The drawer then pushed it a distance, to be coupled up with the rest of the hutches. From that point trains of hutches were hauled out to the pit bottom. In early mining this was done by ponies with a 'pony laddie' in charge. Some of these animals never saw the light of day, the lucky ones were brought up to the surface on national holidays, strike days or lockouts. Ponies were still in use in Lothian mines until 1954.

It was brutal work, conditions in the confined darkness aggravated by a lack of good ventilation, worsened when shots were fired to blast out new coal deposits and dense clouds of smoke and coal dust filled the air. Lung disease was a common fate of the miner. The terms silicosis from stone dust and pneumoconiosis from coal dust were medical conditions only given labels in a later age. Knotted scabs along the backbone were common as the miner's back rubbed along the low roof or the wooden bars supporting it. Safety in the mines improved after the industry's nationalisation but it still remained one of the most dangerous occupations with high rates of accidental injury and major occupational health issues.

Women's lives at home were also hard. All water for cooking had to be boiled on an open coal fire with a movable iron swey (or bar) on which kettles and pots were hung. Few houses had a separate laundry room but in some cases a communal wash house was provided and individual families were allocated a day for their washing. When the family's pit workers returned home, they would be black with caked coal dust and sweat. Stour or moleskin trousers would be soaking wet and muddy. The zinc bath was placed on the hearth and filled with water heated on the fire for a succession of bathers to remove the day's grime. It was always the woman's job to clean up the mess and empty the dirty bath water into the open sheugh (or drain). The rag rugs would then be returned to the hearth and wet clothes hung up to dry in front of the fire. Miners received an allocation of coal as part of their remuneration, a practice which continued into the 1970s and 1980s. When the clothes were dry they were beaten and brushed outside the house. Boots were cleaned and left at the door to air.

Women started work early in the morning around 5am and would prepare a piece (or sandwich) box and tin flask for each of their menfolk to take with them to the pit. These usually consisted of 4 slices of plain bread, with cheese or jam as the filler and a scrape of butter. The flask was filled with tea. After the menfolk were away, the wains (children) were roused for school, fed and clothed for the day ahead. Depending upon the distance to school, more *pieces* might need to be prepared. In the evening the meal would often consist of soup, followed by boiled beef and tatties (potatoes).

Most women were responsible for the financial management

of the house, making sure the rent was paid and keeping the Cooperative book clear. If menfolk were ill and off work no money came into the household. Only if the family's situation became dire could they apply for Parish Relief. Later, Friendly Societies were established which in return for weekly payments allowed claims to be made if a doctor's note was obtained. Managing the house, and the usually large family, was a fulltime job and few wives held separate employment. A typical home consisted of one room, sometimes two, with on average six family members living there.

Ramsay and Margaret Armstrong moved to Haywood between 1914 and 1920. Margaret had lived in Loan street as a child, she was recorded as living there in the 1891 Census aged 4, with her parents and brother William. My father was born in Loan Street in 1920 and his youngest brother, Ramsay, three years later.

Both would have attended the village infant school. Here boys and girls were segregated, and the playground was divided by a wall. The children sat two to a desk. Lessons included learning multiplication tables by heart and reading aloud. There were bible lessons, from which Catholics were excluded. Playtime for the boys might include marbles, football, hide and seek, and cowboys. While there was no school uniform, better clothes were worn and had to be removed on getting home. The Headteacher, Mrs Lamie and her assistant, Miss Goddard, made up the staff. School was an extension of home and discipline ultimately involved use of the 'belt'. Away from school one of the children's contemporary chants was; *'Haywood is a bonnie place; It stands upon a hill; The only thing that's wrang wi'it; Is auld Jean Lamie's skule'*.

Haywood Wanderers, the local football team, were an intimidating outfit unbeaten at home for 14 years and regarded with local pride as 'the dirtiest team in Scotland', a reference to game play rather than cleanliness.

In 1922, the first Miners' Institute in Britain was opened in Haywood, built under the Miners' Welfare Scheme. It was a simple corrugated iron building with an asbestos slate roof. Inside was a wood lined hall, retiring rooms and toilets. Within a few years of its opening, the Haywood pit had closed.

At its peak Haywood had its own railway station, post office, police station, village hall and cooperative store. The nearby West Calder cooperative had opened in 1875 utilising disbanded union funds and was entirely in the hands of local colliery men. The cooperative in Haywood opened in 1894 and in Forth in 1925. As well as village stores the society gave a van delivery service to local homes. A former farmhouse became the Haywood's licensed hotel *Big Annies*, named after Annie Little the last landlady of the establishment. The ruins of that building contain a stone carving made by my father's brother Ramsay, who was also born in the village; *'Oh Annie wert thou here tae see, A waeful wumin thou wad be'*. The ruin was a regular destination, in later years, for older walkers from nearby Forth, bringing back for them memories of childhood days.

Wilsontown

In 1929 the Armstrong family moved from Loan Street in Haywood to Quality Row in Wilsontown, about three miles away. Wilsontown was named after the brothers Wilson who founded there in the 18th century a major ironworks. Their foundry depended upon local mineral deposits of iron stone, limestone, coal and fire clay. Problems of drainage had to be overcome to facilitate the mining of those minerals and this involved a great feat of engineering to divert underground water into the Cleugh burn (river).

Wilsontown is now a small hamlet but had once had a population of 2,000 with most of the menfolk working at the ironworks and adjacent colliery. The ironworks was founded in 1779 by three brothers: John, William and Robert Wilson. John and William were living in Cleugh House in the hamlet of Forkens. As the ironworks prospered, the name of Forkens was changed to Wilsontown. A second blast furnace, forge and rolling mill were added under Robert's management. Production was not only of pig iron but of iron used for shot, pipes, ballast for ships and the beams for steam engines such as those in the New Lanark textile mill.

In 1785 John and William, after a disagreement with Robert, bought out his share. This did not result in the harmony hoped for and the brothers continued to disagree about the running of the business leading to acrimony, litigation and, in 1812, bankruptcy. The Wilsons had brought experienced ironworkers, miners and tradespeople to Wilsontown. By the time that the business fell into bankruptcy there were 450 homes in situ to house the workforce. The ironworks even had its own company store and employees were obliged to use it for everything from food and clothes, to coffins. Nine years later the business was bought by William Dixon at a fraction of its former value. Production of iron was thereafter sporadic, closing for good in 1842, but coal extraction continued.

Quality Row and Pleasance Row were two of the main streets in Wilsontown with the latter at the entrance to Dixon's Wilsontown colliery.

After the collapse of the ironworks, coal mining became the main industry of Wilsontown, but remained small in scale until the arrival of the railway in 1860. As the lines extended, mining expanded to Climpy and Haywood. A further large Wilsontown pit was sunk in 1898 and it was here that, subsequently, many of my relatives worked. It produced high-quality metallurgical coke that was being used in the iron and steel industry elsewhere. Some of the Wilsontown pit workers broke the 1926 general strike and this caused deep divisions in the Forth and Wilsontown communities. Eventually the colliery was closed in 1955 when most of the economically mineable, deep coal seam was exhausted. However, privately owned companies continue to exploit some of the surface seams using 'open cast' methods of extraction. Wilsontown now consists of a few houses and an industrial heritage site that commemorates its once great ironworks. Also in Wilsontown is to be found what was St Paul's Church, now a holiday accommodation let, and its cemetery where many Armstrong and Ritchie family members are interred, including my grandparents.

Ramsay and Margaret Armstrong moved to Wilsontown in 1929 when my father was nine but in 1935 they made their final house move to Carmuir, a street in a new council house development in nearby Forth.

Forth

The name Forth is thought to originate from the old Scots for 'the open air'. Early inhabitants were handloom weavers and local trades, like blacksmiths, servicing the needs of those working on the land. Farming was focused on cattle and sheep rearing rather than crop cultivation. The village sits on higher ground overlooking the Lanark area to the south. On a clear day the hill Tinto is visible in that direction. The village is surrounded by settlements at Climpy, Braehead and Wilsontown, with Haywood, Woolfords, Auchengray and Tarbrax lying to the east of Wilsontown. All these, including Forth, were in the parish of Carnwath. Forth was the main beneficiary of migration as the surrounding villages fell into decline. The council built 754 new houses to accommodate the growing population. By 1951 half of the inhabitants of the parish were in Forth and its population had risen to 3217 from just 600 in 1901. Like Haywood, and Wilsontown before it, Forth was, in the first half of the 20th century, very much a proud mining community. The Miners' Welfare building opened in 1930 and survived until 1995. As the village grew cultural and recreational facilities were added with music, football and bowls given priority. The Wilsontown Masonic Lodge remained an important cultural centre even after much of that village's population had migrated to Forth. After World War II a branch of the British Legion became the social heart of the community with regular weekend evening performances of live music, often contributed to by some of the more musically gifted members of my Scottish family. With the closure of the Wilsontown pit and consequent loss of employment, Forth's population contracted and now stands at around 2000.

William Ritchie Armstrong

My father was given the Christian name of both his maternal and paternal grandfathers. His middle name was his mother's maiden name. He was brought up initially in Haywood and then Wilsontown from the age of nine, moving to Forth when he was 15 years old.

He passed his eleven plus examination and went to Lanark Grammar School, attending from 1931. He was a member of the Boys' Brigade up to the age of seventeen. The Boys' Brigade pre-dated by some 40 years the more famous Baden-Powell Scout Movement and had been founded in Glasgow by William Smith in 1883. On leaving school my father became an apprentice electrician at Wilsontown Colliery, Pit No 3, passing a qualifying course at the technical college at Coatbridge in 1938.

He was baptised by the Reverend Rae at St Paul's Church in Wilsontown on 21st March 1939. The timing suggests that this was prompted by the coming war. In April that year he joined the RAF and was then trained in aircraft electrical and radio maintenance at various bases around England. In November 1940 he sailed for Egypt via South Africa. By the end of December he was in Cairo, visiting the pyramids of Giza briefly, before moving on to Sudan with the No 1 South African Air Force Squadron. His diary dated November 1941 describes an enemy air attack on the base where he was stationed; *'reveille this morning was given at 4am by the AA (anti-aircraft) guns opening up on enemy bombers. As we had no shelter Lofty and I stayed in bed. The noise was terrific: the boomp of Bofors AA, the rat-tat-tat of Lewis guns and the crump of bombs some distance away. It was like hell let loose. After the fire had died away we crawled out to view any damage which might have been done. There was none. The bombs had dropped near the foot of a fortified hill three miles across the drome from where we were. I crawled back to bed and slept until 7am'*. From Sudan he moved to Abyssinia and a year later was in Benghazi. By March 1943, he was with the No 47 Squadron and then held the rank of corporal. He appears to have regularly sent home money to his mother. By April 1944, he was temporarily back home in Carmuir, before being posted to 120 Squadron at Ballykelly in Northern Ireland. A year later he was back home in Scotland to receive a 10 guinea award from the Wilsontown and District Welcome Home Fund. In April 1946 he was elevated to Master Mason at the Wilsontown Masonic Lodge.

After the war, when he was demobilised, a friend introduced him to Hadfield and Waterside mill where he sought employment and subsequently met my mother. His career there progressed steadily to senior production management by way of weaver, apprentice overlooker (production supervision) and work study officer. He stayed with the firm until the mill closed. Garside's had sold the business to English Sewing Cotton in 1968 and the new owner progressively transferred production to other factories before closing down what remained in 1976, bringing the mill's 200 year history to an end. My father then found employment with other local textile mills until his retirement in 1985.

Lanark Grammar School and New Lanark
Lanark Grammar School is one of the oldest schools in Scotland and can trace its roots back to foundation in 1183. It was originally a fee paying single sex school for boys. In 1884 a larger building enabled it to become co-educational and this is the school building which my father attended between 1931 and 1935.

The school's origin long predates the killing of the English Sheriff of Lanark in 1297, in an uprising led by William Wallace. Robert the Bruce became Lanark's Sheriff in 1303 and was King of Scotland from 1306 to 1329. He re-secured effective Scottish independence from England following the Battle of Bannockburn in 1314.

Lanark, or its near neighbour New Lanark, a village on the River Clyde a mile or so to the south of Lanark, also had a major claim to fame during the Industrial Revolution. Its location is in close proximity to the building occupied by Lanark Grammar School in the 1930s, when my father was in attendance. New Lanark was founded in 1785 by David Dale who built a cotton mill and housing for workers in partnership with Richard Arkwright. Arkwright had played a key role in the development of the cotton industry in Lancashire and later in Derbyshire. His invention of the spinning frame, a multi-spindle water driven machine, and carding engines were important steps in the development of large-scale manufacturing in cotton mills, at the birth of the Industrial Revolution.

The use of waterpower was key to this and the River Clyde was that local source in New Lanark. In 1800 Dale sold the mills, land and village to Robert Owen who was his son-in-law. Owen was a Welsh philanthropist and social reformer who greatly contributed to the development of New Lanark as a social experiment. In Owen's time 2,500 people lived in New Lanark, many having migrated from the poorer districts of Edinburgh and Glasgow. He set up an Institute for the Formation of Character and also paid particular attention to the 500 or so children living in the village. He opened the first infant school in Britain in 1817. New Lanark became celebrated throughout Europe, attracting many visits from statesmen, reformers and royalty. They found a healthy industrial environment with a generally contented workforce and a prosperous viable business. New Lanark mill village is today a UNESCO World Heritage Site.

In 1825 Owen sold New Lanark and left Britain for the USA to start the, ultimately unsuccessful, experimental socialist settlement of New Harmony in Indiana. He returned to London two years later where he continued to champion the needs of the working classes. His work led to, amongst other things, the development of cooperatives and the trade union movement.

Wilsontown Masonic Lodge St John 236
The true origin of the Masons can be difficult to distinguish from the mythological narratives that have been created over time. The group is believed to have been founded in Scotland under the reign of King James VI. The guild was part trade union and part trade body. It laid down standards that helped control quality in stonemasonry by both training and restricting membership. The first lodge was founded in 1598. The organisational foundation of the Masonic Order is the lodge, this is where meetings are held and membership administered.

In the 1640s Robert Murray was a major Scottish influence in the evolution of Freemasonry away from being simply a trade related organisation. Like the famous London City Guilds the trade protection criterion was at some point jettisoned and the masons became an exclusive, predominantly male, club or fraternity. Murray also helped create and reinforce the ritual and mythology which became part of Freemasonry's tradition, along with rites, regalia and secrecy. Beyond the lodge there is usually an overarching national body to which the local lodge is affiliated, but there is no recognised international body that holds authority beyond national level.

The Grand Lodge of Scotland is the relevant body for Scotland and its first Grand Master (Mason) was William St Clair of Roslin in 1736. His ancestor William Sinclair founded Rosslyn Chapel in 1456. What started as a 'working class' trade body/union was infiltrated by, and then led by, the aristocracy. The current Grand Master in Scotland is still of aristocratic heritage. In 1752 the first American lodge was founded and had George Washington as a member. Masonic emblems on the US dollar bill and elsewhere indicate the importance of masonic influence. The masonic ideal of the 'brotherhood of man' did not quite extend to Americans of African origin.

They eventually formed their own black lodges. By the 1950's 13 of the 33 Presidents of the USA had been freemasons. Back in Scotland in 1781 one of the famous sons of freemasonry was Robert Burns, his humble origin an indication that, in Scotland, working class men were still an important part of membership. His masonic contacts were influential in getting his poetry published. Burns and Scottish masonry are closely entwined right down to one of its famous international legacies, the Burns Supper. In Scotland, more so than neighbouring England, masonic membership retained a strong working class element; it is estimated that one in ten male adults there in the 1920s were masons. Wilsontown Lodge St John 236 was chartered in 1810, with the lodge being housed originally in the Wilsontown store.

This, in what was predominantly a mining community, perhaps an indication that the lodge was built on local mineworkers' membership. In 1851 it moved to a small hall behind The Inn in Main Street, Forth. It wouldn't be until 1926 that the lodge acquired a more substantial home on the other side of the same street. Following the ancient Guild format, membership of the masons was traditionally based on three degrees. If one's application to join was agreed by the existing membership one was admitted, with accompanying ritual, as an apprentice member of the craft. The next degree required knowledge being acquired and further ritual to reach journeyman or fellowcraft status.

The final stage with more knowledge and ritual resulted in elevation to 'master mason'. Criteria for membership of the masons varies by jurisdiction but generally requires belief in a Supreme Being. It is not a religious organisation in itself and is open to many faiths. In fact the discussion of politics and religion is often prohibited by local lodge rules. Other common principles or landmarks have eluded clear definition and there are many variants of masonic structure around the world. The 'Scottish Rite' variant, not necessarily applicable in Scottish lodges, has no less than 33 degrees.

A great deal of mythological history has been created in the masonic tradition, some parts more generally accepted than others. A common theme traces masonic history back to the Temple of Solomon and its chief architect Hiram Abiff. His murder is central to various aspects of ritual in which those seeking membership and elevation are required to participate.

The oaths of secrecy required have given rise to a number of conspiracy theories related to the masons over the years. Many of my Forth based Scottish relatives, over many generations, were active members of Wilsontown Lodge, participating in its annual public walk on 24th June, Festival Day of St John the Baptist, which visited the site of the first lodge building, Wilsontown store. My father became a master mason of that Lodge in 1946, shortly afterwards he moved to Hadfield and, as far as I know, never participated in any masonic lodge meetings in England thereafter.

My Scottish Family

Scotland played a major part in my childhood. My grandparents' role was less than that of my uncles and aunts. I have limited memories of my grandmother who died when I was 10 years old but from recollection, and what others recount, she was hard working and kind. She ran an evening newspaper distribution business for a number of years.

That involved receipt of papers en masse at 64 Carmuir and then organising home delivery paper rounds, employing, amongst others, many of her grandchildren. My grandfather was always a benign presence but his deafness and reticent nature did not invite any real closeness. An abiding memory of him is sitting by the coal fire, smoking his pipe and occasionally making use of a tin can spittoon.

My uncle Ramsay was always the main source of entertainment on our visits as children. He was no higher than four feet tall. The explanation given was that, as a child, his mother had applied to his side a red-hot poultice to cure some ailment. This resulted in an extensive burn to his torso, confirmed by a large scar on his side. It was thought that this shock to his system caused his growth to be arrested. I have no idea as to whether that explanation was true, but it was always offered as the reason for his diminutive size. It seemed also to affect his physical maturing. He did not shave, and his voice never broke in adolescence, otherwise, he was physically normal, just small in stature.

Mentally, he was intelligent and well read. An avid reader of mainly library books. Ramsay was the youngest child of five children born to Ramsay Armstrong and Margaret Ritchie. Their eldest was a daughter, Mary, then four boys followed: John (nicknamed Corrie, derived from the Gaelic for left-handed), Robert (Bert), William (my father) and finally Ramsay. John and Robert were coal miners. Mary married Tam Rae and in turn they had five children, two girls Margaret and Mary and three sons Ramsay, Robin and Tom. Uncle Tam and his son Ramsay were both coal miners. My father escaped Forth and the pit by moving to Hadfield. Uncle Ramsay, despite being able bodied, never took up any regular employment although he did hold some local menial posts for short durations. He lived with his parents until they died, then with his elder brother, John, who remained a lifelong bachelor. Ramsay in effect kept house for him. Most of the men folk were well read and intelligent. They were inclined towards left leaning politics and no doubt had an influence on my own development.

I was baptised as a baby in my grandparent's house in Carmuir alongside my cousin John, son of my father's brother Robert (Bert) and Hannah Armstrong. He was their third child after Anne and Robert. Before the age of one I was entrusted to the care of my grandparents while my mother gave birth to my brother Alan. Most annual holidays were taken in Scotland, initially by train, then by car. I remember on several occasions locking myself in the train toilet on departure from Carstairs, as it came time to say goodbye, not wishing for my tears to be seen – parting was such sweet sorrow. As I got into my teens I would travel up to Forth on my own, by bus or train, to stay with Ramsay and John, always visiting Averton where my Aunt Mary and Uncle Tam lived.

Armstrong and Ritchie Family Trees

The immediate forebears of Ramsay Armstrong and Margaret Ritchie follow.

Roots

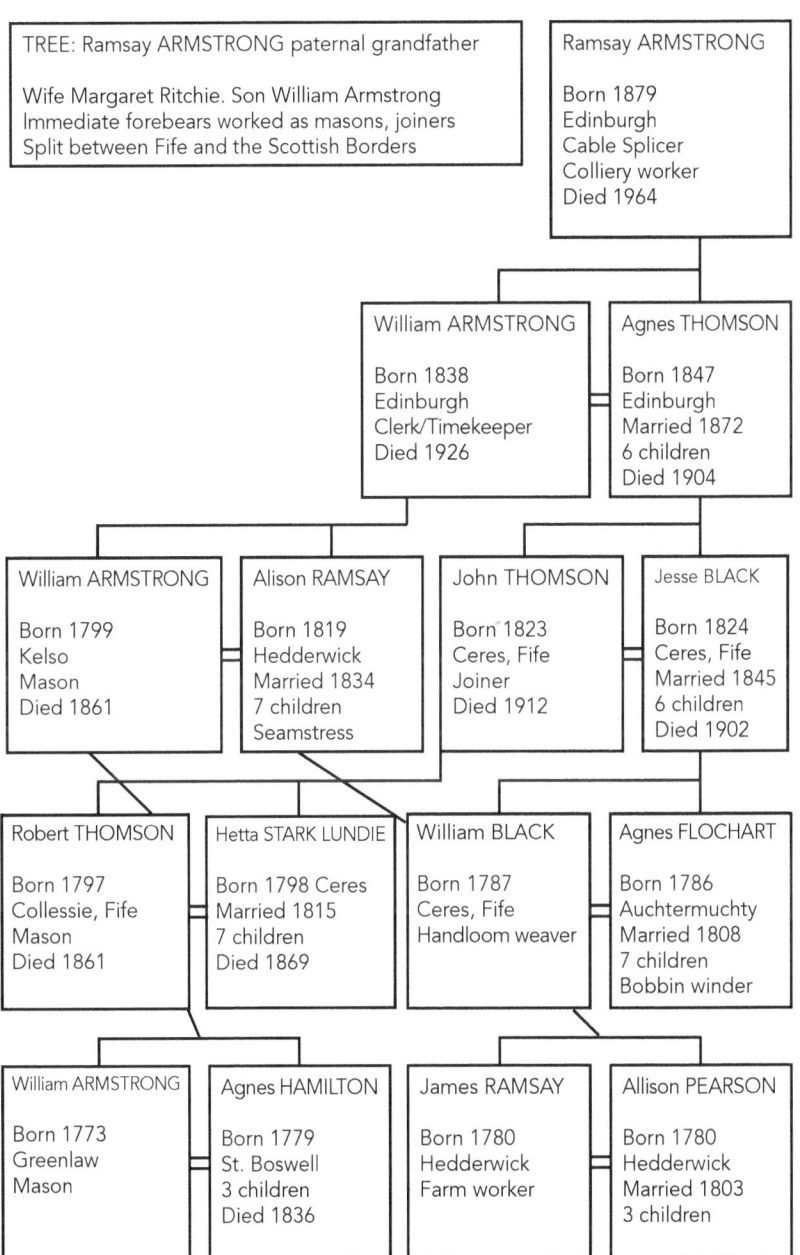

A Life in Perspective

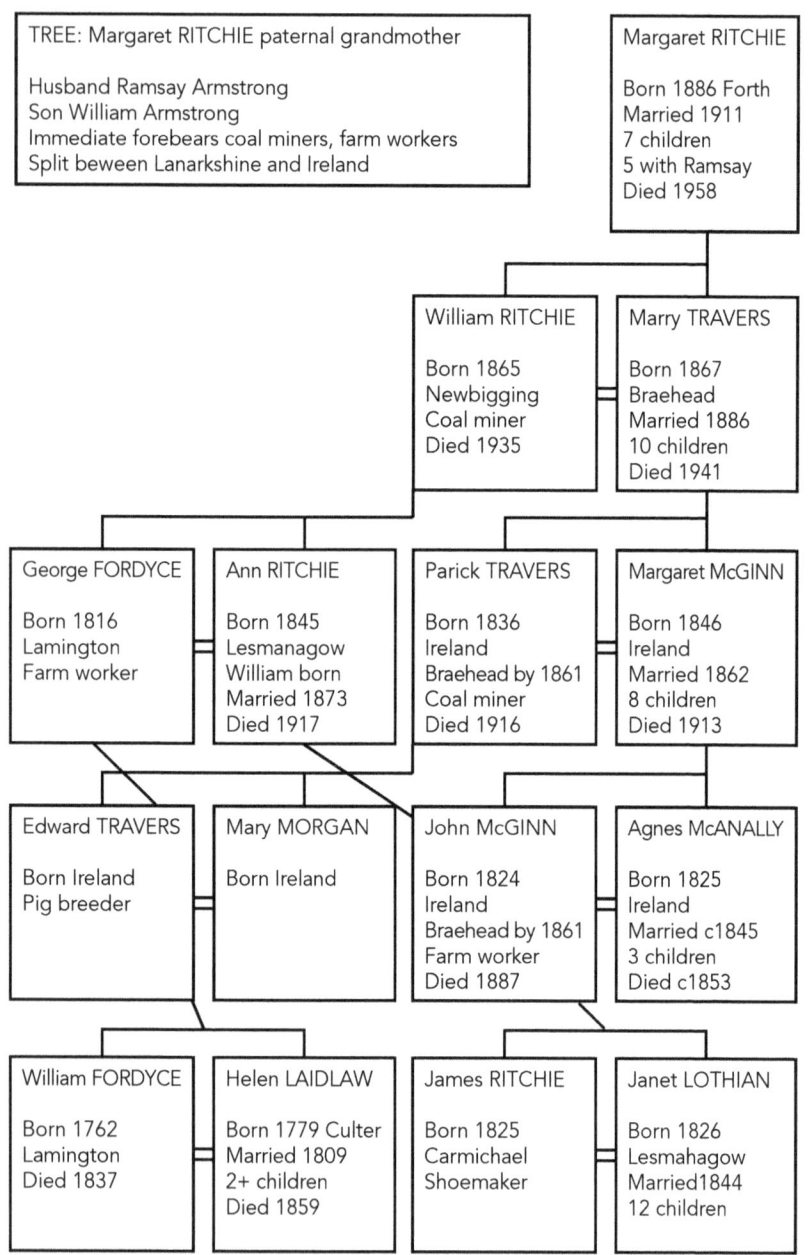

Part 2
Formative Years

Chapter 1 Leaving School, Finding Direction
Chapter 2 College, Career and Marriage

The period between 1964, when I left school aged almost 16, and 1972 when I married and joined the company Spicers, was an important formative stage in my life. I left school with little sense of future career direction. Socially I had never been out with a girl and was plagued by lack of confidence in relation to the opposite sex. This manifested itself in excruciating blushing episodes that in turn gave rise to thoughts of suicide. It was a period of intense introspection and through diaries and letters became the most contemporaneously chronicled part of my life. That reflective and written response was facilitated by my parents' move to a larger council house in 1964 which provided me, for the first time, with a bedroom of my own. It was here that my thoughts were recorded, with no detail too small to capture, and secreted from the potentially prying eyes of parents and siblings. These years saw schoolboy preoccupations morph into interest in current affairs and politics, folk and classical music, religion and philosophy, the latter then much influenced by Bertrand Russell's writings. Reading was my principal gateway into expanded interests but the political era unfolding under Harold Wilson led me to engagement with the Labour Party and to establishing, with one of my school contemporaries, Glossop Young Socialists.

The general lack of confidence I felt extended beyond girls to my comparative academic achievement and this eventually led me back into full-time further education in 1968. That was in part courtesy of the student grant system of the day. Technical college and polytechnic were the institutions that provided my further full-time education, albeit now vocational. That path led to meeting my future wife, B, and to my eventual move to Cambridge where I looked for work and found Spicers. This part of *A Life in Perspective,* drawing on my diaries of the day, chronicles in some detail those formative years that profoundly influenced the shape of my future life. It is divided into two chapters, one setting out the period after leaving school and the other after my return to full-time education.

Chapter 1
Leaving School, Finding Direction

Following my return from Norway I had a short break before starting my first job with a firm of chartered accountants in Manchester. That job prompted acquisition of a new suit priced at £13.6 shillings and raincoat £6. To become an articled clerk at the firm required commitment to the Institute's examinations and study by correspondence course. That course required more GCE 'O' levels than the five that I had acquired and so I undertook to re-take two of the papers I had failed at school. By the November date of those exams I had decided that I did not wish to return to the firm of accountants and instead wanted to follow my real desire, a career in the Royal Air Force. The passion for flying had grown throughout my childhood and may have been triggered by my father's wartime spell in the RAF. Newspaper articles on aircraft had been avidly collected, as had developments in space travel, with cuttings carefully mounted in scrap albums.

Observer books on aircraft and a subscription to *Flight* magazine were further sources of information. That solitary pleasure flight from Southport beach in 1962 may also have helped cement my passion. The interest was definitely about flying rather than any mission that the RAF might have. At the time you had to be 17 years old to join an RAF aircrew training programme but an application could be made in advance of that so, in the autumn of 1964, I applied for assessment at Biggin Hill in Kent.

Delivering Sausages

In the meantime I resolved to find a job without career potential that would pay reasonably well. I started at Walls' factory in Godley near Hyde on December 1st as an assistant salesman. The pay was £7.1 shilling a week. The role involved working with salesmen/drivers of vehicles based at the Godley factory that produced sausages, pies and other meat based products. Each van called upon a fixed round of retailers, in the greater Manchester area, whose displays of Walls' products were replenished from the stock carried on the vehicle. The salesman took the order and my job was to fetch products from the van and remove out-dated stock from the retailer's display. Most payments were then in cash and at the end of the day a reckoning-up was done that had to be reconciled with the balance of stock returned to the factory.

Each day, Monday to Saturday, I would leave home at 6am, take a train to Godley and on arrival at work be allocated a particular van for the day. I was home by 6.30 pm, sometimes earlier. The process of ordering, replacing stock and collecting cash was wide open to manipulation by the van salesman, often justified by the inability to balance the books at the end of the day. I worked with many different salesmen and quite a few succumbed to this temptation, involving me as the van-boy. Much of that manipulation came to an abrupt end, shortly before I left Walls, with the dismissal of two salesmen.

There was much talk, by other salesmen, of a strike in support of their sacked colleagues but that all came to nothing.

Writing Room

In October 1964 my parents' application for a larger council house on Whitfield Avenue was approved, their case no doubt helped by having three teenage sons. The new home was a semi-detached house at the top of the road with three bedrooms. I, as the eldest, was allocated the smallest bedroom which accommodated a single bed and small desk.

It was to become my haven. My younger brothers shared the slightly bigger room next door. The house-move was undertaken by physically carrying many items from our old flat at number 13 and my father obtaining use of a works vehicle for heavier items. My mother acquired a second hand cooker to supplement the Raeburn range installed at number 36. Our new neighbours were the Shawcross family. They too had had three children but the eldest boy had been killed in a bicycle accident outside our front door at number 13 sometime before we moved. Shortly after we moved my mother's sister, Doris, obtained a similar house directly opposite ours. The two families had arrived in Whitfield together in 1951 and made the transition from flats to larger houses together.

Also in October the first Labour Government for 13 years was elected under Harold Wilson's leadership. A sign of the times was his return to a Yorkshire accent from the clipped received pronunciation of his years as President of the Board of Trade in the post war Attlee administration. It felt as if a tide of working class opportunity was at last coming in. However, Labour's parliamentary majority was wafer thin and the deposed ruling establishment would prove ever adaptable in their quest for a return to power.

Flying Crash

On the 20th January 1965 I made my way by train and bus from Glossop to Biggin Hill in Kent for two days of tests and assessments to determine whether I was suitable for RAF aircrew recruitment and training. Two days later I made the long journey back to Glossop with my ambition and passion crushed.

The journey gave me my first taste of London, involving navigation of the tube system. I arrived at Biggin Hill at 1.30pm Wednesday and met some of my fellow candidates. I noted that a number had been members of their school's Air Training Corps, not something that existed at my school. We were subjected to 10 written and 3 physical tests over the next couple of days, as well as a medical examination. Tests involved hand/eye coordination and hearing. The medical included a test for colour blindness. On day two I was informed by the Medical Officer that my test results made me unsuitable for air crew and many ground crew roles. Would I still be interested in other possible roles? Yes. Then I faced an interview by the 'Board' who asked me lots of questions about myself and current affairs. Why did the RAF have a base in Aden and who was the potential enemy? I didn't have an answer for that. Eventually I was put out of my misery and told that I wouldn't be considered for recruitment and further training. I subsequently read that about 25% of candidates are recruited for aircrew as a result of the Biggin Hill process and then undertake 48 weeks of training. Of 20 student pilots at that time, and I do not know whether this was typical, 17 were from grammar schools, 2 from secondary modern schools and one from public school. I returned home despondent, my flying fantasy at an end. Back to reality and no clear path ahead. A small consolation awaited me, I had passed my History and Art 'O' level examination retakes.

On Monday I returned to Walls at Godley to discover which van route I had been allocated for the day. What lay beyond the wall of Walls was now a source of anxiety.

A Girl (pen) Friend

Besides writing up detailed notes of my experiences at the time I also found amusement in tape recording music from the radio using a reel to reel recorder purchased on hire-purchase from Currys. That involved 65 weekly payments of 6 shillings (30 pence). The music was largely of the pop variety, then all the rage amongst teenagers, occasionally I would venture to the Home Service for lighter classical pieces. My appetite for classical music had been whetted when I recovered an LP of Tchaikovsky's first piano concerto from our Paranjotti neighbour's clear out, as they prepared to return to India.

Dr Paranjotti was returning home to help in India's second (following partition) Kashmir war with Pakistan. The radio I used for recording gave me access to the shortwave transmission band which in turn enabled a much wider listening spectrum. In May 1965 I wrote to Mr Zee, host of a radio broadcast *Breakfast in New York* that I had managed to pick up. My letter was a plea for a 16 year old American teenager prepared to enter into a pen pal relationship with an English 16 year old. My bait was Glossop's proximity to Manchester and my letter listed all the pop groups from the area that might be known in the US, including Herman's Hermits and The Hollies. I did not hear it but Mr Zee must have broadcast my appeal, for within weeks I had not one but two responses from US teenagers, both, as luck would have it, female. Carolyn Kuster from Omaha, Nebraska and Linda Weiss from Durand, Wisconsin. The former correspondence lasted somewhat longer than the latter (Kuster's last stand) extending into 1967 and included the exchange of tape-recordings. It was the nearest I had so far come to sustained communication with a member of the opposite sex. Most of my eye-locking flirtations at work, or on the commute thereto, never got beyond staring and the occasional blush.

Putting things in writing, as opposed to verbal communication, would prove to be a lifelong preference. Self awareness of my introverted nature was growing, albeit then more often self-interpreted as an inferiority complex, however that consciousness did not lessen the anguish I felt at my inability to communicate with the opposite sex.

Home and Work

Life at home had its ups and downs despite my bedroom sanctuary, as illustrated by my diary entry of 25th May 1965, a Sunday. 'Woke at around 10.30 with the sound of shouting downstairs. Lay there thinking of the future and past. Would hurry-curry (*hari kari* or suicide) solve all? Got up at 11.30 washed, dressed and went downstairs. Told mum I would like to buy a casual shirt. I wouldn't have mentioned it had I known what the result was to be. I was cursed, slandered in the most revolting way. Accused of not giving her enough money, of saving £5 a week and was told to leave home as soon as possible. I was ignorant, furtive and the worst and lowest type of human. All this served to confirm my thoughts on waking about suicide or, at least, leaving home.' In contrast, three days later my diary records that I purchased a table lamp present for my mother's birthday at a cost of £4.10 shillings... 'mum seems quite happy with her present'.

Following the disappointment of Biggin Hill I applied for various jobs with career prospects, that is to join training schemes with larger employers. Those applications all failed, adding to my depressed state. In May my brother Alan applied for a mechanical engineering apprenticeship, to be taken up on his leaving school that summer. The firm was Mather and Platt, a large engineering company based at Newton Heath, north east Manchester. Its origin was in Salford in 1836 when two Mather brothers set up a business to supply equipment to the textile industry. Mather and Platt (M&P) formed in 1853 and evolved to become a manufacturer of pumps, dynamos and sprinkler systems, eventually adding overseas operations. Its move to Park Works, Newton Heath began in 1900 and it was to become an enormous manufacturing plant and major local employer.

In 1944 L.S. Lowry produced a painting titled *Factory workers going to work at Mather and Platt, Manchester in the snow*, a print of which I was to later acquire. Both Alan and I were to find employment at Mather & Platt, he as an engineering apprentice suited to his mechanical aptitude, I as a commercial trainee. My own employment there was thanks to my father's intervention following my various failed attempts at traineeships elsewhere. He had suggested that I write speculatively to the company following Alan's application, not only that, he drafted the letter of enquiry which I duly copied out and sent. He then drove me to the resulting interview. He had not planned to attend the interview but somehow did so. I have no doubt his interest and involvement helped me secure an offer of employment at the end of the interview, an offer I readily accepted. On the 28th of June my employment began, involving a journey by train to Ashbury's station and then a bus to Park Works. I was to enjoy my work at M&P but it was not to become the gateway to a career that I had then anticipated.

Driven

In May 1965 I applied for a provisional driving licence, at the same time as my mother, so that I could begin to learn to drive. Early lessons were with my father but by the autumn he booked for me a 10 lesson plan with Solly, the local driving school he had himself used. Also in the autumn Alan and I began looking around for possible transport that could take us both to and from work at M&P.

With our father's help in October we located a vehicle at the Three Wheeler Company. It was a second hand blue Isetta bubble car costing £85 and we made the £30 deposit to secure our first jointly owned car. The Isetta was of Italian design, had three wheels and was entered from the front by a single large door which opened to reveal a bench seat that could accommodate two adults. As the door opened, the attached steering wheel pivoted out with the door. It was left hand drive, suggesting continental European manufacture, and the gear stick was in the wall of the car. A 300cc BMW motorbike engine was in the back providing modest power but excellent fuel economy, approximating 100 miles to the gallon. The overall vehicle structure was 'bubble-like' with good all round visibility and it even had a sunroof. So our first car was to be a BMW, or so we declared to those easily impressed. The engine and power meant that the car was classified for driving and tax purposes as a motorbike which also helped insurance costs, first premium £8.13 shillings. It was to be a few months before I passed my driving test and teething problems with the vehicle were sorted. Alan's natural mechanical ability was to prove regularly necessary, helping compensate for my own lack of mechanical aptitude. By March I had passed my first, nerve-racked, driving test and we were regularly commuting to work in the Isetta.

However the car was not to survive 1967. On a return journey from M&P with Alan, as we neared home passing Turnlee paperworks, I misjudged our road position on a right hand bend, probably in part due to the left hand drive seating position. A car coming in the opposite direction may also have been too close to the centre of the road. It was a glancing blow but enough to rip off one of the two front wheels of the bubble car, so we were down to two wheels as the car veered across the road, fortunately avoiding any other oncoming vehicle. No injuries were sustained, other than my pride, but the Isetta was a write-off and third party insurance meant, after a long correspondence battle with the two insurance companies involved, that no recovery of vehicle value was obtained.

Petty Larceny

In the year after our move to the top of Whitfield Avenue an incident occurred, indicative of the times, and was duly recorded in a separate detailed diary entry titled 'Petty Larceny'. At 10pm in the evening, having finished watching *Panorama* on TV, I moved to the kitchen to make a toast supper before going to bed. The mains cooking gas had run out so I located a shilling (5 pence) to go and feed the gas meter, that being the way the gas supply was maintained. This entailed a visit to the house extension outside, adjacent to the back garden, comprising external WC and separately a coal-hole that was usually left unlocked and which contained the meter. I noticed that the padlock on the meter coin drawer had been broken off and the contents of the drawer removed. I called my father to be told not to touch anything to allow for fingerprinting and he and I went off to Glossop police station to report the break-in. We were informed a member of the CID would be up by 11.30pm. That did not happen but by 9.30am the following morning two CID officers did turn up and asked a lot of questions. A further visit occurred in the evening to take a statement from my father. I do not think that the investigation resulted in any arrest as two months later a neighbour's gas meter was also robbed, but the cash box was taken for fingerprinting. Householders were required by the gas supplier to make up any missing money. Worthy of note was the level of police attention. That compared with the current era when police may record burglaries and car theft but give up investigating half of all crimes without visits, often within

24 hours of notification, if they deem there to be little chance of making an arrest.

Grooming

A further separate diary entry in 1965 detailed the marriage of my cousin Tom Rae to Margaret Hassan in Scotland and my minor role in proceedings. The wedding date was fixed for Friday 24th September and was to be held in Wilsontown St.Paul's Church.

Tom's elder brother Robin was best man and I had been asked earlier in the year to be the solitary groomsman. That entailed some duties, such as reading telegrams at the reception, but also paired me with one of two bridesmaids, both younger teenage sisters of bride Margaret. Another frustrated infatuation was born.

The family travelled to Scotland on Thursday evening in good heart with lots of singing in the car and a fish supper en route in Penrith. When we arrived in Carmuir at 11.30 only Ramsay was home, Uncle John being on night shift at the pit and my grandfather having died in 1964. Sleeping arrangements were that much easier as a result. Early the following morning we decamped to my Aunt Mary's (Tom's mother) house on Averton.

There we found a very nervous Tom and some of his assembled family. I handed over my personal wedding present, of tablecloth and napkins, to receive in return cufflinks and tie-pin, as thanks for being a groomsman. Also I tried on for the first time, in trepidation, the morning suit that had been hired for me and was relieved when it fitted reasonably well. A bus arrived to take all the others gathered at number 7 Averton to the church.

Tom, best man Robin and I awaited the wedding car, downing a dram of whiskey to calm growing nerves. Robin dispensed pennies to the waiting kids as we exited the house, that being the local tradition. Wilsontown church was familiar territory, its graveyard containing the headstones of many generations of Raes, Ritchies and Armstrongs. Our arrival at the church was an opportunity for me to be briefed on what was to come, given that I had missed the rehearsal earlier in the week. A false start inside the church, with the first *Here comes the bride* having to be aborted, broke the growing tension.

Shortly afterwards Margaret did arrive on her father's arm and the ceremony got underway. It was soon over and we were accompanying the bride and groom into the vestry to sign the wedding register. My role to pair Mary Hassan, junior bridesmaid. That pairing was to continue at the reception held at The Royal Oak, Lanark, where following a meal, speeches and telegrams, the bride and groom took to the dance floor, shortly thereafter followed by best man and groomsman with allied bridesmaids. I may have held Mary in my arms, I may have felt her to be beautiful and graceful but I could not find that elusive small talk to put her or more importantly myself at ease. And that is how the evening proceeded, a groomsman unable to groom. A conflicted, infatuated evening of teenage angst. Even the alcohol intake seems to have made little difference.

Eventually, following the departure of the bride and groom, a return to Forth, where I found I was to be billeted at my Aunt Mary's house. A sleepless night ensued to be followed by a day of teasing on the morrow as family members came and went.

Somewhat relieved the evening came and as arranged with my cousin John, we went off on the bus into Lanark for a pub-crawl. John was the youngest son of my father's elder brother Robert (Bert), we were of similar age and in fact had been baptised/christened together as babies in our grandparents' home, 64 Carmuir. A latish return to Forth with John and to the *Miners' Welfare* for a last drink. On leaving there we were set upon by a group of lads who seemed more interested in getting John than me. The last I saw of him was a clean pair of heels as he outpaced the following pack.

The following day the family returned home to Glossop. A week or so later we were joined at Whitfield by the bride and groom after their honeymoon in Scarborough. A trip into Manchester with them and the following day a long walk brought the wedding adventure to an end and they returned to Scotland. My diary comment on their departure 'I think Tom & Margaret will make a great pair – I hope so anyway'. So it was to prove. They had no children, moved away from Forth for a number of years but returned in retirement, their house half a mile from that same Wilsontown Church, then decommissioned and a holiday let, and across the road from 64 Carmuir. Each year in retirement they holidayed in Scarborough. As older generations passed they and their house became the focal point for geographically dispersed family reunions, bringing folk back to their roots in Forth. I was very pleased to be able to attend in 2015 their 50th wedding anniversary celebration, held in the town's British Legion hall, along with a large gathering of family and friends. Tom and Margaret are likely to prove the last personal connection to Forth for the diaspora who attended. 'A great pair' indeed with their ever warm welcome and kindness to one and all.

Serial Murder

A short distance between Godley, Hyde where I worked for Walls in 1964/5 and Mottram in Longdendale, where LS Lowry lived between 1948 and 1976, lies Hattersley. With a population of around 5000 it is an overspill estate built by Manchester City Council in the 1960s. It is most famous as being the location of residence and arrest of Ian Brady and Myra Hindley in October 1965. Between

1963 and 1965 they are known to have sexually abused and murdered at least five children/teenagers. In October and December 1965 Brady aged 27 and Hindley aged 23 appeared at Hyde Magistrates Court for committal hearings in relation to the murders of 10 year old Lesley Ann Downey and 12 year old John Kilbride. Local newspapers reported that 'Chairman of the Bench Mrs Dorothy Adamson, a grey-haired woman of dignity, has been a JP (Justice of the Peace or Magistrate) for more than 20 years and is the wife of a local industrialist. When she has anything to say, which is rarely, she says it in a crisp businesslike way. She is supported by Mr S B Redfern, a retired baker and confectioner and Mr Harry Taylor, a retired trade union official. Both are grey haired, soberly dressed and quietly attentive.'

They and those members of the public able to gain seats in court would hear details of some of the most despicable and sadistic crimes ever to be reported in an English courtroom. Hattersley and Saddleworth Moor, a few miles to the north, where bodies were buried, would thereafter always be associated with the notorious Moors Murders.

The magistrates passed the case to Chester Assizes (now Crown Court), Hyde then being in Cheshire, to be tried the following April. There the jury took little time to find Brady and Hindley guilty as charged. That was made easier by Brady's hubris. He had developed a taste for reading about depraved acts from history and created a small library of such material. This he used to educate his co-worker Hindley who became increasingly infatuated as the relationship developed. He became obsessed with committing the perfect murder. Hindley was to play a vital part by enticing victims into her car and leading them to their fate at Brady's hands. Not satisfied with rape and murder Brady took satisfaction in photographing victims and burial locations. He also tape recorded the final moments of Leslie Ann Downey as she pleaded for her mother. A suitcase containing all this material was recovered from a left luggage office that Brady no doubt thought was a secure location, as part of his perfect crime fantasy. His attempt to co-opt Hindley's brother-in-law, first with reading material, then with involvement in a murder led to his downfall when David Smith went to the police.

The death penalty being ruled out, having just been abolished, both perpetrators were given 'life' sentences. Life can mean many things under English law, not necessarily life. After 19 years in prison Brady was belatedly diagnosed a psychopath and transferred to a secure hospital. He never sought release from incarceration but did seek transfer back into prison. In part he believed this might facilitate his suicide by hunger strike, or other means, whereas in hospital he was watched and forced fed. He died of natural causes in 2017. Hindley constantly sought release from prison, unsuccessfully, with politicians periodically intervening to extend her sentence, as was then allowed. She died in 2002, was cremated at Cambridge crematorium and her ashes scattered in Stalybridge country park, a few miles from Hattersley, by her lesbian ex-prison guard lover. The relatively new Hattersley estate house where Brady and Hindley murdered and were arrested was finally demolished in the 1980s.

At the time and for many years thereafter, as more bodies were sought on the moor, these crimes deeply disturbed not only the local community but a much wider segment of the population, raising, as they did, fundamental questions about the nature of evil. Another local case later added to those questions.

Hyde and Mottram, either side of Hattersley, were again to feature in another notorious case of serial murder which came to light in 1998. That case involved perhaps the most prolific killer in British criminal history. Harold Shipman, a general practitioner or doctor, working in Hyde from 1977, was retrospectively believed to have killed around 250 of his patients, in the main elderly women. He committed 'perfect' murders over a period of 20 years or more without suspicion being aroused. Eventually he was reported to the local coroner, by a worker at his practice, because of the disproportionately large number of his patients, relative to other doctors, who died and were then cremated.

That police investigation got nowhere, however later that year, following the death of yet another patient and the uncovering of a forged will, he was finally detained. At the time of his arrest he lived in Mottram. He was convicted in January 2000 of having murdered 15 of his patients and sentenced to life imprisonment. The public inquiry that followed revealed that he had been prosecuted in 1976, following his first spell as a GP in Todmorden Yorkshire, for drug offences, including the forging of patient prescriptions to feed his addiction to opioids. Subsequently the regulatory body responsible for registering doctors, the General Medical Council, decided against striking him off their register. His killing spree may even have predated his Todmorden employment when he began his medical career in Pontefract General Infirmary after graduating in medicine in 1970. For the vast majority of the killings his motive remained unclear. He had the means, the opportunity and the power and the latter may have been key. As it might also have been in the case of Brady who described, in retrospect, his murder spree as 'merely an existential exercise'. Shipman was not deemed insane and four years after conviction managed to hang himself in his prison cell.

Forlorn Infatuation
My detailed teenage diaries contain numerous entries describing frustrated feelings for pretty girls seen at work or on the commute

to and from work. My bridesmaid-groom experience at Tom and Margaret's wedding was typical of the pattern. The interest was not, consciously at least, sexual in nature. It was of the unrequited, romantic love variety. Solace was found in books like Henry Williamson's *Dandelion Days* and *The Dream of Fair Women*. The intermittent correspondence with American penpal Carolyn Kuster had little or no effect on my confidence with the opposite sex.

One particular infatuation lasted around three years, all without any real engagement with the object of my adoration. The first record of my seeking out the 'blond goddess' on the Ashburys to Glossop train was in November 1965. This entailed boarding a particular carriage where she might be found. The young woman was tall and slim, had shoulder length blond hair and classical high cheekbones. I was smitten. On that particular journey my diary entry noted 'our eyes met' but 'who knows what goes on beyond that mask of bronze'.

On leaving the station I noted the direction for her homeward walk but that was it, other than periodic sightings on my commute, with the occasional locking of eyes. By March 1966 I had become much more involved with the Labour Party and was part of its General Election canvassing team in Glossop. Canvassing simply involved knocking on doors and asking whether the occupants were likely to be voting Labour, this to facilitate getting out our vote on election day. Part of my patch was the street I had seen my blond goddess head for, on leaving the station. That filled me with hope, hope that came to fruition when she opened the door to my knock. She was called Margaret and lived with her parents. The conversation did not extend beyond my official Party enquiries and a query she raised regarding her parents voting eligibility, given their recent move to Glossop. Three months later I was to see Margaret with her little boy at the station and then later arm in arm with what I took to be her partner. She boarded the train, chose to sit opposite me and waved goodbye to him. 'My eyes looked out of the window, but I did not see'.

A year later my infatuation had not dimmed when I found her on the train and saw that she was pregnant, my diary concluded wistfully 'I guess married life must be suiting her'. A further year on from that I saw her in the Labour Club, by then a regular haunt for me, this time with what I took to be her mother. Again no words passed between us and I avoided making eye contact. Colleagues at the bar commented on my quietness, this I managed to divert by attributing it to a stomach upset. I will never know what Margaret made of the strange boy, quite a few years her junior, patently infatuated with her. Maybe pity is the best that can be hoped for. In some ways the unrequited obsession was reminiscent of another I experienced at infant school with Mary. The failure of confidence and engagement resulted in much torment and anguish. Also a real despair that I would never surmount the mental barrier built, over so many years, between myself and any member of the opposite sex to whom I was attracted.

Politics and Reflections

Labour was elected to govern in the autumn of 1964, after 13 years in opposition, with a tiny majority in the House of Commons. In February 1966 I attended my first Party meeting involving volunteers in the All Saints ward of Glossop where I lived. It introduced me to local activist Ken Bracewell with whom I discussed the possibility of setting up a branch of Glossop Young Socialists (GYS). Later that month I linked up with two old school friends, John Slinger and Steven Cavanagh, who expressed interest in starting up a GYS branch. That was all put to one side, at month-end, when Prime Minister Harold Wilson, frustrated by his small parliamentary majority, called a general election for the end of March. It was then a question of all hands to the pump and I became actively involved in canvassing Labour support wherever required in Glossop.

The town was part of the High Peak constituency covering north Derbyshire, rural with the exception of the Glossop, Buxton and New Mills conurbations. It was a constituency that had regularly returned Conservative MPs since the popular decline of the Liberal party after the first world war. Glossop based industrialists had once monopolised the seat. Samuel Hill Wood was Conservative MP from 1910 to 1929 and before him Oswald Partington had held the seat for the Liberals. Peter Jackson was Labour candidate for the 1966 election and I was to meet him on a number of occasions during my canvassing duties. Glossop Labour Club was the main meeting point for party workers and became a regular personal watering hole over the next few years. The general election result was a resounding victory for Harold Wilson and his parliamentary majority mushroomed to almost 100. Not only that but High Peak was to have its first ever Labour MP in Peter Jackson. The local Tory vote actually increased on the 1964 result but a collapse in the Liberal vote gave Peter a slim majority.

Local party morale soared and I was drawn further into that community which included members, councillors, aldermen and the MP's constituency agent. Through it, and Ken Bracewell in particular, I was introduced to folk music and local clubs. Organising folk music evenings became a fund-raising precursor to forming Glossop Young Socialists in the spring of 1967, initially under John Slinger's chairmanship, then mine. That entailed joining the party and organising both meetings and fundraising activities. I was also a regular attender at Hyde Folk Club, whose resident group were the excellent *Pennine Folk*. One of their most notable evenings included guest artists *The Corries*, a Scottish band of national reputation, my diary entry of May 18th gave a fulsome review of that 'wonderful evening'. GYS folk evenings were not quite in that league but were a source of funds and recruitment. We struggled to gain membership but a high point was the unscheduled appearance of Peter Jackson MP at our June meeting and his agreement to become GYS President. Also in June John Slinger and I attended a regional Young Socialist weekend school in Blackpool where we were exposed, for the first time, to more radical elements in the party's youth movement.

The Labour victory in 1966 had been despite the Conservative Party moving away from its normal, privately educated, aristocratic leaning, leadership. Edward Heath was a grammar school boy, not exactly with a 'common touch' but definitely a reflection of changing times. The Labour administration enabled a number of significant social reforms. The death penalty was abolished, male homosexuality decriminalised and divorce made easier for ordinary people. Vocational education was boosted with the establishment of 30 polytechnics and adult further education enhanced by the creation of the Open University. A move away from the eleven plus examination for children got underway and many grammar schools became comprehensive schools.

These changes were made despite significant economic turbulence. Balance of payment deficits and their financing implications led to a devaluation of sterling relative to the US dollar. This, in an era of fixed exchange rates, was one means of correcting overseas trade imbalance, by reducing the prices of exported goods and increasing the price of imported goods. It was regarded as a national humiliation by many and particularly the Tory dominated press. Similarly Wilson's explanation of the mechanism, to the economically uneducated general population, and statement that devaluation did not mean a fall in value of the 'pound in your pocket' was lampooned as a 'lie' by the press, because of the increased cost of imports. Inflation, as measured by the Retail Prices Index (RPI), did increase in the two years after devaluation to an average of 5.3% per annum but that compared with an average of 4.1% in the two years prior to devaluation. So a 15% devaluation of sterling had a marginal impact on the 'pound in the pocket' of consumers. Fifty years later, with floating exchange rates and governments 'printing money' indiscriminately, economic prudence had disappeared and the mainstream press was silent.

Wilson accepted the UK's diminished economic and military role in the world and saw the increasing importance of the continental European economy, in particular the growing strength of the Common Market, powered by France and Germany. His attempt to join that club was spurned by France, then led by Charles de Gaulle, who famously said *'non'* to the country that had provided him with a home in exile 25 years earlier. Ted Heath would later prove more successful in cultivating French approval.

As well as facing up to the economic reality of the time Wilson was also more realistic about the UK's diminished military significance in the world. He dispensed with some of the remnants of the British Empire, for example abandoning the military colony in Aden, unfortunately too late for my unsuccessful Biggin Hill interview. As the UK empire shrank so the US empire grew and serving the new empire provided consolation to a British establishment reluctant to accept its lessened status in the world. Wilson was not of that establishment and was the only post World War II British prime minister to decline to provide the US administration with the 'legitimacy cloak' it frequently sought when embarking on overseas interventions. He refused to provide military support in Vietnam, much to President Lyndon B. Johnson's displeasure. By the time of the next lengthy Labour government of 1997, ironically under a privately educated Tony Blair, support for US intervention in Iraq would receive uncritical UK involvement, regardless of its legality under international law. That intervention, widely applauded by the UK national press of the day, was to permanently tarnish Blair's political reputation.

My involvement with the Party continued over the next few years as Labour's fortunes deteriorated from the high of the 1966 general election. Seats were lost in both local elections and by-elections with the occasional bright spot. One such was the by-election victory of Ken Marks in Gorton, between Hyde and Manchester, over Winston Churchill, the grandson of his namesake. The latter had attracted a lot of 'big gun' support from the Tory hierarchy which Labour had matched along with a flood of ground troops from the surrounding area, including a contingent from Glossop. A close result, involving a recount, meant the final declaration had to wait until 12.15am. I was in Gorton Labour Club for that and the subsequent singing of *The Red Flag* as the new MP Ken Marks arrived shortly after the count.

Meanwhile that day Labour began its long retreat in Scotland with the loss of the Hamilton by-election to Winnie Ewing of the Scottish Nationalist Party. That was to mark the beginning of the end of Labour's political dominance in Scotland, the rise of the SNP and subsequent long term trend towards Scottish separation from the UK. That trend continued despite the 1990s Labour government's attempt to head-off independence by a referendum and subsequent implementation of a devolved administration for Scotland. If anything that only served to strengthen national identity, despite the UK Prime Minister Tony Blair and his right hand man, Gordon Brown, being Scottish born.

Blair had announced on his arrival in Downing Street that his government's priorities would be three 'education, education and education'; that being seen as the road to the empowerment of the working class. One of his priorities was to expand university places and make higher education for the majority the norm. That educational aspiration was more oriented towards the academic rather than the vocational. Many polytechnics and technical colleges became universities. Gradually, obtaining a degree became the expectation of many if not most school children. Funding this student expansion was to entail the taking on of personal loans so that most working class students, unable to depend on their parents, ended their degree courses with a large debt.

As expanded universities chased student numbers so entry requirements were to effectively fall, this in part facilitated by an inexorable trend towards examination grade inflation. The law of unintended consequences came into play. Deteriorating educational standards and large numbers of graduates expecting their education to be a springboard to a better paid career found that no such opportunity awaited them at their course end. Only the reality of an enormous debt. Similarly it can be now argued that the effective abolition of grammar schools deprived brighter working class children of a route out of more mundane employment. That is not to justify selection at age eleven but to acknowledge that the general watering down of standards was a result of the prevailing motivation that no pupil be regarded as a failure. Ironically private schools having dominated the higher echelons of the establishment and then been in retreat in the 1960's and 70's. found themselves once again in the ascendant. This in an era of apparent social mobility and meritocracy, thus proving true that perennial proverb; the road to hell is paved with good intentions.

Mather and Platt

I was employed as a commercial trainee at Mather and Platt in June 1965. That involved rotating through a number of administrative departments at Park Works and being given one day a week, plus evening, of vocational training at Manchester's College of Commerce. I sought advice from the head of M&P trainee administration as to what I should study and was recommended an accountancy qualification course involving the examinations of the Association of Chartered and Certified Accountants. Accountancy had and would be a recurring, yet almost reluctant, theme in my career development from leaving school up to and including my employment at Spicers. Ironically, or maybe predictably, by the time I finally completed a recognized accountancy course in 1977 my Spicers' employment had moved on to commercial operations.

My work as a trainee at M&P was mundane and generally involved repetitive tasks in various departments, however I gained knowledge of some of the administrative work necessary to support a large manufacturing concern. The pay scale of the nine trainees then employed started at £6.10 shillings a week at age 17 rising by annual increments to £13.5 shillings at age 23. My brother Alan joined M&P on leaving school a few weeks after my arrival. He was an apprentice mechanical engineer and subject to a different regime, shop floor based. An incident on that floor's 10 Bay in late October received both an office perspective, then a shop floor view courtesy of my brother. An ambulance arrived at Park Works at 12.30 and our office was told that a young man had been killed in a factory accident. That came as a shock. On seeking out Alan that afternoon on 8 Bay more detail was added to that nondescript word 'accident'. A 19 year old lad's overalls had got caught on a rotating boring machine table, that table had then dragged him around four times smashing his body against steel supports. The foreman had had difficulty switching off the machine as the boy's body kept knocking him back. A number of workers who saw the boy's battered head and body, when the machine was eventually stopped, fainted and were sent home. Alan fortunately had not seen the aftermath of the accident.

By the following March, having passed my driving test, Alan and I were commuting into work using the Isetta bubble car. It was an exciting but not necessarily reliable means of transport and Alan's skill was frequently called upon to keep us on the road. Spring also brought my first exam results from the College of Commerce. Rather than book-keeping it was in law that I excelled, topping the class with 70%. A year later my enthusiasm for the course had dimmed, as had my work rate. In January 1967 I decided that I would drop out of the accountancy course and consider a career in a more socially worthwhile field. An application to the Blood Transfusion Service got nowhere. In a subsequent discussion with the head of trainees at M&P it was suggested that I stick with day release from September but take an HNC conversion course. The Higher National Certificate in Business Studies was a vocational qualification that could be studied for part-time. Completion of the conversion course was a one year alternative to gaining an O(ordinary)NC over two years. The training manager also undertook to remove me from the trainee scheme and find me a permanent job. That resulted in a move to a relatively new M&P division, Contracting, at the beginning of May 1967. A couple of the draughtsmen there, with whom I shared an office, were keen trade unionists and I felt at home. I was even co-opted into the department's football team for inter-departmental competition, described on the locally generated match programme as 'a young, fast, fiery winger, not afraid to cut in and score goals'.

In July 1968 I received a psychological boost when I received my HNC conversion course results. They were much better than I expected; law 80%, economics 81% and accounting 84%. For reasons not clear to me the College of Commerce advised that I would be unable to progress that autumn to the HNC course I had planned to pursue, I would be obliged to wait for another year. This was a disappointment so I explored another option of doing an HND (diploma) sandwich course instead. This entailed continued employment for a segment of the course but then required full time study for the remaining segment. It transpired, however, that M&P would not support that option. A flurry of activity during the summer resulted in my winning a place on a full-time, two year, HND course in Business Studies at Stockport Technical College in September. That was enabled by my obtaining a state grant to meet tuition fees and maintenance costs.

The parting from Mather and Platt after three years was sad but I was excited at the prospects of becoming a full-time student and obtaining what I regarded as a significant vocational qualification. My diary entry on departing M&P captured the moment; 'I have enjoyed my last 15 months in Contracting. I've been given a great deal of freedom to impress my own ideas on an embryonic organisation. I would like to have grown with the department but always nagging away at me has been the feeling of dependence on M&P. I need some good solid qualifications to back me up and give me interfirm freedom.' By a series of unplanned and unforeseen circumstances I found myself back in full time education, now aged twenty.

Family Matters

Besides obtaining a grant my decision to become a full-time student was made easier by my brother Philip leaving school. He obtained from Glossop comprehensive school, as it was then, the necessary GCE 'O' levels to secure employment with Lamport and Holt and a potential career in the merchant navy. That was a relief given that two years earlier my diary recorded that he had received a beating from my parents as a result of their discovering that he had not only been playing truant from school, but entertaining his absconding friends in the house. Philip had an independent nature which he was to retain throughout his relatively short life. His navy career removed a source of cost from home life as did Alan's employment income from M&P. This made my decision to stop working easier as that involved the removal of my modest contribution to family coffers.

In July 1968 Philip returned from his first sea voyage which had involved travel to exotic South American destinations. In Buenos Aires he witnessed the death of a shipmate who fell from a gangplank, but that experience did not dim his enthusiasm for a seafaring life.

The navy gave him access to cheap cigarettes and alcohol and he took full advantage of both those benefits. Maybe the latter contributed to his relatively short naval career. By the time he returned home a couple of years later he was effectively an alcoholic and that he remained thereafter, despite several attempts to break free. Philip was widely read, courtesy of Glossop's library, and inherently intelligent. Whether failure to get into grammar school at 11 years old blighted his life, or access to cheap booze in the merchant navy, no one can say. In the end he made the choices he did and rarely, if ever, complained about his lot. He never, to my knowledge, had a girlfriend, nor did he seem homosexually inclined. Alcohol helped him mix socially, as it did for many an introvert, but at some point it took control of him. He was never aggressive when drunk and was by nature placid and undemanding of others, requiring of them only freedom to tread his own path without interference.

Alan was also introverted by nature. Whereas Philip read widely and was politically inclined Alan was more practically oriented. His love was for all things mechanical and he would spend countless hours over the years on scooters, motorbikes, bubble cars and cars, the workings of which were a complete mystery to me should they fail to do what was expected of them. He was to complete his apprenticeship and satisfy his vocation in a career involving machine maintenance in factory settings. Girlfriends came late for him but he was fortunate to find in his second serious relationship a partner, Carol, who would prove a lifelong anchor for him. They settled down to live in Glossop, buying a house in Wood Street, and did not have any children. Alan developed health problems in late middle age that resulted in early retirement and a premature death.

My mother had been the youngest of the seven surviving children that her parents produced. She spent much of her adult life estranged from her father, her mother having died a few months after her marriage. She had grown up close to her elder sisters and in particular to Doris who was the next eldest. She was not intellectually inclined, rarely if ever reading a book, but was physically and mentally strong. She displayed honesty, determination, courage and common sense. She played hockey into her twenties, worked hard most of her life despite having to bring up three children, all born in quick succession. She rarely felt sorry for herself and was proud as a person, preferring not to show vulnerability. Occasionally she would break down and that was always painful for me to see and brought out a protective response. That loyalty was occasionally undermined if she favoured my brothers over me, particularly when I may have believed that I was doing something in her interests rather than my own. She had been brought up in childhood under a regime of physical retribution for wrongdoing and that same mentality carried through into her method of managing the transgressions of three, often squabbling, boys. She was not a gregarious person by nature but had at various stages a limited number of reasonably strong female relationships. She was much loved in Scotland, drank in moderation and smoked cigarettes from an early age, as was then the norm. Her health was generally good until her 50s when various ailments began to manifest. She was to die aged 63 following a series of strokes.

My father was of a more intellectual nature and much less physically inclined than my mother. He was the penultimate child of five born to his parents. Two of his brothers were also more academically inclined, his sister and other brother less so. He was a conscientious worker who advanced his career by vocational training and progressed into senior production management at the cotton mill where he spent most of his adult life. He was keen that his children progress academically but rather lost hope when sons two and three failed their eleven plus examinations. He could indulge in physical chastisement but more rarely than his wife. I do recall my mouth having to endure a bar of soap after he had heard me utter some expletive outside the house.

My father too was quiet by nature, had no strong male relationships that I knew of and rarely if ever brought anyone to the house, other than relatives from Scotland. His health was generally good despite having been, since an early age, a smoker of cigarettes. He drank in moderation. Stress produced stomach ulcers in midlife resulting in one incident of hospitalisation. Dentistry of its time meant that he had all his teeth removed by his mid 40s somewhat later than my mother who suffered that fate by the time she was 30. False teeth were a common accessory of the era and accepted by many as normal. Otherwise my father's health was good. It was a surprise when he died a few months after my mother. The death certificate said *emphysema* but I suspect he lost the will to live on the premature death of his younger wife.

Recreation for my parents was mainly provided by the television. On our move to the top of Whitfield Avenue they would regularly frequent the *Beehive* pub on Hague street. Family outings by car took the form of day trips to various destinations in the north of England. Holidays often involved one or more weeks visiting Scottish relatives. Later my parents would treat themselves to foreign holidays, mainly in Spain, sometimes with Alan and Carol. Books were not generally a feature at home other than by exception. My father took regular delivery of the *Daily Telegraph* newspaper, somehow tolerating its right wing bias. I do not recall any classical music being in my parent's collection of records, it was largely made up of popular music.

A new member of the family arrived in December 1967 when I was given by my parents a dog, as a Christmas present. It was enabled by my mother having recently given up work. I got to choose the dog's name and opted for *Luath*, that name coming from a poem by Robert Burns about a conversation between two dogs on the relative predicaments of the working class and upper class. *Caesar* represented the latter and *Luath* the former. I now had an excuse to revisit the surrounding moorland, ideal for my long, once solitary now accompanied, walks. Luath, of mixed breed, was not to last long.

He went missing, first from a local kennels used while the family was on holiday, then on being recovered, and possibly having tasted freedom, from home. We suspected he may have been shot by a local farmer protecting his sheep, but never discovered his fate.

Personal Development

Poetry did not generally provide comfort or inspiration as I endured adolescence. Music did. Pop music sometimes reflected the emotional turmoil felt about the opposite sex. Folk music too could touch on those feelings but also spoke to more political leanings then emerging. Classical music also began to take hold, whetted by that discarded Tchaikovsky LP. By 1967 I had joined the World Record Club which sent by post a monthly record in return for membership fee. That year also I attended with my father and Philip a first classical concert in Manchester's Free Trade Hall where the Halle orchestra performed Mendelssohn's *Scottish Symphony*. In the orchestra were two brothers that I knew who had attended my school. Robin Davies had in fact been in my own class. Also that year I joined a WEA (Workers Education Association) course in Glossop on opera.

That introduced me to Mozart's *Idomeneo* and Wagner's *Die Meistersingers von Nurnberg*. I also acquired 'picked up for a song' my first recording of Puccini's *La Boheme*. That introduction to Italian opera would provide a source of joy throughout the remainder of my life. The language may have been incomprehensible to me but the impassioned human voice, joined with deeply moving music, touched something buried within that was beyond reason.

My reading widened from Dickens and the classics to Henry Williamson. He captured the angst of growing up with his life of Willie Maddison in a four book series *The Flax of Dream*, a semi biographical narrative that resonated with my own inner turmoil.

Williamson followed with the fifteen novel story of Phillip Maddison under the collective title *A Chronicle of Ancient Sunlight*. In these books I found comfort. Comfort that my own predicament was not unique, that the mental anguish periodically experienced was not necessarily terminal. That there was hope. Books rather than interpersonal dialogue were my way to salvation. Yoga, meditation and philosophy also entered the scene facilitated by library membership. Bertrand Russell's books helped put things in perspective and appealed to the rational predisposition that was to be my lifelong preference. Not necessarily in denial of a spiritual realm but a bedrock I always returned to when assessing competing narratives or beliefs. My periodical reading occasionally extended to the *New Statesman* and *Listener* weekly journals.

The handwriting and prose of my diary entries between 1964 and 1968 underwent a transformation. From purely descriptive pieces of the day's routine, to more considered, albeit intermittent, pieces of reflection, with some prose-like flourishes. As work became more engaging and my spare time was invested in political interaction, the preoccupation with self and my inferiority complex or lack of confidence began slowly to diminish. Nevertheless that was to be a long and sometimes painful process.

Chapter 2
College, Career and Marriage

On the 30th September 1968 I began, once again, life as a full time student. That involved a commute from Glossop to Stockport, initially achieved by public transport, later by a jointly acquired vehicle with Alan. The second hand black Austin A35 was purchased privately in Glossop and we were delighted to have negotiated down the asking price from £50 to £40. My diary was very clear as to my two goals at Stockport College; 'The first was to socialise me, to have normal healthy relationships with males and females of my own age, lose my self consciousness and gain confidence and secondly to complete the course successfully. In that order'. A week after starting I began to understand what I had taken on. Over 25 hours a week in lectures, in only two of which were notes provided, and 10 text books to read. I was mentally exhausted by that first Friday, not only with the workload but the constant effort required to initiate and maintain many personal relationships. This had become so overwhelming by the end of the week, that I resorted to locking myself in the college toilet for respite.

Despair accompanied me home, but the weekend calmed me down and resulted in a resolution to consult a doctor rather than devise ways of killing myself. That consultation never happened. Solace was sought instead in my reading and periodic scribblings. Bertrand Russell's autobiography with its references to his 'years of adolescence being very lonely and unhappy' and his realisation that 'introspection far from being morbid was the road to a great deal of important knowledge' gave me hope, albeit I was now beyond adolescence and in my 20s. Further encouragement came with the results of the course's first examinations held in December. Across the six subjects taken I had averaged 85% and had come top of the class in four.

Death, Politics and War

My diary entry of early April 1968 begins with a quotation from Oscar Wilde following his first visit to the United States 'the only country to have moved from barbarism to decadence without the intermediate stage of civilisation'. The event that prompted my entry was the assassination of civil rights leader Martin Luther King in Memphis, Tennessee. My diary recorded, 'that America shuddered in anticipation and sure enough one city after another erupted. Negro ghettos became battlefields of looting and violence'. 'It was all a rather poor, no sad, farewell to the man who stood above all for peace'. Two months later I learned that Robert (Bobby) Kennedy, brother of John and contender to become the Democratic Party's presidential candidate in the 1968 election had been fatally shot in California. The forces of darkness seemed to be closing in. My diary… 'something will have to be done about the gun laws…but will they do anything…will Robert Kennedy be forgotten in a month's time as were Martin Luther King and John F. Kennedy?'.

One of my early political involvements as a student was participation in the Vietnam War protest held in London in October 1968.

In March that year 10,000 protesters had marched on Grosvenor Square, home of the US Embassy. That protest had resulted in 300 arrests and 86 injuries as police, on foot and horseback, had sought to control protesters with some intent on violence. It was described as a 'riot' by the right wing press. Peter Jackson MP raised a question in Parliament about 'unnecessary violence by police'. The demonstration I attended in October with the same destination was much bigger, an estimated 30,000 people, but was a more peaceful affair with only 11 arrested. My diary recorded that 'the demo was good humoured and enjoyable, the majority of demonstrators were what I would call on another day extremists – anarchists, communists, Maoists, Marxists. Violence on the main march was sparse. Crowd provocation was the main cause of trouble. The police behaved very well'. I had travelled to the event with fellow students who had hired a van. It was my first experience of London, other than the underground rail network. My impression was favourable, 'we arrived at 8pm, had one or two drinks, and presented ourselves at the Earls Court flat of fellow socialists. Our hosts were extremely pleasant and warm-hearted and we spent the evening discussing the demonstration and wider political issues'. After two late nights the *raison d'etre* and then a return journey to Stockport, arriving back at 3am.

Vietnam War History

Vietnam was part of the Indo-China conquests of Imperial France in the nineteenth century. During the second world war Japan occupied this territory but post war it reverted to French control under a client regime. A movement to liberate the country from colonial rule arose under the communist inspired leader Ho Chi Minh. He gained power in the north and following a decisive military victory in 1954 accepted an international treaty to halt hostilities and temporarily split the country into two. That treaty anticipated a nationwide election in 1956 with the goal of re-unifying the country. Leadership of the South, with increasing US military intervention or 'support', abandoned that election promise and became increasingly repressive of those sympathetic to unity under communist rule. This prompted renewed fighting between North and South. Under Presidents Eisenhower and Kennedy the US became increasingly involved in the conflict, claiming the need to halt a 'domino effect' in South East Asia, if Vietnam was 'allowed' to fall to communism.

In 1962 there were 9000 US troops stationed in Vietnam. When Johnson stepped into the shoes of the assassinated Kennedy US involvement dramatically escalated. That was a result of the 'Gulf of Tonkin Resolution' passed by the US legislature. It effectively gave carte blanche to the sitting US President to 'defend US forces in the area'. A USS destroyer Maddox stationed in international waters off North Vietnam and involved in that country's surveillance was 'attacked' by North Vietnamese patrol torpedo boats. This followed various South Vietnamese seaborne attacks, supported by the US, on the North. The Maddox suffered no damage unlike the patrol boats that approached it. That incident passed without an official US response. Two days later a further 'attack' resulted in Johnson seeking powers under the Gulf of Tonkin Resolution. Classified documents released by the US in 2006 raise serious doubt as to whether the second attack ever happened, although the Maddox commander, maybe mistakenly, reported such. The resolution passed was in effect a declaration of war on North Vietnam.

The commander of a second USS destroyer in Tonkin Bay described the outcome as 'the launch of war under false pretences'. The escalation of US involvement had grave consequences for

Vietnam and severely damaged US credibility at home and abroad. Between 1962 and 1975 over 7 million tons of bombs, including napalm, were dropped on Vietnam and neighbouring neutral Laos. That is three times the total tonnage of bombs dropped in the whole of the second world war. Cambodia too was illegally invaded. Chemical weapons were deployed against large tracts of forest/jungle ostensibly to deprive the Vietcong of aerial cover. An estimated two million people died and three million were injured. Twelve million people were displaced and became refugees.

The US introduced conscription at home to feed the ever growing need for boots on the ground. Draft dodging became an art form and the US saw a large scale domestic war protest movement develop. Over 500,000 US troops were eventually committed and allies Australia, New Zealand, South Korea and Thailand were persuaded to provide manpower. On behalf of the UK Harold Wilson declined to do likewise, much angering Lyndon Johnson. The war brought a premature end to Johnson's grip on the White House. He opted not to stand in the 1968 election and paved the way, with Bobby Kennedy assassinated, for President Richard Nixon, who continued to prosecute this 'crusade against communism'. It was a losing war despite a face-saving 'peace agreement'.

The defeat was graphically illustrated in a 1975 photograph showing the ignominious exit by helicopter of US staff from the CIA Saigon station roof, as the city fell to the forces of the victorious North Vietnamese. The city was then immediately re-named after Ho Chi Minh. 58000 US military died and many more were injured in the conflict; those numbers were dwarfed by massive Vietnamese casualties. Local victims received little attention in America but the regular sight of military coffins returning home, draped in the US flag, had a profound impact on domestic sentiment. That would affect how future US interventions were managed if not the imperative to intervene. The dominos did not fall as predicted. The largest communist domino in the region, in the form of China, after suffering Mao's disastrous 'cultural revolution', embarked upon economic reform, embracing aspects of capitalism but retaining communist party control. In a generation its economy outstripped all others and its gross domestic product is on course to exceed that of the USA in the immediate future. The latter's wealth in treasure and reputation having been, in the meantime, squandered on numerous other foreign adventures, for mistaken or misrepresented noble goals. In 2021 after 20 years of war in Afghanistan US and client allied forces, including the UK, were again defeated by another local 'primitive' but determined enemy. Once again the US military cohort, after another face-saving 'peace agreement', were pictured fleeing Kabul as the Taliban took control of their capital city. It was confirmation that 'those who fail to learn from history are condemned to repeat it'.

Torment and Breakthrough

The examination results received in early 1969 boosted my self esteem but I noted that 'my confidence did not hold and my hopes faded as the days passed'. The immediate reason was duly recorded. I had developed a growing bond with three fellow male students on my course and, over a casual coffee with them in the refectory, I was asked by Robin whether I had a girlfriend. That question I deflected but found acutely embarrassing. Tony, one of those present, clearly noticed my discomfort and I saw him as a future potential tormentor. Instead he proved to be my saviour. After more weeks of self analysis and self doubt in relation to the opposite sex I was cajoled by Robin and Tony to join them at the College May Ball. It had not been my intention to attend. Early in the evening Tony introduced me to a girl he had worked with prior to college. She and I escaped the deafening music of the dance hall and spent most of the evening talking together. Later I dropped Tony off and then took Linda to her parent's home, there to be invited in for a coffee. We talked until 3am and plucking up my courage I asked her for a date the following evening. That date almost did not materialise.

Alan and I spent the afternoon struggling to change a shock-absorber on the A35 and at 4pm I had given up hope of being able to get to Stockport. Fate then intervened to conquer that resigned expectation. Our date was a combination of the film *Dr Zhivago*, at the Davenport cinema, followed by a meal in a Chinese restaurant. My nerves were contained, although a great deal of sweat was expended, Linda taking the initiative in holding a no doubt damp hand. I delivered her home by 11.30 where her mother was still up and provided tea for an hour long chat. On my departure Linda gave a positive response to the suggestion of a follow up date a week later and again took the initiative with a goodnight kiss in the doorway. That first date came as an enormous relief, as my diary recorded 'my confidence has been boosted, in fact I feel a great deal better than I have for a long time'. I am not sure that Tony appreciated what he had achieved or that I, at the time, fully appreciated his role in my salvation. By June 21st the seven week relationship was over but it had played a vital part in overcoming a deeply entrenched female phobia.

Linda, it transpired, was just 16 years old. Our relationship had developed to the petting stage in which she was an enthusiastic participant. My diary noted the limits of exploration acceptable to her enthusiasm. A number of dates followed but as she talked of a future together I realised that that was not something I wanted. I did not find her stimulating in anything other than a physical sense, 'she has intelligence but does not appear to have any thirst for knowledge'. So at the end of one such date I rather brutally asked her how she felt and told her that I did not feel particularly strongly about her. She said she was shocked but added the rider 'why couldn't you have waited a few weeks and I chuck you'. That provoked a smile. My diary entry acknowledged that we had probably 'used each other'. She gained being taken out and having money spent on her, I gained experience of something I craved but had built a mental barrier around. A later reflection noted 'at first I thought her main reaction was that of hurt pride, a point on which I tried to reassure her. It then seemed as if there may have existed some affection, which it hurt me to see so affronted'. In being blunt and honest I successfully escaped a growing commitment that I did not wish to pursue but almost immediately regretted the wisdom of my decision and was 'left to stew in my own pessimism and depression'. My final sentence of that diary entry lifted the mood a little 'I have no doubt my morbid thoughts will pass within a few days and once again life's challenges will be accepted'.

As One Door Closes…

Shortly after parting from Linda I received my first year examination results, they were generally good with more work needed in law and economics. That prompted a visit to Manchester to acquire economics textbooks plus other reading material for the summer that included books by Tolkien, Sholokhov, Mailer and Heller. I had opted not to return to Mather and Platt for a summer vacation job and instead found temporary work at Gallaher's *Senior Service* cigarette making factory in Hyde. It was housed in an old cotton mill and operated over several floors. It was here that I met my fellow student and future wife, B. She also had a summer vacation job there secured for her by her mother who had permanent employment in the factory. My first diary description of B 'she is 18, has just left school and has a very playful character which evokes a warm response in me'.

On my 21st birthday 'summoning all my courage' I asked her out on a date. We agreed to meet in her home town of Ashton-under-Lyne the following Saturday evening. I waited patiently at the point of rendezvous at the time we had agreed. No B. My heart sank and had almost given up hope when I saw a familiar figure hurrying towards me. She arrived close to tears and I ushered her towards my father's borrowed car. As she calmed down she related the evening's sequence of events. Her parents had refused her permission to go out, then relented, then changed their minds again as she was about to leave. The reason presented was 'her mother, working in the same department as myself, would find it embarrassing if her daughter and I were to go out together'.

My diary recorded 'such obstacles are the food of romance'. The date was not a great success. The only seats left in the cinema were on the front row and we left after 45 minutes with stiff necks. We looked for somewhere to eat as B had had no tea, eventually finding an Indian restaurant. The meal was not very good but it gave us an opportunity to talk before she thought it best to return home, having defied her parents and escaped the house. I dropped her off at 9.30pm. Dates followed on a regular basis throughout the next few weeks without B revealing to her parents my involvement. That was so until we both departed *Senior Service* and she was freed of her mother's objection and possible embarrassment. One obstacle was to replace another. By the end of September she had taken up her place at Cambridge College of Arts and Technology to study for a degree in modern languages and I had returned to Stockport for the final year of my HND course.

My diary entry of September provided the following analysis;

'Our relationship has matured as was to be expected. She is now aware of my feelings about her giggling and promises to control herself. That is by far her biggest fault. She has a sense of fun that died in me many years ago. She seems to me in some ways prudish, as if her values have been adopted directly from her parents. She is not however 'genteel', that is although her parents are overprotective she is not dependent on them for the running of a house – she can cook, sew and knows hard work. I think living away from home will bring maturity and her own sense of values. I don't think I love her. I don't know what love is, so really I shouldn't use the word. I know I have had more intense feelings about Margaret and Mary, whether part of my feeling for them was frustrated infatuation I know not. In seeking the same feeling in a mutual relationship perhaps I am being immature'.

Stockport Final Year

This was to be a year dominated mentally by my relationship with B. More on that troubled tale follows later. Academically the year was vitally important if I was to secure a good final HND qualification and that partly depended on examination results and in part on a lecturer assessment of an extended essay.

The autumn of 1969 provided some distraction from both factors by my involvement in student union elections for a new executive and president. A team was put together from the HND Business Studies course under Robin Parkinson's leadership using the party banner *Unity*. My role in that team was deputy to Tony Barnes' treasurer candidacy. It was a hard fought election, professionally conducted compared with those of recent years, but resulted in our defeat by an *Action* team under the leadership of an HND Graphics student. That autumn I also strengthened my relationship with fellow course student Rana Salim from Sialkot in Pakistan. He had married a local girl, Jean, and B and I got to know them both as the year developed. It was Rana who came to Whitfield Avenue to enquire in January 1970 why I had missed the first week of term.

This mistake on my part came as a great shock after having spent my Christmas vacation preoccupied with B. What should have been a confident return to my course in January, given excellent interim examination results (including a 75% result in economics which, according to Tony, was the highest mark Miss Cheetham, our lecturer, had ever had to give to any student, an accolade I unfortunately missed in person due to my week's absence), turned out to be a less than smug return. My diary 'to do' list on finally ending the Christmas break was 'not to spend so much money and do more college work' in future breaks. Both entailed restricting what was becoming an all consuming commitment to my new relationship.

In February my mind turned to what I should do on completion of the HND course. I had identified a one year full time Diploma in Management Studies (DMS) course as a logical extension to my vocational training. It involved more detailed study of practical business functions as compared with HND's higher level economic perspective. It was a step down from an MSc or MA in Business Administration but that option looked unlikely to be open to me, given only an HND qualification. By May I had narrowed available options down to focus on a DMS at Brighton Polytechnic with the diary comment 'I don't expect that I shall be flooded with career offers if I should obtain a DMS but other factors have convinced me of the need for a year away from home'.

The extended essay I was required to submit as part of my final HND assessment was on the subject of the containerisation of freight. This 40 page typed paper described the growing importance of containers in moving goods by sea, land and air. Noting that its greatest impact had been on marine freight, the paper stated that it marked a decisive move away from labour intensive methods to a mechanisation of the transport chain and that although this resulted in unemployment in the docks, employment elsewhere was being created. The final conclusion was that 'containerisation between industrialised countries is here to stay and we have yet to see it reach its full potential'. That essay and the resulting interview earned me an assessment of 62%, somewhat less than my average final examination mark across six subjects which yielded 78%. The overall result was an HND pass with distinction. It seemed that the two objectives noted in my diary on embarking on the course had been largely achieved.

Peace of Mind

I may have hoped that having made progress it would bring peace of mind, after years of self questioning and doubt. It was not to be my fate. B and I saw a lot of each other after finishing at *Senior Service* and before the call of our colleges separated us. A day at Chatsworth house prompted a confession of my love for her, despite my earlier misgivings. A meeting with my parents went well. Then we parted. At the beginning of November I travelled to Cambridge in the A35 to spend a weekend with her. She was obviously very happy in her new environment and that raised doubts in my mind, prompting the question; 'Are you tired of me?'. This produced a flood of tears and then talks long into the night about the mysteries and torments of love and life. The following day I accompanied her to church where, coincidently, the sermon covered similar themes to our late night discussion. It proved too much for B and we exited the service early with her again in tears. Nevertheless my diary records the weekend as 'the happiest three days of my life'. My return journey to Glossop suffered the idiosyncrasies of an aged car of that era. Periodically, as I was motoring along, the car's electrics would cut out, the headlights would extinguish and the car grind to a halt. That proved most disturbing in the dark on the winding Snake Pass between Sheffield and Glossop. Unlike Alan I had little clue as to what was happening but miraculously found a shake of the wiring under the bonnet would, for a while anyway, bring the little black car back to life. It was almost like a metaphor for the up and down relationship with B over the next few years. The course of true love never runs smooth, as Shakespeare observed in *A Midsummer Night's Dream*. One form of angst was to replace another, with intermittent moments of blissful happiness. In December I was back in full introspective mode, describing myself as locked in a prison of my own making. I had the key 'to engage with others, facilitate their happiness or growth and in so doing free myself from the preoccupation with self, but as I approached the prison door the key grew ever heavier'. I despaired that my occupation of this cell had now lasted six or seven years and observed that 'the candle of hope has not long to burn'.

In this depressed state I resolved to end my relationship with B during the Christmas break… 'I suspect that neither of us is in love, more likely that we are in love with love. I certainly need her but do I love her? How can an unhappy person offer anything to one who is basically happy? I found solace in a long walk after a despairing diary confession, then later encouragement in reading *He and She* by Kenneth Barnes. My natural tendency towards being judgemental, not only of myself but of others, was much in evidence as the Christmas vacation unfolded. B and her parents were the subject of such scrutiny. Despite all this critical analysis going on in my head B, surprisingly, claimed that her feelings had crystallised over Christmas and that 'she now loved me' having had doubts in the autumn. The turbulent currents of Christmas calmed as we once again approached separation. Little wonder that my mental state had resulted in a serious miscalculation of term start date, resulting in that missed week at college.

Bertrand Russell and Belief

At the beginning of February Bertrand Russell died. He had been born in 1872 and orphaned at age 3 to be brought up by his 'severe but stimulating', 'liberal but puritanical', grandmother. The bible she gave him aged 12 had the following text inscribed on the flyleaf 'thou shalt not follow a multitude to do evil' a sentiment he later claimed had a profound influence on his life and work. After graduating from Cambridge in mathematics and moral sciences he became a Prize Fellow at Trinity College. In 1908 he was made a fellow of the Royal Society and two years later published, in collaboration with A.N.Whitehead, his magnum opus *Principia Mathematica*. In 1910 he was appointed to a lectureship at Trinity, a post from which he was subsequently dismissed as a result of publishing in 1916, in the middle of the first world war, a pamphlet for the *No Conscription Fellowship*. His pacifism also led to his prosecution and imprisonment for six months in 1918 during which he wrote *An Introduction to Mathematical Philosophy*. His catalogue of philosophical work was later placed in the canon of Descartes, Leibniz, Locke, Hume, Kant and Mill. He was also known for his socialism, feminism, pacifism, anti-clericalism and finally anti-communism. Russell made no claim to infallibility and his four marriages suggest significant upheaval in his private life. He received the Nobel Prize for literature in 1950 and later played an active part in the Campaign for Nuclear Disarmament. In 1963, shortly after the Cuban Missile crisis, he established two foundations, one to better understand the cold war mentality that dominated international relations and the other the basis of large scale hunger and poverty in a world of growing prosperity. In 1967 aged 95 he published a book *War Crimes in Vietnam*. He believed that ultimately the only guarantee of peace in the world would come from some form of world government.

My diary comments on his passing, 'he loved humanity knowing its defects', 'he in turn was loved and respected yet he was a rebel'. I felt loss at his passing and reflected that my own life by comparison 'will prove totally insignificant'. 'I have already embarked on the road to conformity. Everything seems to point me towards joining a society whose fundamental values are misguided. Values based on exploiting man's weaknesses rather than his virtues. Isn't 'management', my chosen field of study, instrumental in that exploitation? The greatest weapon in the hand of conformity is that of isolating its enemy. Loneliness is unhappiness'. This reflection resulted in a kind of personal manifesto; 'my first problem is to arrive at a critique of contemporary society, including the role of business and management, then find how best my life can be used in pursuing ideas arising from that critique. I must not isolate myself from society, I must be part of it but not part of it, not an easy task, but necessary for happiness'.

In the months between February and July my relationship with B underwent regular trauma. She became more involved with Christian groups at college and that challenged me to consider my own belief system. The logic of religion had some appeal. I felt God, as an ideal or principle to encourage me to be better than I was, made sense, given my own (and mankind's) fallibility. However the story of Christianity, with Jesus as the fundamental intermediary between God and humanity, I found difficult. If God made us all, why would He invite some to immortality and condemn others? Would God demand our love or failing that ensure our damnation? Was this a logical God of love? By May B and my relationship seemed on the brink of collapse. Numerous letters flowed between Glossop and Cambridge each would be analysed on receipt for indications of warmth or detachment. Longer letter intervals would be noted and occasionally phone calls would seek to clarify feelings. When weekends were spent together potentially dying embers would be reignited. Those Cambridge weekends brought talk of full sexual intercourse, beyond kissing and petting, also talk of marriage and the place of sex in relation to that institution, in the context of Christian teaching.

Holiday from Hell

The summer college break then came into prospect. Part of B's course involved a stay in Italy that summer, along with some of her fellow students, to improve fluency in that language. Her father, who was self-employed, subsequently developed an ambitious plan to drive to Greece, spend time there with his wife's aged mother, and on the return journey drop B in Siena, Tuscany.

Mr B had met his wife in a devastated Greece towards the end of the second world war when he was part of the British Army deployment there. Greece had been occupied by the Axis powers in 1941 and suffered one of the worst death rates of any country impacted by that war. Around half a million or 9% of the Greek population died, a similar percentage to neighbouring Yugoslavia. That compared with less than 1% of the British and 0.3% of the US population, both also dwarfed by Poland's devastating death rate of 17% and the Soviet Union's 14%.

I was invited to accompany them on the 6 week trip, along with B's younger brother. I foolishly accepted. How our relationship survived that six week ordeal I will never know. It must have been ordained by fate.

The journey started in excitement. It was only my second trip abroad and the prospect of seeing so many countries whetted my appetite. Day one involved a long drive to the channel ferry port, a crossing into Belgium then further drive into what was then West Germany. Here I was impressed by the autobahns and terrain. We were to spend two nights in Germany sleeping in the car at suitably large lay-bys. Crossing Austria followed with its magnificent scenery and deteriorating road surfaces.

Next came what was then the country of Yugoslavia. I had in advance of arrival at the border been bombarded with, what I felt to be bigoted, descriptions of life under communist rule by B's parents and looked forward to seeing the country for myself. My diary, taken with me on the expedition, recorded.. 'I remember being very surprised at seeing peasants using cattle drawn carts to carry the fruit of their labours. My surprise soon passed however as the sight became increasingly common. The road in places deteriorated into cobbled surfaces and cars seemed relatively scarce. The main users of the roads were massive lorries with *Albania* or *Bulgaria* written on the side. We spent our first night in the country in a comfortable hotel. The people there were very friendly and we had a meal of spaghetti Milan style. It was so nice to sleep in a bed for a change.

The following day called for an early start as we were attempting the long road into Belgrade. The heat now began to become oppressive. We stopped every few hours for a drink or something to eat. Just as we were leaving Belgrade we ran into a massive hold up. A Skoda car and lorry had been in collision and there was very little of the car left.

The traffic just piled up, we amongst others travelled up the wrong side of the road to the front of the jam. It was fortunate that the man in the Skoda was dead and not just injured, for I doubt whether an ambulance could have reached him very quickly. We spent the night not far out of Belgrade in a motel. Not long after we arrived there the heavens opened. I have never seen a storm like it. Lightning was flashing continuously and the wind went mad. First the electricity went off, then came on again, only for us to find the water was now off. Nevertheless I still slept soundly that night.'

'Late the following day we reached the Greek border. The Customs checks here were far more meticulous than anywhere else we had encountered but we were fortunate and the car was not searched. One was in no doubt that the army was in charge of the country. Soldiers abounded wherever one looked. Posters everywhere recorded the army takeover (coup). After one overnight stay on our transit across Greece and having late the following day skirted Athens, we arrived at the city's port Piraeus. Here we caught a small ferry to the island of Salamis and there quickly located B's grandmother's (*mama*) home, which she shared with local fisherman Nicole, her partner after the death of her husband. They lived in a one room apartment in a largish property and shared a small courtyard where one can sit in the shade under a small cone tree resting one's feet on the well '.

'I have had just over a week on the island now and things have settled into a somewhat monotonous routine. We tend to get up about 10, or I do anyway, wander over to *mama's* for breakfast, perhaps have a walk round, have lunch, go for a swim, back to the hotel, change, have a walk, have dinner and then go to bed. The hotel isn't at all good.

We have two rooms opposite each other; B's brother and I take one, B and her parents the other. Each room has a sink with a tank water supply. It wouldn't be so bad if the sinks drained but they are forever clogging up. If we want drinking water we must take a bottle downstairs to the cafe and fill up there. There is no bath or shower, not even a communal one. The communal lavatory is filthy. It flushes once in half a dozen times.

The door cannot be locked so one stands a very good chance of being 'caught in the act' if one uses it. Even in this crude state it is still centuries ahead of *mama's* hole in the ground, which I had to make use of on my second evening there.'

'We spend as little time as possible at the hotel, most of the day we are at mama's or on the beach. I am a little sick of all the oily food now but we have had some very tasty dishes this last week. We have yoghurt most evenings before dinner made from goat's milk – I really love it though it has a tart taste compared with our domestic variety.

Another dish I love is stuffed tomatoes and peppers; we've had them twice now and they are really delicious. It is the fruit that really makes one's mouth water. Massive peaches full of juice, melons which taste of banana splits and water melon served ice cold. Fish is one of the main dishes we enjoy with Nicole being a fisherman. We have tried octopus and two types of small fish. I wasn't really keen on the octopus although it looks edible enough. The fish are really too small, when one has removed head, tail and backbone there is little more than a couple of mouthfuls left.'

My relationship with B throughout the holiday was typical of our first year's courtship, some times of happiness punctuated by regular intervals of disharmony, if not full blown argument. Throughout much of the holiday I was determined to end the relationship on my return to the UK. The situation was not helped by her parents delegating their son to accompany us everywhere as an involuntary chaperone. This eventually erupted into a serious confrontation as I rebelled against the constraints being imposed. It got close to physical violence with B's father but fortunately this was avoided. Some freedom resulted from the altercation, with

B and I released to visit Athens, first with a local relative, later on our own. The battles were not limited to myself. An argument arose between B's father and *mama*. He refused to eat food prepared by her because he had seen her tasting from the pot. That became a major incident and resulted in angry exchanges and a tactical withdrawal from *mama*'s yard. No doubt all parties were suffering from the claustrophobia of too much time together and inescapable heat. This finally resulted in a plan to depart Greece earlier than anticipated and tour Yugoslavia before heading for Italy where B was to be dropped off. A tent was procured to limit expenses and avoid sleeping in the car.

Our journey home took us to the north Greek border with Yugoslavia. Yugoslavia became, following the second world war, a communist state under its wartime resistance leader Tito. It was not part of the Soviet Union and operated a more liberal economic model. It consisted of many ethnic groups and was made up of a federation of political administrations, each with delegated power but held together under Tito's enlightened dictatorship. On his death in 1980 the forces of fragmentation began to gain momentum, descending into armed conflict in the 1990s. Our journey to Italy involved one other country after Greece. Today that journey would involve five; Macedonia, Kosovo, Montenegro, Croatia and Slovenia. We passed through, or by, Titograd (now Podgorica), Budva and Dubrovnik. The weather was generally wet, causing us to have to abandon the tent one night, but when the sun shone it was hot, very hot. A day's drive into Italy got us to Tuscany and Siena where B was to meet up with some of her fellow students. Siena is famous for its annual *Palio*, a bare-back ridden horse race around the central Piazza del Campo. That race dates back to mediaeval times and is between the various districts that make up the city. One race is in July and the second in August. As luck would have it we arrived in the town just before the second race in mid August and so got caught up in the trials and race preparation. Eventually we met up with the fellow students and parted company with B; it was not a tearful farewell. Four days later I was home and as my diary recorded, after my six week adventure and ordeal, 'home, home sweet home'.

Leaving Home

I had a month in Glossop before departing for Brighton and my DMS course. I found temporary work at a local factory and got closer to fellow young socialist, John Slinger. We were able to commiserate with each other about girlfriend woes. The letter exchanges with B were perfunctory, not touching on a troubled relationship. On her return to the UK we met again and eventually it was sexual intimacy that rekindled warmth in what had seemed a doomed affair. We began to value each other's company again and also met up twice with Rana and Jean. All this in time, inevitably, for separation as our respective colleges beckoned.

In late September I arrived at my pre-arranged digs in Brighton. This accommodation proved of short duration. After two weeks I, with a fellow student resident, moved into an apartment in nearby Clyde Road; a single room bedsit with twin beds conveniently situated over the top of a launderette. One wall was made up of storage cupboards containing a sink, an electric Baby Belling cooker with twin hobs and small oven, and adjacent wardrobes. The room was next door to a communal lavatory and separate bathroom. Ned was a little younger than myself and came from Mumbles just south of Swansea in Wales. His nature was at times quite overbearing and he was far better at talking than listening. His overt confidence in some respects counterbalanced my natural reservation. My subsequent analysis of his make-up was perhaps more insightful 'I now see his talkativeness and assertiveness to be a means of keeping confidence in himself.

Indications are that he is very much a mother's boy and used to being heavily praised by his parents. He has little respect for anyone else and constantly has to prove his superiority to those around him'. Living together in a small apartment proved trying at times but my resilience was no doubt helped by the experience gained on my European trip which had involved even more confined spaces. As the weeks passed my own confidence and assertiveness grew. Ned's habit of heavily poking people in the chest with extended forefinger, to make a point, stopped when I responded with a surprise knee nudge to his lower assets. Over time his rather shy girlfriend appeared to succeed in tempering his superficial arrogance and their formal engagement appeared to help his need for security. Somehow we survived the nine months of my course. We shared a love of the potato and regularly purchased a 56 pound bag, carefully stored by the cooker, to provide one of the main ingredients of our student diet. We also both shared a taste in pop music. At that time The Moody Blues were my favourite group. They had come out of Birmingham, struggled for a while and then found a distinctive and successful 'sound'. Their LP *Days of Future Passed* with its mix of rock and orchestral pieces was followed by *In Search of the Lost Chord* cementing their growing appeal. A mystical element in their lyrics appealed to me and that student generation.

My observation about my own insecurities at the time contained a glimmer of hope. 'I do believe that living away from home is going to be beneficial. I seem to be quite frequently confronted with psychological crises and these will, I think, bring on maturity more quickly than the shelter of home'.

My stay at Clyde Road was punctuated by weekend meet-ups

with B in Brighton or Cambridge. Her perceived ambivalence towards me reduced when a long term potential relationship in Cambridge ended. She had been drawn, since her arrival there, to a fellow student only to realise, eventually, that there could be no romantic future as he was gay. That realisation on her part helped strengthen our bond. I had my own flirtation in Brighton on joining the local young socialist group. That was short lived. By November I observed that; 'B radiates love and good sense, her concern for others is touching. She looks outward rather than inward, which is refreshing, but can be self-righteous. She has many qualities that I lack and my feeling at present is that we could perhaps be happy together'. A carefully expressed hopeful note that did not mark the end of doubt or turbulence in our relationship.

The Course

My course was delivered in an annexe building of Brighton Polytechnic, a large one-time domestic residence adjacent to Preston Park, a short walk from Clyde Road. The DMS course was designed to improve practical knowledge of business management. It involved the study of functional management such as marketing, production, accounting and personnel as well as looking at corporate strategy and the economic environment.

Assessment was by examinations at the end of term two and evaluation of a major case study submission. Term three was devoted entirely to this individual project, under college supervision, in a local business. My project was with a Burgess Hill manufacturer of recording instruments, Hersey Sparling Meter Company, and the terms of reference related to improving the cost accounting system. The project began on May 3rd and ended on June 18th, it involved working with local management, in particular the business's head of finance. I never found out whether any of my recommendations were implemented but received a kind of compliment at the end of the project when I was offered a job by the financial controller. More important for me, at the time, was that my college tutor's assessment contributed to my obtaining a final overall DMS qualification 'with credit', one up from a pass, one down from a distinction.

I enjoyed the course very much and it proved to be much more practical than the HND course in Stockport. I developed a friendship in the latter part of the course with Bob Dunn, a fellow student. He was a fellow northerner from Swinton, Greater Manchester although he had lost much of his local accent. That might have been the result of his politics and dedication to the Conservative party. He had working class roots, had failed his eleven plus examination and left school early, but returned to further education to do a degree at Manchester Polytechnic. My comments at the time 'he cuts an impressive figure, very much a talker but is not as confident as one might think... he hides behind his mouth... nevertheless he has considerable qualities of intellect'. We got on despite our political differences and enjoyed many walks on the Sussex Downs as well as days out in London, one of which involved visiting the Houses of Parliament. We argued for hours about politics but always good naturedly.

My note at the time 'he has been very active in the Tory party, more concerned with the cut and thrust than the cause. Will probably make an admirable politician if he can control his temper. He lets his prejudices dominate on occasion but if guided by his intellect could be quite liberal. I think the snobbery in the party nauseates him at times but he gauges everything in relation to a future political career'. Bob and I lost touch in the year after the course ended, our letters slowly declining in frequency. His was the only correspondence I ever received which incorporated the DMS letters after my name; that always brought a smile. On leaving Brighton Bob started a course at Salford University but abandoned it to get a job in the buying department of Sainsburys. His political passion still burned brightly and he became Chair of Eccles Young Conservatives, later travelling south to seek election as an MP. He had to make do with being elected to Southwark borough council in 1974 but was finally elected MP for Dartford in 1979, when the Conservative party under Margaret Thatcher triumphed to form a government.

Bob became an arch Thatcherite and was appointed under secretary for education in 1983. He proved to be less than happy at the despatch box and struggled under that spotlight. In 1986 he offered to resign his post having had his declared educational qualifications 'at Salford University' exposed as false, an offer the Prime Minister rejected. However by 1988 he had lost office and then chose to become an active back-bencher resulting in election to the executive of the 1922 Committee. He retained that role until he lost his Dartford seat in 1997 to the Tony Blair 'New' Labour onslaught. He subsequently became a Dartford borough councillor and died of prostate cancer in 2003. His obituary described him as 'a fundamentalist Tory and privatisation champion, good humoured and often witty, he was liked as well as respected for his honesty, robust common sense and care for his constituents'.

Self and Beyond

My psychological crises mentioned earlier, recurrently faced, were crises of confidence in my own self-worth. The year in Brighton saw a return of doubts I thought I had mastered. Being subjected constantly to new situations and attendant appraisal by others was wearing, given my introverted nature, and brought a return of blushing and profuse sweat generation. I had learned that escape lay in focusing on others and rising above self analysis to make practical plans for the future. In other words moving from feelings of helplessness to gaining control of self and environment. I was helped by reading books such as White's *Lives in Progress*, about personality development, and that produced more balanced diary reflections and gave reassurance that I was 'work in progress' rather than of doomed fate.

Relations with B oscillated between blissful happiness and moody negativeness. In early 1971 I visited Cambridge 'the weekend began with gentleness and love... never have I experienced such love for B... and she in turn loved me. I cannot explain the beauty of the experience.. it was total. The sense of oneness was consummated with B's willingness to make love... I could not love anyone more than I now love her'. It was to mark the beginning of the end of our virgin-hoods. The weekend drew to a close with a visit to Great St Mary's Church in Cambridge's market square, there to hear a talk by Bishop John Robinson. Sunday evening lectures by renowned thinkers, rather than sermons, were then a regular feature at that church. John Robinson was regarded by many in the Christian church as a heretic with his move away from the idea of God as 'Father', the anthropomorphic metaphor used by Jesus. His book *Honest to God* confronted some deeply entrenched beliefs and emotions. Listening to his talk concluded a happy weekend but one that still failed to eradicate my inner doubts.

With full sexual intercourse, and lack of contraception, came the inevitable fear of an unintended pregnancy. Late periods produced great anxiety. By Easter and our return to the north, to see families, we were talking to our respective parents about our ultimate intention to marry, hopefully following a formal engagement period rather than precipitated by an accidental conception.

My May diary entry began 'I have just finished writing a letter to B. A letter of goodbye. My heart isn't filled with regret, anxiety or any of the usual feelings associated with troughs in our relationship. Nor do I feel elated or free. More a feeling of adventure imminent'. I had travelled to Cambridge the previous weekend on completion of exams.

My mood was somewhat depressed, fearing for the result of those examinations. B too was not her usual sunny self. Two letters followed from B expressing her view that it was essential that I become a Christian, not in the notional label sense that many apply to themselves or others, but involving a deep commitment to doctrine and an overt profession of 'faith'. A letter expressing doubt about our relationship and saying how she missed 'that little something' she had with Christian friends was the final straw. 'I hadn't been thinking of a break before today's letter but it was the only thing that brought any satisfaction. I half expect that we shall be together again but not on B's terms. I can take it if we don't make it, all the same'.

The next diary entry of early June began 'Thankfully my letter did not bring the relationship to a close. One minute of the love I now feel for B is far more precious than so called freedom. B visited me a week after my letter. She was distraught to say the least. I have seen her cry on many occasions but never have I heard such anguish in her sobbing. Nor do I ever wish to again'. Our correspondence thereafter was more reasonable and understanding of each other's needs and feelings. An early return visit to Cambridge completed the healing process. Both the psychological and sexual union grew stronger in tandem or maybe one dependent on the other. B's take on Christianity, in part fuelled by the literalist group with whom she mixed at Cambridge, no longer came between us. As expressed in my diary 'my God is and has been, an abstract concept – love. The bible is to be read in this light – Jesus was the personification of love'. We now seemed able to respect each other's interpretation of Christian belief. It would not be the last time I wrestled with what I believed or what form my acceptance of Christian doctrine took. My journey of discovery would encompass a moment of 'conversion', albeit temporary, then take me into more esoteric Christianity before moving beyond its confines to understand and embrace other interpretations of spiritual reality. Synthesis would be a lifelong quest.

Having received some expenses from my DMS Hersey Sparling project I splashed out in June on a number of books including Bertrand Russell's books; *Marriage and Morals*, *The Conquest of Happiness* and *Power, A New Social Analysis*. Also in preparation for my future career I bought the irreverent and pithy book on management by Robert Townsend *Up the Organisation*.

Brighton Conclusion

My diary entry of June 23rd sought to draw some lessons from my year in Brighton. 'First I have managed to live in the same room with a stranger for nine months. This required far more patience than I would have guessed. It will be an excellent introduction to living with B next year. She is different in that I love her but nevertheless I imagine patience will still be required.' 'I have made a friend in Bob Dunn, as near a friendship as is possible from this point onward. Childhood friendships are different and these I never did conquer'. 'I have discovered a few more of life's secrets. I know how to overcome my self-consciousness and inferiority complex, not that these have been vanquished but are relegated to spells of shorter duration.' 'I have managed to make the break from my parents and although I haven't found that difficult, it is an achievement'. 'I have learned something about people. There is much more to learn. My awe of 'degree' persons and the 'academic' generally is much reduced. I have a sounder basis on which to judge individuals. Perhaps I am still a little too harsh in my judgments of others. Overlooking certain faults I find very difficult'. 'I've learned to work with others in a group and accept leadership by others. I've learned that to lead one has to prepare well and work hard, that impressions count a great deal for most people – one must always present oneself with the appearance of confidence even if doubts are present in one's mind'. 'I have completed a project in a new environment on my own and without making a fool of myself. I was quite pleased with the result. My attitude to career seeking will as a result be much more selective.' 'I have discovered the beauty of making love. How rich this becomes when love is in one's heart. Thank heaven I met B and didn't first taste intercourse for purely selfish reasons. Love in a more general sense has proven itself to me as a powerful and fundamental way of life.'

Home to Crisis

My feelings about my parents back in Glossop underwent some change viewed from the distance of Brighton. After an Easter visit home my diary noted 'only now am I beginning to appreciate the love and wisdom of my own mother. Whether I have been blind in the past, or whether the passing years have brought her insight I cannot say, but I do know that I still have much to learn from her. My father has knowledge and much intelligence but he knows little of people. My mother is in harmony with life. Love is her way'. Courage, honesty and common sense were also my mother's hallmarks. Her lack of academic attainment diminished in importance as my own experience of life expanded.

At the end of my course that summer I returned to Glossop and the family home before setting off with B on a hitch-hiking and hostelling holiday in Cornwall ... 'glorious sunshine and magnificent scenery, wheatfields bending to the wind, seagulls wheeling above the rocks at home in their element, a kestrel motionless in the air its eyes scanning the ground for movement'.

A month later my next diary entry, late in August, noted my 23rd birthday had passed and opened 'family life underwent a violent upheaval a week ago, an explosion of smaller proportions brought the whole mountainside down'. My mother had discovered that my father had been taking a woman from work out for lunch for several months.

'Family existence for the last few years crystallised in that second for her. The lack of communication, the boredom and monotony of evenings at the Beehive, the worry about her children, particularly Philip, the absence of cash, the illness of change of life and weariness of late nights and early morning work. All the sores burst simultaneously, self pity she initially managed to contain, anger came rightly to the fore'. 'Father was crushed, pitiful, pathetic'. 'I came home on Sunday evening with B, my mother told me of what she had discovered within two minutes of my entering the house. I took B and Alan's girlfriend home and returned. Father and mother sat waiting in the living room.

My father's front had vanished and he sat there in the raw, with no substance, no character he was like a child caught doing something he knew to be wrong, completely without defence'. What followed in the immediate aftermath was then spelled out in my diary 'mother has given up her work, things in the house have changed quite drastically. Mum and dad are together a great deal. Excursions to the Beehive have been reduced to two or three times a week. The TV is being switched off far more than I ever remember (although my mother did note in one letter that the family had acquired their first colour television). We are talking to each other without much difficulty.

Mother has taken control of the money coming into the house. Things have changed and I hope that happiness touches their lives again. A little care works wonders'.

The eruption at home led to my learning more of the skeletons in B's father's cupboard. These made my father's indiscretion miniscule by comparison. However relatively minor, that breach of trust deeply affected my mother and over the next few months my support was important, particularly when self doubt overtook her. My diary recorded 'my mother needed support and I provided it. She no longer needs this knowing she is in the right'. Two days after that optimistic entry 'my mother broke down, engrossed in self pity and took some settling. Reason and good sense eventually prevailed'. Over the next few months I received a series of long letters from my mother. In them she explained how she was constantly encouraging the others in the house to communicate honestly with each other. Alan and Philip were still living at home and so my mother was surrounded by adult males who generally are much less likely to discuss their feelings, or personal matters, than women. She would no longer allow things to fester, as they had in the past, or be swept under the carpet. Those confrontations caused friction but also helped create a healthier, more open atmosphere in the house, even if it was achieved with some pain for the likes of my father.

Adding to the domestic turbulence was Philip's state of mind. He was back home having returned after his short spell in the merchant navy. He showed no interest in a new career or in developing relationships. He was an avid reader of library books and undoubtedly intelligent. His letters often conveyed wit and erudition. My mother despaired of his aimlessness. I constantly tried to communicate with him, as much to relieve my mother's anxiety, as to try and understand what was going on in his head.

One diary entry … 'he is basically insecure, frightened of

people but it is not in his nature to try to overcome this fear. Instead he is cynical and revels in trivia. He is unable to talk about himself, he also seems incapable of serious thought. Now I recognise the symptoms for I have been in a similar state but I don't think I was ever resigned to accepting my state as my fate'. A later moment of confidence between my mother and Philip revealed that he thought he had contracted venereal disease in the navy. He lived with that for years, doing nothing to confirm it or otherwise, despite it being the reason he used to justify, to himself, his non pursuit of relationships. My mother's reaction to the revelation; 'she felt as if someone had given her a pile of money'. It appeared to explain much about her son's mentality that she could not understand. The blood test, then arranged, showed no sign of the disease in his system. That brought hope that a change of outlook might result. Initially there was progress and he began to communicate better with mum and myself. However the effort he made proved short-lived. His dependence on alcohol, initially to bolster his confidence, then facilitated by duty-free naval provision, grew as time went by and he remained a source of worry for my mother until her early death twenty years later. It seems that many, if not most, mothers are never free of concern for their children's wellbeing. My mother's mother had died early 'her work done' when she saw her youngest daughter, Phyllis, married.

That mother's love, a source at times of great joy, is also at times, seemingly, a curse.

Cambridge

At the end of August with the situation stabilising at home and B off to Germany for a month, as part of her modern languages degree course, I decided to travel to Cambridge and search for accommodation and temporary employment. The summer had depleted my funds and I arranged a £30 overdraft from NatWest bank. Somehow my temporary work objective changed and instead I found full time employment with British Domestic Appliances in Peterborough. BDA was the result of a merger between GEC and EMI's domestic appliance businesses and manufactured products under the Hotpoint and Morphy Richards brands. The role was in their export finance department and had career prospects, albeit involving, yet again, more study to qualify as an accountant. My chosen accommodation was in Cambridge, to be close to B for the final year of her course, and involved a short walk to the railway station for my daily commute by train.

At Christmas, having spent a great deal of time in each other's company, B and I got engaged and made a commitment to marry in the second half of the coming year. She had planned on completion of her degree course to do a one year teacher training course in Birmingham, but that was shelved as our marriage plans took shape. We fixed a November date for the wedding and began to look for somewhere to live together in Cambridge. We found an excellent privately rented flat on the ground floor of a detached house in Arbury Road. It was luxury compared with the bedsit world of the last two years, having a kitchen, dining and sitting rooms, bedroom and bathroom. That summer I had also decided to try and find employment in, or nearer to, Cambridge. That search eventually bore fruit with a job offer to join Spicers (Stationery) Limited in August on a salary of £1600 per annum. The trainee position was in the accounts department and the company provided free bus transport from Cambridge to their base at Sawston. After all the uncertainties of the recent past the autumn of 1972 delivered some much needed stability and clarity as to my future direction.

Back in Whitfield I was still concerned for my mother's mental state and tried to encourage her to have a telephone installed so that we could talk regularly, given she was not a great letter writer. B and I also managed to persuade Philip to leave Glossop and join us in Cambridge, this in the hope that a different environment might stimulate a new frame of mind. He obtained work locally and rented a caravan in Chesterton, close to where we lived, in the grounds of a public house.

The wedding duly took place in Albion Congregational church, Ashton under Lyne, B's home town, with a reception in Glossop centre at the Norfolk Arms Hotel. John Slinger was my best man. We had grown closer since my move away from home and had enjoyed an active correspondence, and occasional weekends together, to exchange views on life, politics and woes. The wedding party was largely made up of extended family, including many of my Scottish relatives. I remember the day as being a very happy one with B and I departing the Norfolk Arms late, having enjoyed the food, music and dancing, to find our accommodation at the Olde Nags Head in Castleton. The one night stay there was followed by onward travel to Scotland for our honeymoon.

Part 3
The Spicers Story

Chapter 1   Foundation and Growth
Chapter 2   Apprenticeship
Chapter 3   Leadership
Chapter 4   The Final Years

This is the story of the Spicers business; its birth in 1796, long history, my employment there and the company's death some 14 years after my departure.

Spicers started as a paper making business with capital passed down from the family's previously generated wealth. It grew as a privately owned concern and that involved several subsequent generations of the family. Eventually it sought outside investment, however the share structure then created still retained family control. Funding helped it become international in scope with overseas expansion in Britain's empire of old. As that empire began its long retreat, the company's fortunes faltered. That was coincidence rather than cause. The family eventually relinquished ownership control and in the early 1960s the business was sold to a large papermaking and publishing company. The new owner then proceeded to break up and restructure the business it had acquired. A slimmed down Spicers, mainly involved in manufacturing stationery products, was the result and that was the business I joined in 1972.

Over the next eighteen years the business transformed to become predominantly a wholesaler of a wide range of office products. That was the result of a small acquisition followed by rapid organic growth and gave UK market leadership by 1990. The next eighteen years saw expansion in Europe, with wholesaling operations established in Ireland, France, Germany, Spain, Italy and Benelux, to become Europe's largest, broad range, office product wholesaler. Twelve years after that, in 2020, the business was liquidated, a victim in part of a changing marketplace and the management's response to those changes, but also the result of a predatory form of capitalism, less concerned with long term wealth creation than with short term wealth extraction.

I joined Spicers as a management accounting trainee. The accountancy body setting those examinations was originally called The Institute of Cost and Works Accountants and that was a good indication of its original purpose. 'Chartered' accountants tended, in general, to be in separate firms and focus on auditing company accounts and helping businesses with tax and other matters, or alternatively, doing the books of smaller enterprises. Cost and Works (later Cost and Management) accountants were employed mainly in manufacturing businesses and focused on improving productivity and general efficiency by providing managers with relevant information.

My background qualifications, a Higher National Diploma in Business Studies and Diploma in Management Studies, gave me some Institute examination exemptions. To qualify as an accountant still required me to take numerous other examinations and gain practical experience of relevant work in industry. Spicers, at the time I joined it, had a very good accountancy training scheme with several trainees rotating through various accounting disciplines in order to gain relevant experience. The scheme was led by chief accountant Peter Frost. He was to be my first boss, principal inspiration and mentor between 1972 and his departure from the company in 1986.

Spicers main business in 1972 was on a site in the middle of a 550 acre farm, adjacent to the main Cambridge to London railway line, at Sawston a few miles south of Cambridge. Its principal focus then was the manufacture and sale of commercial envelopes and other stationery products such as manuscript books and pads. It was on that site that I began my career with the company as an accountancy trainee and on that site 34 years later, in the Homewood head office building, as chief executive of a European wide business, that I ended my career.

Chapter 1
Foundation and Growth

Spicers is named after the Spicer family. That family's known history stretches back to the Norman Conquest when as gentlemen-volontiers or merchants, they traded in spices. This is believed to be the origin of their name and Exeter was their then base. John Spicer was the mayor of Exeter in 1273 and many of his family descendents held that and other senior city posts into the early eighteenth century. The Spicer family arms can still be seen in the City's Guildhall.

In around 1660 Edward Spicer started paper making in a mill at Chepping Wycombe, Buckinghamshire that subsequently became known as Hedge Mill. The family were therefore amongst the earliest English papermakers. Predating Hedge Mill was a paper mill at Sawston that is thought to have been in existence by 1600, a mill which Spicers would eventually acquire.

Edward Spicer's great grandson, John Edward (1766 – 1845) founded the Spicers business that was to develop into the company that I joined. John's uncle, also a papermaker, bought for his nephew Alton Mill in Hampshire in 1796 and it was that date that was subsequently used as the foundation date of Spicers.

John Edward's parents were both dead by the time he was

ten years old and his uncle brought him up. He developed deep religious convictions and was influenced by non-conformists John Wesley and George Whitefield. His ambition to follow a career in the church was abandoned as a result of speech impediment. His religious beliefs informed his business principles and patriarchal approach to employees. He instituted a regular short Monday morning service for the workforce, a practice that the business would continue until 1922.

Papermaking at that time was a handmade process using pulverised rags of cotton, linen, wool and silk as raw material. John Edward concentrated on making a high quality product and his mill's growing reputation led to it receiving from the King the accolade *Royal Mill*. His success encouraged John to adopt a take it or leave it attitude to his customers, who were in the main London book publishers. Pride comes before a fall and the depression following the Napoleonic Wars hit his business hard, as did the onset of new, more mechanised, methods of producing paper at a lower cost. This resulted in the mill being closed for a time. John then moved his family to London and established in 1824 a new business as wholesale stationers and rag merchants. This business took product from a later reopened Alton Mill, now managed by one of his sons, but also from other mills and stationery manufacturers. The return load to his mill suppliers took the form of rags collected in London. The new business thrived and in 1835 he founded J E Spicers and Sons. His customer base expanded to include printers, publishers and stationers. In 1844 John Edward retired leaving the business to his sons and it then became known as Spicers Brothers.

The consumption of paper grew rapidly in the Victorian era as prices fell, a result of new machine processes and the move to use wood pulp as raw material. Between 1860 and 1903 annual production of paper increased from 100 to 773 thousand tonnes.

Disagreements between the Spicer brothers led to a breakaway business being formed, James Spicer and Sons. Both businesses were successful. In 1889 Spicers Brothers formed a limited liability company facilitating the raising of capital to expand the business, as well as providing protection of family wealth in the event of business failure. In 1901 a Stock Exchange listing for the business's preference shares followed, ordinary shares, and control, were still in the hands of family members. Edward Spicer was the first chairman of the limited company and remained so until his death in 1912. He, like his father, was actively involved in the Congregational church and was politically a Liberal. Under his chairmanship the business opened its first branch and warehouse in Manchester in 1889 and then a second in Birmingham in 1897. Glasgow, Leicester, Dublin and Newcastle followed. In 1901 the business bought a factory in Union Street, Southwark, to manufacture stationery. By 1909 the factory employed a workforce of 270 people, mainly women. In that same year the paper mill at Alton, where the Spicers business had started in 1796, closed and production was transferred to another Spicer owned mill at Eynsford in Kent.

Meanwhile James Spicer & Sons separate business had grown equally successfully. It too was driven by 'Christian Feudalism', a description coined by James's grandson to describe the business philosophy. The underlying principle maintained 'that in exchange for material benefits in life, there was an obligation to do service in the community'.

James's public service included being; a magistrate in Essex, a deputy Lieutenant for his county and the City of London, twice Warden of the Fishmongers Livery Company and treasurer of the City Liberal Association. He also played an important part in his local Congregational church. His business was not involved in the manufacture of paper but acted as a wholesaler/distributor and exporter of paper, for example it supplied newsprint for *The Times* newspaper. It also owned factories that manufactured products from paper. James's second son Albert was regarded as the principal architect of the firm's expansion. His two primary management principles were; to never hesitate to delegate, and always to seek the views of his managers before forming his own opinion. From the late 1870s branch offices were opened in Bristol, Leeds and Belfast and warehouses in Birmingham, Manchester and Glasgow. Albert Spicer then opened offices in India, Australia and South Africa. The business became James Spicer & Sons Limited following its incorporation in 1910.

An Employee's Perspective

Here is a James Spicer & Sons employee's contemporary account of his work in Upper Thames Street offices in the winter of 1895. 'All we saw, day after day, was a field of miniature icebergs across the Thames. The high office stool was universal. Electric light was available but each of us had a candle for use when the supply failed. The Export department had introduced the first typewriting machine. It was operated by a rather dim male clerk. The Packers department was the centre of wit and humour, a really Dickensian scene. At times the backchat between Messrs Love and Booty, the department's custodians, was as good as any you would hear in the Music Hall '. In 1914, then aged 37, the same employee commented on his weekly budget. 'I found I am keeping a family of three on 37 shillings and 6 pence (£1.88) per week, managing to live in a semi-detached house in Ilford, to afford a season ticket and to find time to study literature and art as well as take an interest in church life and politics. The harmony in office life was worth a great deal to us'.

Sawston and Merger

In 1917 Spicers Brothers acquired Edward Towgood and Sons business at Sawston, near Cambridge. Paper had been produced at the mill there since the sixteenth century and the acquisition included an estate of 269 acres, later expanded by further land purchases. Some of Spicers' stationery manufacturing operations were subsequently transferred to Sawston from the greater London area. Major investments were also made in a new paper making machine and the installation of electricity.

Sawston village had had a long beneficial relationship with the Towgood family and it was to be followed by equal commitment from the Spicer family. Towgoods had rebuilt Sawston National School and Spicers later donated land on which Sawston Village College was built. Likewise, Sawston's sports ground and cinema utilised land given by Spicers. The business owned numerous houses in the village and later added to them to accommodate key workers when the envelope factory was moved from London.

In the years after the first world war trade generally suffered and unemployment grew dramatically. The two Spicers businesses were not immune to this recession. In 1921 discussions began between directors of the two businesses about an amalgamation and this came to fruition a year later, giving birth to Spicers Limited. Control of the business, now with a large worldwide workforce, still lay with the Spicers family shareholdings.

Albert Spicer chaired the combined business initially but soon retired to be replaced by Harry Spicer, who also took on the role of managing director. It was he who led the process of rationalising the merged businesses.

The 1930s saw a gradual increase in the manufacture of envelopes and books and pads at Sawston, this against a backdrop of difficult markets, rationalisation of operations and cost cutting, including wage reductions. Management of the business became fraught and Harry Spicer lost the confidence of the board of directors, resulting in his powers being heavily circumscribed. His occupation of Homewood, a large detached house on the Sawston site that he had adopted as his country home, was compromised by his being obliged to share it with six war-evacuated staff from London. He spent most of the second world war years at Sawston and died in 1944.

He was followed as chairman by Leonard Spicer who set up in 1946 a 'committee of reorganisation' led by his son James Spicer who later became managing director (MD) of the whole business. At the time Spicers Limited comprised many diverse businesses in addition to its UK paper based manufacturing and merchanting operations. It was headquartered in London and had sixteen UK branches, factories at Union Street, Red Cross Way, Sawston and Haddenham, major overseas operations in Australia and South Africa as well as branch offices around the world. The workforce exceeded 4000 and the family controlled over two thirds of the voting shares, however, that was destined to fall to 7.5% by the early 1960s as the business's fortunes faltered.

James's reorganisation committee decided that the focus should be on the merchanting operation which was the biggest and most profitable part of the business and was principally involved in the sale of cut paper. Lancelot Spicer was given responsibility for manufacturing and export operations.

In 1946 Giles Witherington, absent the Spicer name but a cousin of James Spicer, joined the company following a distinguished career in the army. Two years later he was appointed manager of the Edward Towgood paper making business at Sawston and moved into the Homewood house on the estate. The paper mill at Sawston was losing money and to address that it was decided to invest in a new paper making machine which finally became operational in 1960.

The stationery manufacturing business on the Sawston site was seen to have growth potential and In 1955 the London Union Street factory operation was relocated, with key workers transferred and housed in Sawston. Despite investment and rationalisation the manufacturing operation remained unprofitable. In 1958 the Spicers Board decided, in principle, to close the Sawston factory but by 1960 had reversed that decision.

Management of the two businesses at Sawston, in the fifteen years post-war, was inconsistent and problematic. Following the death of James Spicer in 1960 Giles Witherington was appointed joint MD of the whole business alongside Charles Austin, the non-family financial director. In 1962 Spicers Limited sales were £28.8m and a profit of £836 thousand was generated. That result paved the way for Spicer family ownership to come to an end. In 1963 Reed Paper Group, a large UK based paper, packaging and publishing business, bought the business for £13.6m.

Reed Ownership

Reed's managing director, Don Ryder, wanted Spicers to retain its identity within the Group but focus on merchanting and stationery manufacturing. Paper making was to become part of the Reed structure and accordingly the Edward Towgood business was removed from Spicers' control. The business with its long history stretching back to around 1600 was subsequently closed in 1971.

Reed acquired in 1966 the Scottish paper group Alexander Cowan and proceeded to merge its merchanting operation with that of Spicers to form Spicer-Cowan. It reported into Reed Group, thus removing merchanting operations from Spicers' control. Likewise, control of Spicers' overseas operations were brought together with Reed's other overseas businesses to form Reed Consolidated Industries. The old Spicers Export business became Spicers International and accounted for half of Spicers' turnover, its revenue coming from paper and the sale of printing machinery, manufactured by others. In 1974 Spicers International reporting switched to Reed and shortly afterwards the business was sold.

Although the scope of the Spicers business became significantly smaller under Reed it received major investments in stationery manufacturing, both at Sawston and in a new envelope factory that opened in 1970 at Washington, Tyne & Wear, This was an area of high unemployment, with the local coal industry in decline, and consequently attracted substantial government grants covering 40% of Reed's £1m investment.

Chapter 2
Apprenticeship

I joined Spicers at Sawston in 1972 and took on an accountancy trainee role. At that time, because of the relatively remote location, the company bussed in employees from the local area. Car ownership was still limited and I, like others, took advantage of free transport from Cambridge where I lived. The company's paternal approach to employees extended to a Sports and Social club on site, with tennis and squash court facilities. The next stage of the Spicers story was to become part of my personal history. I in turn was to play a part in the development of the business, particularly as my responsibilities grew. The long established company was to enjoy a final significant flourish before it met its end in 2020.

Almost immediately after joining the accounts department I was appointed budget officer. Preparing budgets involved visiting all parts of the business to determine, with cost centre managers, detailed plans for their area of responsibility. These were the building blocks for compiling an overall business plan for the coming financial year. One of my earliest memories with the company is of visiting Ledbury in Herefordshire, the smallest of our three manufacturing locations, along with production director,

Gerry Peters. The Ledbury operation was part of Reed's acquisition of the Cowan business and had subsequently become part of Spicers. It specialised in small runs of handmade envelopes and other paper based products of every conceivable shape and size. It was managed by Jack Mallen who was a major employer and figure in the Ledbury community. He had set up the factory at the behest of his employer Cowans in 1946 and had developed the business successfully. Jack and his wife Joy are named on a plaque on the wall of St Katherine's Chapel, Ledbury. The plaque records a bequest made for the upkeep of the hall and clock made in memory of their only child, Lisa, who died aged 16 in 1981. Jack's right hand 'man' was in fact a woman, Anne Gladwin, who ran the factory, employing mainly women, and was a key part of the success of the business. It was the most profitable part of Spicers envelope manufacturing business at that time. I would accompany Gerry Peters on his visit to the factory, involving a two and a half hour drive from Sawston, there to reach agreement with Jack Mallen on his planned sales, margins and detailed costs for the coming financial year.

Gerry Peters

Gerry was to be my main personal connection with the old Spicers family regime, a regime that had been systematically dismantled after the business was taken over by Reed in 1963. Gerry's father Peter had joined Edward Towgood in 1922, five years after that business had been acquired by Spicers. He was head gardener on the Sawston estate and led a team of seven gardeners responsible for the numerous vegetable patches, greenhouses and gardens. Gerry was born in 1919 and went to school in nearby Whittlesford but spent many hours on the Spicers estate with his father. At the age of sixteen he secured a job in the book factory. On outbreak of war in 1939 he enlisted in the Royal Engineers and after training in various locations around the UK set sail from Liverpool in October 1941, not knowing the ship's destination. After crossing the Atlantic to Nova Scotia it sailed down the US coast to the Caribbean and back across the Atlantic to Cape Town, then on to Mombasa, Bombay and eventually Singapore. They arrived in January 1942 just sixteen days before the British garrison there surrendered to the Japanese army. Singapore was the UK's major military base in south east Asia. It was called the *Gibraltar of the East* and was regarded as impregnable. That claim proved catastrophically mistaken. The Japanese advanced down the Malayan peninsula and it took them just over a week to overrun Singapore. Having captured 50,000 allied troops in Malaya the Japanese added a further 80,000 on taking Singapore. Winston Churchill called the defeat 'the worst disaster in British military history'.

Gerry was to spend over three years as a prisoner of war. The Japanese paid little attention to international conventions on treatment of prisoners and Gerry was subject to deprivation, illness, beatings and long hours of hard physical labour. He worked on the infamous railroad between Thailand and Burma, a railway that British engineers pre-war had considered but had regarded as impractical because of the terrain. It was nicknamed the 'Death Railway' and was made famous to a wide post-war audience as a result of David Lean's film *Bridge on the River Kwai*. Gerry suffered many hardships and illnesses, malnutrition was the norm and dysentery almost killed him, but he survived when many of his fellow prisoners did not. Towards the end of the war he was shipped to Japan to work in a sulphuric acid plant and, when that was destroyed by an earthquake, on to a chrome producing blast furnace. The Spicers estate idyll must have seemed like a different lifetime. Two atomic bombs dropped on Hiroshima and Nagasaki brought the war against Japan to a sudden and decisive end. Eventually Gerry returned home in August 1945 via the Philippines and then Canada. He and other British ex-prisoners were treated royally in Canada before finally crossing the Atlantic to home.

A more sober welcome awaited there, a ration card rather than the luxuries of Canada, and a standard letter from King George rather than cheering crowds. The British had celebrated Victory in Europe (VE Day) back in May and those returning from the Far East received a more muted welcome home. His real reward was to return to Whittlesford to be reunited with his family and his job at Spicers.

Gerry related none of his traumatic war experience as we made the long commute between Sawston and Ledbury. I knew he had been a prisoner of war but it wasn't until he published an account of 'his' war in 1987, for his grandchildren, that the full horror of his experience became clear to many who worked with him. He was, for us, a mild mannered, thoughtful, gentle-man. His graphic account of being a prisoner of war was all the more compelling because of its absence of emotion or bitterness.

Management Accountant

My role as budget officer progressed into that of management accountant by June 1974. I was then responsible for preparation of business plans and operating budgets as well as the supply of control information to management. The latter took the form of monthly accounts, direct labour reports and sales analyses showing detailed comparison with plan by cost centre. This involved managing a small team and as my subsequent CV stated 'the work entailed close liaison with all levels of management and called for interpretation and communication skills'. In the early 1970s computers played a relatively small part in the mechanics of producing information. In those days at Spicers a large team of girls in the accounts department were comptometer operators, each working all day with a mechanical device that facilitated calculations. A comptometer, invented at the end of the 19th century, had around 100 keys and required dexterity and concentration for accuracy. Typing pools typed invoices, as well as other documents, comptometer operators calculated invoices and did other routine computations.

By the early 1970s Spicers had become predominantly a UK based paper converting business. Paper making, paper merchanting, overseas businesses and export had or were being progressively hived off by Reed. As a result, Spicers profits, despite investments like Washington and acquisitions like Ledbury, were little better than when Reed had acquired the business back in 1963. In 1971 Reed appointed Bob Challoner as general manager of the Stationery division, the main part of the Spicers business. Giles Witherington, the last of the Spicers family clan, remained chairman of Spicers Limited until 1977 but from 1968 onwards had become progressively more involved in Reed Group management rather than in Spicers day to day operations. Bob Challoner's brief was to grow the business and its profitability, his analysis suggested that that could be achieved by putting greater volume through the business's existing distribution infrastructure. The resulting strategy was to bear fruit but was many years in the making. The 1970s were to prove as turbulent for Spicers as had been the 1960s under Reed management and the 1950s under Spicer family control.

The Birth of Wholesaling

In 1973 Spicers bought Gutteridge Sampson (GS), a wholesaler of a wide range of office products with regional bases in London and Glasgow. The business was owned and run by the

Gutteridge family. It had been established in the early 1930s by Mancel Gutteridge and he was joined after the war by his son Jack. Two important exclusive distribution agreements helped build the business, with Philips Dictation Machines and Imperial Portable Typewriters. One of the company's main marketing tools was its annually printed, full colour, catalogue which displayed a wide range of products consumed in offices. Most of that range was held in stock. The catalogue was sold to office product dealers and was then personalised by overprinting on the front cover the dealer's own name. This catalogue was then distributed by the dealer to his own customer base, usually offices in the immediate vicinity. It was a powerful marketing tool already in 1973 and had the potential for substantial growth if the model could be successfully rolled out across the UK. That potential would ultimately be realised, with UK annual catalogue sales eventually exceeding one million copies, but only after considerable difficulties were overcome.

The acquisition of GS and ambitious growth strategy resulted in a review of Spicers organisation structure. The business head office was moved from London to Sawston and two new divisions were created; Manufacturing and Emgee, the latter to manage wholesaling operations. Emgee was Gutteridge Sampson's house brand, or private label, the name taken from the initials of Mancel Gutteridge. In 1974 the first new regional distribution centre (RDC) was opened in Glasgow and it combined the existing distribution activities of GS and Spicers Stationery. Unfortunately the growth plans were not matched by the administrative systems necessary to manage service to customers.

The catalogue business model depended on dealer confidence; that should he receive an order from his customer, across the range in his catalogue he could promptly deliver that order, ideally in one consignment. Dealers generally carried in stock on their own premises a limited range of faster moving products. For the wider range of slower moving products, displayed in the Emgee catalogue, the dealer depended on Spicers not only having the product in stock but giving a reliable delivery service. If Spicers failed, then the dealer failed and the result was an unhappy end user and unhappy dealer. So getting Spicers service right was critical to confidence and dealer commitment to Spicers. That service proved inadequate. Not only that but the duplicated infrastructure cost of two divisions, Stationery and Emgee, each with its own accounts department and other functions, drove the business into loss. Bob Challoner left Spicers in 1975 and a new MD, Chris Behrens, restructured the business to improve accountability and cut costs.

My budding career with Spicers took a step backwards when it was decided to merge the two divisions into one 'Office Services Division'. I had been management accountant (MA) of the original Stationery business and then moved across to become MA of the Emgee division, having understood that business's growth potential. My new role became redundant when the Emgee accounting function was folded back into the established department. A position of project accountant was created for me but, seeing this as a 'non-job', I chose to leave Spicers in July 1976 to join Newmarket based United Photographic Laboratories. My departure was to be short lived.

Chris Behrens recruited Eric Smith onto the Spicers Limited board as sales and marketing director where he sat alongside Gerry Peters as production director and Ian Chalk who managed two Spicers subsidiary businesses, Spicer Hallfield and Alacra. Ian replaced Chris Behrens as Spicers MD in 1977 and in the same year Giles Witherington stepped down as chairman, severing the business's final link with the Spicer's family. The regular chop and change at the top of Spicers had done little to help a struggling business. That was about to change under Ian Chalk's calm and thoughtful leadership. Customer service was identified as the key to success as a wholesaler and that became the focus of company strategy. In the financial year ended March 1977 the business reported a loss.

Two years later a profit of £1.7m was achieved on revenue of £27m of which £10m was attributable to the wholesaling side of the business. That result gave some confidence in the strategy being pursued and provided motivation for further investment in the business. It was recognised, however, that substantial growth would depend upon the efficient management of customer service. Handling large volumes of low value orders required good systems, as did maximising stock availability. A great deal of effort, over several years, went into developing bespoke computer systems that could meet those demanding service requirements, at an affordable cost to the business.

Commercial success depended not only on having efficient systems and detailed information but also on having competent management of both information and the frontline staff delivering the company's service. That was to be another important pillar of future success, as was getting the right distribution infrastructure in place. The south east of England was the largest market Spicers could serve as a wholesaler in the UK. The inadequate mix of warehousing in London was finally closed in January 1979 and relocated to two regional distribution centres (RDCs). Each carried the full catalogue product range, one at Park Royal in north west London and the other at Bermondsey in the south east. Other RDCs had already been established in Birmingham, Bristol and Leeds in addition to the original Glasgow investment.

Apprenticeship from Accounting to Commercial

My return to Spicers was fortuitous. I had left the business on good terms, in particular with my boss Peter Frost, then chief accountant. He approached me in early 1977 to advise me that an analytical role had arisen in the marketing department and that I should apply, if interested. That would entail a move out of accounting, the role I had taken up in Newmarket, and coincided with my completing the examinations of the Institute of Cost and Management Accountants. I decided to apply. The position reported to the marketing manager, David Gutteridge, one of two sons of Jack Gutteridge still employed in the company. I was interviewed by him and his boss, Eric Smith, and was offered the job. One of the perks of marketing jobs at that time was provision of a company car, a substantial benefit, and that was one reason I promptly accepted the offer.

My new analytical role was short lived and I became envelope product manager a year or so later. The job description explained the purpose of my role 'to develop, with regard to production constraints and competitors' activity, a marketing plan for envelopes, whereby sales are increased, market share maintained and maximum profitability achieved'. This was an era when the use of fax machines in offices was growing rapidly.

That appeared to have major possible implications for future communications between businesses with consequent impact on the consumption of commercial envelopes, Spicers' principal market. I undertook a major project to consider how this might affect the business. That entailed travelling the country alongside the head of Spicers' industrial salesforce, Ron Pulford, whose team sold envelopes directly to large users, such as banks. We visited many major envelope consumers and mailing machine manufacturers, machines that inserted content into envelopes, to obtain their views on future trends. Ron was both manager of the sales team and their shop steward. They were some of the very few white collar employees in Spicers who were unionised and somehow Ron managed his role of 'boss' and 'worker representative' without alienating the company or his team. After many miles travelled, Ron's phlegmatic conclusion on the threat posed by new technology prevailed. This could be summed up 'as one door closes, another will open'. Direct mail promotional material at this time was growing strongly and he saw that growth opportunity as more than offsetting any technologically driven decline in business envelope usage. My report to Eric Smith in late 1978 may not have led to any change in Spicers' marketing strategy but it undoubtedly helped raise my profile and in consequence may have shortened my stay in the marketing department.

At the end of February 1979 I attended, along with twelve other managers from across Spicers, the first 'management assessment seminar' held at Wadenhoe House near Kettering. The purpose was to give the directors of the company an opportunity to meet and judge candidates' suitability for future management vacancies. We were split into teams and over two days given a number of exercises to work on, many involving real issues that had faced the Spicers business. The faculty included MD Ian Chalk, Eric Smith sales & marketing, Gerry Peters production, Dennis Sutherland finance and Stanley Bradley personnel. A few months later I was encouraged to apply for the role of sales manager at Park Royal RDC, this, I was told, 'to help your development as a manager'.

The role involved managing a field sales force of six people who had geographical territories extending from Hampshire to

Norfolk in an arc around the north west London RDC. It was a job I would never have dreamed of applying for. I had no experience of sales and felt I had little aptitude for a sales role, being introverted by nature. On top of that Park Royal, one of the two new London RDCs, had inherited an atrocious reputation for customer service. The job would entail uprooting my family, wife and daughter, from Cambridge and relocating to within commuting distance of Park Royal. I had severe doubts about applying for the job which depended on an interview with my current boss's brother, Michael Gutteridge, the other family remnant of the Gutteridge Sampson legacy. He was London region manager, responsible for the two RDCs, but was also effectively RDC manager of Park Royal, so the role of sales manager reported directly to him. After much anguished consideration I decided to apply and was subsequently offered the job.

It was to be one of two really traumatic job changes I undertook at Spicers, yet it was probably the most important move I made in the development of my career with the company. It immersed me, for the first time, in the commercial reality of the business and introduced me to that oft forgotten key to any business's ultimate success – the customer. It would also prove to be my last job application, all subsequent roles and increases in responsibility were offered without application. I will never forget being introduced to the field salesforce, on taking up my new job. The averted eyes and look of despair on their faces. They had been without a direct manager for 18 months, every day they were harangued by customers for service failures or invoicing issues and now someone had decided to put an accountant, with no experience of sales, in charge of them. Their lack of confidence was only matched by my own. The difference was that I could not afford to show mine.

The Customer Comes First

Michael Gutteridge was quite different in temperament to his brother David. The latter lacked confidence and was never very comfortable directing Spicers' marketing effort, other than in championing the catalogue which had been the principal commercial inheritance from his father's business, Gutteridge Sampson. Michael was, outwardly at least, a much stronger character, confident to the point of arrogance in certain respects.

Unhappy customers tried him sorely. One famous incident illustrates both these points. He received a phone call at Park Royal from yet another disgruntled customer who ended his less than sympathetically heard complaint, by threatening to close his account. Michael's response, which he was happy to relate to others later, was to tell the customer that he would close their account before they could. Neither Michael nor David Gutteridge survived at Spicers. David went off to set up his own dealer business and became a customer of Spicers. He famously had two cars, a rather modest one in which he would visit his customers and a more prestigious one kept for domestic use.

Shortly after I arrived at Park Royal Michael went off to become sales director of Antocks Lairn, an office seating manufacturer supplier to Spicers. His replacement as London region manager came as a very pleasant surprise for me, it was Peter Frost, my old accounts department boss, who had decided to make the leap into the commercial side of the business. We were to be reunited and together played an important part in transforming a still poorly performing operation, into the UK's leading office product wholesaler. In 1980 the division's sales were around £10m and market competition was considerable. Birmingham based John Heath was national and the UK's leading office product wholesaler, Neville & Gladstone, another competitor, was growing strongly having been set up in the 1950's by an ex-employee of Gutteridge Sampson. In turn an ex-employee of Neville & Gladstone, Roger Murphy, had set up a new regional wholesaling business in Luton that he named Murfax.

What did two accountants do to help change the fortunes of Spicers? They patiently listened to unhappy customers and set about overcoming the numerous service related issues causing that discontent. Peter installed on the wall above his desk an embroidered plaque containing the words THE CUSTOMER COMES FIRST. Nobody could doubt where the focus would lie in the months ahead. It is of course one thing to set an objective and another to make it happen. That is where the disciplines of management accounting came in. All the elements making up customer service were analysed; from order fill, what percentage of lines ordered by a customer were filled first time, to picking accuracy, to on time delivery and correct invoicing, to query resolution. Every aspect of service was measured, accountability made clear, targets set for improvement and weekly reporting of performance against those targets actively monitored. Good performance was acknowledged, poor performance was revisited until it improved. The adage was 'what gets measured gets done'. And it did. Service over the succeeding months was transformed. It was instinctively believed that if we got the service right, higher sales growth and better profitability would follow. And they did. This quickly resulted in happier customers and happier Spicers' employees, who were no longer having to field large volumes of complaints. So what might appear to have been simple disciplines soon transformed London region's service and then the rest of the country's, as successful methods were emulated elsewhere. It could not have been achieved without the computer systems that had been developed to provide the information needed, nor if the warehousing and delivery infrastructure and its management had not been in place. All were essential in the transformation of Spicers to become a genuinely customer focused business.

Influencing Skills

My role as field sales manager became that much easier as we got on top of service. Face to face contact with customers was a revelation, unimagined when I had previously sat in a marketing department far removed from the realities of the customer 'coal face'.

Understanding what their issues were in developing their own businesses helped inform my future business philosophy. My vocational training was now largely on the job, however I did participate in one notable training course. It was organised through our parent company's in-house training centre, at Reed's Aylesford site, and was under the leadership of their senior training manager Denis Gabbitas. The course on *Influencing Skills* was over several days and it involved 15 or so participants from across the Spicers business. Denis went to great lengths to create an atmosphere of trust and mutual support amongst delegates, with exercises involving role play as well as team building. At the end of the course we were joined by Stanley Bradley, personnel director of Spicers.

Course participants had observed his arrival from an upstairs window, saw his exit from the car and watched him replace his 'driving' shoes with highly polished 'business' shoes, to complete an immaculate presentation. A circle of seating was formed with a place for Stanley to sit alongside Denis. Stanley kicked off proceedings with an open question to the group 'how have you found the course? '. One participant, probably expressing a view common to most, volunteered 'it has been the best course I have ever been on, it has been thoroughly enjoyable'. Stanley's response was instant and instinctive 'you have not been here to enjoy yourselves, what have you learned?'. The carefully constructed atmosphere of mutual confidence and goodwill instantly evaporated, a look of despair crossed Denis's face as he silently watched his work demolished in a few seconds and saw participants' guards hastily re-erected. Fortunately the lessons of the course and in particular the principle that influencing begins with listening, was not lost on me or, hopefully, others there.

Growing Sales and Experience

As service improved so did sales growth. With growth came opportunities to further improve service. Dealers who had previously enjoyed two deliveries a week from Spicers now justified daily deliveries. Order cut off times for next day delivery were systematically pushed back until orders could be taken until 6pm and be reliably delivered the following day. Shift working grew in the warehouses to accommodate the new demands. The product assortment too was expanded. Most dealers would buy faster moving product from manufacturers and carry those in stock but the ever growing 'tail' of product, represented in the Spicers catalogue, were sourced from the wholesaler.

With later ordering cut-off times and early delivery slots the dealer could integrate items from his own stock with those sourced from the wholesaler and make a single delivery to his customers. At last we were in a position to really exploit the key marketing tool we had in the Emgee catalogue.

The development of computer technology also fuelled the growth of dealer purchases from Spicers. As the catalogue range was also the dealer's own range, Spicers pricing was critical to the dealer's own pricing to his customer. Spicers sought from their suppliers fixed prices for, initially, 3 months at a time so that price list changes could be limited to four a year, this in an era of relatively high inflation. Dealers were supplied not only with printed price lists but with a digital price file, in the form of a disc we branded *Spicerfile*, that could be used to update their own systems. Computer links directly into Spicers' system were also developed, this in the early 1980s long before PCs had been invented or the internet. Modified TV sets along with keyboards were rented to dealers and enabled them to view live stock holdings in their local RDC and to order that stock instantaneously. In one dealer's words *Spicerlink* was a window on their other warehouse and enabled them to make reliable commitments to their own customers. By the mid 1980s hundreds of *Spicerlink* terminals were in use by dealers around the country.

In 1983 Peter Frost was promoted to sales and marketing director of the business, as Eric Smith moved up to replace Ian Chalk, and in turn I was promoted into the role of London region manager, responsible for Park Royal and Bermondsey RDCs. It proved to be a relatively straightforward transition, given my previous involvement in many RDC processes.

The strong sales growth the overall business was now experiencing created a need to increase warehousing capacity nationally. The network of RDCs then included the two London locations, Bristol, Birmingham, Leeds and Glasgow. In 1981 a new enlarged Birmingham RDC was opened, a Salford location was added in 1983 and in 1985 Bristol was relocated to larger premises and Belfast RDC came on stream. Also in 1985 a 120,000 square foot central warehouse (CDC) was opened on the Sawston site.

Operating with a CDC had many advantages and it became a core strength of the business. The majority of suppliers now delivered larger orders to a single warehouse and as a result were happy to improve Spicers' buying terms. The central warehouse made a single delivery, across the product range, to most RDCs within 24 hours and that delivery was presented in such a way as to facilitate receipt and putting away of products. This helped dramatically improve RDC goods-in productivity. The depth of local stockholding could now also be significantly reduced, without impacting stock availability, because of the service being received from CDC, and this effectively extended the life of RDCs during a period of dramatic sales growth.

Back to Sawston

After two years as southern region manager Peter Frost offered me a return to Sawston to become marketing manager of the business, which I accepted. In that role I was responsible for catalogue production as well as general promotion of Spicers increasingly sophisticated range of marketing and system tools for dealers. One of the first things developed under my management was an alternative annual catalogue in a different format to the September publication. As circulation had grown we had begun to meet dealer resistance to taking the catalogue because of its prevalence in some local marketplaces. Our new January *A to Z* catalogue, with its alphabetic and generic product layout, addressed that dealer concern. It enabled higher total circulation to be achieved as dealers could choose between two catalogues, albeit with the same product range, as their primary marketing tool. Supplementary, range specific, catalogues were also developed covering computer consumables and office furniture, enabling the dealer to compete with specialist range suppliers. The marketing of Spicers' growing range of dealer services became increasingly sophisticated under the strapline 'Helping Your Business Grow'. That slogan was also aimed at the company's suppliers, increasingly anxious to access Spicers' growing market share.

Trade Association

The UK stationery and office products industry had its own trade body to which most manufacturers and distributors belonged. It had formed in 1905, becoming the *Stationers' Association* in 1912, and provided a range of services to members as well as enabling a forum to discuss areas of common interest. Initially much focus was on pricing protection but this was abandoned after the abolition of Retail Price Maintenance in the 1960s. For many years the association was based in Wimpole Street, London and derived much of its income from an annual industry trade exhibition, *Statindex*. In 1985 the industry body, now called the *British Stationery & Office Products Federation*, began to make an annual 'award of excellence' to one business of outstanding merit within the industry. Spicers was the first recipient of that award and was subsequently to win on several occasions. Each year, also, the Federation organised an industry conference, involving two or three nights away at an hotel venue, and at which many of the industry's leading executives would be present. These socially enjoyable conferences were also informative with guest speakers from across the world of office products and they undoubtedly helped unify the industry. In 1989 I was to chair a *Federation Review Committee* that recommended and implemented a new structure, with separate boards of wholesalers, retailers and manufacturers, and a new overall body name that incorporated the growing importance of systems; *BOSS Federation* (British Office Systems and Stationery).

Golf Day Shock

In 1986, much to my surprise, Peter Frost chose to leave Spicers and join one of our biggest London based customers, *Copygraphic*. I was totally ignorant of this until I was quietly taken aside by Eric Smith, Peter's boss, at a customer golf day in the Midlands.

He explained Peter's planned departure and offered me his job. In shock I asked for time overnight to think about the offer, which he was happy to give me. On 16th June 1986 my appointment as sales and marketing director was announced. My surprise was mirrored by general surprise within the company and the industry. I was 37 years old and much younger than most of those destined to report to me. Many were sceptical of my ability to fulfil the responsibilities I now shouldered, of a business growing rapidly and beginning to play a much more important role within the industry. I did not experience any of the serious self doubt I had felt on taking on the sales manager role at Park Royal seven years earlier. I believed I had gained valuable experience since then that had equipped me to face the undoubted challenge that lay ahead. My rise over a relatively short period had involved no job applications or interviews. It was neither planned nor expected. It was the result of my good fortune in being in the right place at the right time, as well as of considerable commitment and hard work. I had completed my long apprenticeship within the business. Now it fell to me to demonstrate that I could provide the leadership required to take the business forward.

Chapter 3
Leadership

My new role involved becoming a director of Spicers Limited, a legal entity and wholly owned subsidiary of what was now called Reed International plc. Spicers was then chaired by Ian Chalk who had been born in 1931 at Stapleford, near Sawston. He had been educated at Newport grammar school and had joined Spicers in the early 1950s.

He started on the factory floor, then became a foreman and later a company sales representative. In 1961 he was given the opportunity to move to Haddenham to manage Spicer Hallfield, a manufacturer of photograph albums. His success there led to him being given responsibility for Alacra, another Spicers' subsidiary. He was then appointed to the Spicers Limited board and in 1977 became managing director of the total business and played an important part in stabilising the business after years of senior management change. In 1983 he became chairman and stayed in that role until the early 1990s. He provided constancy and clarity of direction, in particular encouraging focus on the customer and promotion of people from within the business to positions of greater responsibility. He was a modest man, honest and reliable. He never moved his family from Haddenham and after retirement in 1991 devoted a great deal of his time to that community with involvement in the parish council, horticultural society and local masonic lodge. He never lost his schoolboy love of cricket and on retirement treated himself to following an English cricket tour of the West Indies. He died in 2020 on his birthday at the age of 89, having had a very good innings.

Eric Smith, my boss, was now titled chief executive rather than managing director of Spicers and had followed Ian Chalk into that role. Job title inflation would be a feature of the years ahead. Reporting to him alongside myself were fellow directors responsible for the manufacturing division, finance and systems and group personnel. All were housed in the old Spicers' family home *Homewood* at Sawston, converted to offices long before.

My responsibility covered the sales, warehousing and distribution, marketing and buying functions of the wholesaling division. At that time the division's sales to dealers were £76m, made up of £56m in bought-in products and £20m in Spicers' manufactured products. It employed 600 people across nine locations and the product range offered to dealers stood at around 7,000 items of which 400 were manufactured by Spicers.

Catalogue sales were then around 800,000 per annum. My team consisted of: three regional managers, responsible for the eight RDCs in Belfast, Glasgow, Leeds, Salford, Birmingham, Bristol, Bermondsey and Park Royal; a central distribution centre manager based at Sawston; a buyer responsible for negotiating terms with suppliers and determining the range assortment in conjunction with a marketing manager who was responsible for catalogue production and the development and promotion of services to dealers. My role evolved later in 1986 into that of general manager (later MD) of the division when it was decided that further separation of the wholesaling and manufacturing businesses could now be financially justified and involved adding responsibility for separated accounting, systems and personnel functions.

The continuing dramatic growth of the business entailed significant expansion of capacity. Park Royal RDC was relocated to nearby larger premises, new RDCs were opened in Chessington, Nottingham and Newcastle and the central warehouse was expanded first from 120,000 square feet to 220,000 and then to 300,000 feet. The full range catalogue circulation grew to exceed a million copies per annum.

Computer services for dealers became even more sophisticated with the development of *Progress,* a stand alone system sold to dealers and on which they could run their own businesses. It was fully integrable with Spicers' own system. Originally developed in-house, the *Progress* project was in 1986 sold off to Spicers' Cambridge based software house. It was subsequently segregated into a separate business, *Interactive Products,* and bought out by Ron Wotherspoon and Peter Barkas. Ron had originally worked for Gutteridge Sampson and then from 1973 for Spicers. He knew the business intimately, understood the dealer's requirements, and had played a key part in the 1970s helping to develop the order processing and stock control systems that were to prove vital to Spicers' later success. Peter was the software creator and had originally worked for Reed. The pair had complementary skills and their partnership worked well in creating a specialist business involved in the development and supply of dealer specific software. In 1988 100 dealer customers were using *Progress* and a further 500 dealers had by then installed *Spicerlink* terminals, connecting them directly into Spicers' system.

By 1990 wholesaling division sales reached £200m, profits were £19.3m producing a return on capital of 43% and the number of employees stood at 1350. Management focus in the 1980s had been largely on maintaining service levels, during a period of dramatic growth, as well as on developing innovative marketing and systems tools. All that growth had been organic. The market had grown to the benefit of all wholesalers, both national, such as John Heath and Neville & Gladstone and regional like Murfax and Kingfield, but Spicers had outstripped them all and had by then over 50% of the UK wholesaling market for office products.

Managing Principles

Many management changes had been necessary during this period of rapid business expansion but the guiding principle, inherited from Ian Chalk, was to promote from within whenever possible. This enabled better selection, given an in-depth knowledge of individual candidates and their discharge of past responsibility, it also resulted in continuity of direction and culture, as well as fostering good morale and motivation. The 1980s had taught me a great deal about management, principles that would be vital in coping with the considerable challenges that lay ahead. Those principles could be summarised as being; the need for clarity of objective, nature abhors a vacuum and if objectives are absent, or ill-defined, people will create their own, often more ego based than business-need based; having defined key goals make responsibility for achieving those goals clear, let there be no uncertainty as to who is responsible and avoid shared goals that might sound laudable, but are responsibility-avoidance fodder for some; quantify as many goals as possible, agree these with those accountable, then measure and monitor performance as frequently as practicable; recognise achievement and give encouragement, rather than criticism, to improve performance; having individuals with the right motivation in positions of authority is key to success, right motivation involves honesty, open-ness, concern with company goals rather than personal or egotistical ones, a sense of responsibility, commitment and industriousness; if you make a mistake in appointing a person who seriously fails the test of right motivation better to replace them than soldier on allowing them to poison the business and others around them; promote from within if you can with the caveat that if you over-promote someone who cannot cope with their new responsibilities you have an obligation to help them by finding a suitable alternative role for them. A key principle was to lead by example not by edict. The belief was that the qualities championed by the leadership determined the business's culture and its success, both in the marketplace and financially.

Recognition of success was institutionalised within the business. Given so many key performance indicators (KPI) were measured and targeted within the business it was logical to have league tables of results across all RDCs. Each year winners would be declared across service criteria and awards made to relevant managers. Numerous awards were made, not only in distribution centres but also in central administrative functions. A *Bright Ideas* scheme encouraged employees to recommend improvements in the business and these were judged and then annual awards made for the best ideas. All these initiatives were designed to encourage and recognise better performance.

Recognition stretched also to customers reaching significant milestones. When Northampton based dealer *Arkle* reached one million pounds of purchases from Spicers their senior management, together with Spicers' senior team, went to Gleneagles in Scotland for a golfing weekend. Supplier recognition of sales to Spicers exceeding £1m could be even more lavish. David Baldrey, head of Spicers' buying function, was involved in organising a succession of celebratory treats. A notable example in the late 1980s was a weekend in Venice for the senior management teams of

Spicers and Swindon Letterfile's Guidex business, a manufacturer of filing products.

In 1989 I was shocked to learn of the death of Brian Lansdown, one of my senior team. He was 42 years old and was Spicers southern region manager, having replaced me in that role five years earlier. Brian had joined the business from sister company Spicer Hallfield. He had died at work of a massive heart attack and had no previous history of a heart condition. What was particularly strange about his death was that found on his person was a letter addressed to his wife, to be given to her 'in the event of his death'. It transpired that he had, in recent years at least, carried such a letter and that some others were aware of his premonition of an early death. This may have been the result of the sudden death of his boss at Spicer Hallfield, Hugh Spence, a few years earlier, but that is speculation. His well attended funeral service was an emotional affair, given his relative youth and the fact his wife was distraught. Her cry of '*I will always love you Brian*', as the crematorium curtain closed on his coffin, left very few dry eyes in the crowded chapel. In memory of Brian the highly prized annual trophy, for best overall RDC performance across a wide range of criteria, was renamed the Lansdown Trophy.

The USA

I visited the USA on a number of occasions in the 1980s, first with Peter Frost then with Eric Smith. Our goal had been to understand how wholesaling had developed there and to build a relationship with the biggest office product wholesaler, United Stationers. A memorable trip in the late 1980s had Eric and I meet up, on completion of our mission, with Ian Chalk, Spicers' chairman, already in New York on separate business. It was Ian that arranged for our return to the UK to be by Concord, the supersonic passenger jet then operated by British Airways. An extravagant treat we would not have dared indulge in without his lead. We learned a great deal from our visits to the US, both about how wholesalers operated and the services they provided to dealers. The US connection and perspective was also going to prove valuable as we entered a new decade and began to experience new forms of indirect competition; this from foreign based intruders intent on taking away business from our traditional customer base.

Spicers' dominance of the UK office product wholesaling market also encouraged us to turn our focus to continental Europe for new avenues of growth. Eric Smith was one of the key ingredients of Spicers success in the 1980s and 1990s. He was born in Wales, had taken a degree in chemistry and subsequently obtained a Diploma in Management Studies, a qualification we had in common. He arrived in 1976 at the age of 35 as sales and marketing director, part of Reed's injection of new management into Spicers. A year later Ian Chalk took over as MD and when Ian was promoted to chairman in 1983 Eric replaced him at the operational helm. He was a charismatic leader with a great sense of humour. That can be judged from the opening of a speech he made at Stationers' Hall marking the retirement of Charles Bessell, head of competitor John Heath. Charles had led Heath to UK wholesaling market leadership. By the time of his retirement Spicers was beginning to overtake Heath in market share. Eric along with others representing Heath's suppliers, customers and competitors was asked to speak at his farewell dinner.

His speech opened *'Friends, Romans, countrymen lend me your ears, for I come to bury Caesar not to praise him'*. Great laughter followed and that tended to accompany most of Eric's speeches. As well as an accomplished orator he was also a skilled linguist, fluent in French and German, and that would prove invaluable in helping fulfil Spicers' European ambition. He was also a great delegator and prompt decision maker. He would give subordinates their head but also have no qualms in removing that head, if they failed or embarrassed him. He was to become a major figure within the industry as Spicers' fortunes rose and his extroverted nature was comfortable with the accompanying limelight. By contrast, my own introverted inclination towards the detail of strategy planning and managing performance, involved less spotlight and a lower public profile. We worked well together.

Management Buyout

In 1987 Reed's paper and packaging interests, including Spicers, were separated and placed in a new division Reed Manufacturing Group (RMG) under the leadership of Canadian Peter Williams. That was the prelude to Reed's disposal of the division as part of its strategy to focus the business on publishing. It later became known as Reed Elsevier and then RELX. Peter Williams and his divisional senior team, including Ian Chalk and Eric Smith, decided to put a management bid together when RMG was put up for sale. The management buyout (MBO) was successfully concluded in July 1988. It was at that point the second biggest MBO recorded in the UK. The new business was christened Reedpack and had a turnover of £909m and profit £75m. Its principal shareholders were the senior management team, however a wider management cohort also became shareholders, with tiered investment levels enabled by a personal loan facility organised by the company. All employees were given the opportunity to invest via an employee share subscription scheme. Over 1000 employees chose to participate. A conscious decision was made by the senior team not to indulge in asset stripping (disposing of company assets), often a tactic of MBO or leveraged buyout schemes. Such schemes, including Reedpack's, entailed a large element of debt being used to fund the business acquisition and a much smaller equity investment by the buy-out participants. Paying down the debt element as quickly as possible is what normally resulted in asset stripping.

Reedpack management decided that they would invest in the business, grow sales and profits and then float the business on the stock exchange. That did not come to pass. In 1990 Svenska Cellulosa Aktiebolaget (SCA), Sweden's second largest pulp and paper business, unexpectedly came forward with an offer to buy Reedpack. The offer, in excess of £1 billion gross, was accepted in June 1990. The price paid involved a significant return on the amount paid for the business just two years earlier. That increase in value meant that all employee shareholders received a payout equal to 34 times their original investment. My own level of investment meant a return of just over £300,000, taken in the form of loan notes issued by SCA and an element of cash. Those loan notes were converted to SCA shares some 10 years later and that proved to be another good investment. The cash lump sum was used to pay for the extension and rethatching of a new home acquired in 1990. As can be imagined, all those that had chosen to participate in the MBO celebrated their good fortune. What was different from most MBOs was that that good fortune had been shared across a wide range of employees.

Shortly after the acquisition the senior management team were flown to Sweden for a company induction visit. SCA owned vast swathes of forest from which wood was harvested for papermaking. The visiting management group were bussed into one such forest, well to the north of Stockholm. Here we watched specialised tractor units cut down coniferous trees, strip off all the branches and log the remaining trunk, all in the course of a few minutes. We were then seated on a tree trunk benched square, around a large fire, and treated to a picnic of barbecued reindeer meat and neat vodka, consumed as snow gently descended on the forest clearing. The assembled group felt warmly welcomed by our new Viking masters.

The acquisition was to result in a number of management changes as individuals of a certain age felt the lump sum payments they had received enabled early retirement. Ian Chalk was one of those. Peter Williams having led the buyout was another casualty, not because of age but because his role had become redundant. SCA quickly set about integrating the paper and packaging businesses of Reedpack into their existing European management structure. The other issue, as far as Spicers was concerned, was that SCA had bought Reedpack for its paper and packaging businesses; owning Spicers, now predominantly a wide range office product wholesaler, fitted neither their business profile nor their future strategy.

The timing of the sale of Reedpack to SCA proved fortuitous for Reedpack shareholders, if not for SCA shareholders. Two major developments were to affect the value of Spicers at the beginning of the new decade. The first was a general business recession in the UK. The wholesaling business, having grown dramatically from around £10m of sales in 1980 to £200m in 1990, was about to experience its first sales decline. Also in the late 1980s it had been decided to seek wholesaling growth in Europe and that was to prove a traumatic experience for business and management.

Europe

Spicers already had a partial presence in the Republic of Ireland, in a joint venture with the company Jefferson Smurfit, largely involving the manufacture and sale of envelopes. Some wholesaled lines were added to the portfolio in 1987 but in order to establish a proper wholesaling operation in Dublin, Smurfit's share was bought out and in 1991 a full product range Spicers RDC was opened. The range mirrored that of the UK and the RDC was serviced out of the Sawston CDC, so the Irish business was in reality an extension of the UK business and used the same catalogue. As a consequence the operation reported to me, albeit that it had its own accounting and legal function to cater for a different currency, taxation and statutory framework.

A far more ambitious plan was also hatched in the late 1980s and that was to establish a wholesaling operation in continental Europe, initially France. This process was led by Eric Smith, his linguistic ability proving to be important. In 1990 negotiations were completed to buy two regional wholesalers, Papeterie de l'Ouest (PDO) and Papeterie Basco Bearnaise (PBB), that operated in the south and west of France. Neither were typical of the wholesaling operation Spicers had developed in the UK. For that reason it was decided to appoint Spicers UK northern region manager to head up development of Spicers France, given his detailed knowledge of the wholesaling model that it was hoped to replicate in France. That proved to be a bad decision, in part due to a lack of sensitivity to differences in the French marketplace and partly due to what might be described as centuries old national and cultural antipathy. The operation entailed developing a French product range and catalogue. New RDCs were opened, one in the all important Paris area at Garonor, another in Tours. In 1991 the operations of PDO and PBB in Bordeaux, Toulouse and Pau were integrated as part of a national infrastructure.

In 1992 the old Toulouse premises were replaced with a new purpose built facility, Pau was closed and a new RDC was opened at Valence, near Lyon. A consequence of setting up that national infrastructure was service disruption and significant losses and cash outflows. In the financial year 1992/3 the business lost £7.6 million on £40.3 million of sales. Eric Smith came under considerable pressure from Spicers' new owner as the value of its recently acquired Spicers business fell dramatically. A decision was made in 1993 to replace the MD of the French business with Eric Schmitt. Schmitt, who shared a name with his new boss, albeit a Germanic version, had been the owner of PBB and had stayed in the business after it was acquired by Spicers. He was French, despite that Teutonic name, and promptly took up residence in Paris, close to Spicers head office, leaving his family living in Pau in the Pyrenees. Schmitt soon got to grips with the many issues facing Spicers France. He was a great deal more ruthless in cost cutting than his predecessor. The business was to become very much a French business with its own distinctive version of the UK wholesaling model. Within three years it was France's biggest wholesaler with sales of £60m and it was by then profitable.

UK Recession

Despite strong growth in the new Republic of Ireland business, as it gained market share, the picture in the UK in 1991 was less rosy as a result of a general economic downturn.

The UK wholesaling division's sales grew marginally in 1990 and then declined by 11% in 1991. After years of expanding capacity to cope with high growth rates the change of fortune came as a shock. It also called for a very different approach to managing the business as profitability declined. In the years of growth the focus had been on service levels and service enhancement. That had often been achieved through considerable overtime working in distribution centres. Those warehouse employees were also unionised and their basic hourly wage rates were commensurate with factory wage rates, a legacy of Spicers' origin as a manufacturing business. Wages were consequently higher, sometimes substantially higher, than competitors such as John Heath, Neville &

Gladstone and Kingfield. My focus as MD turned to the biggest area of cost, warehouse wages, including chronic overtime working at a 50% premium on normal wage rates. In conjunction with Spicers group personnel director a plan was formulated to introduce annual hours contracts for warehouse employees. This entailed employees contracting to work a total number of hours per annum, rather than a fixed number per week. The annual hour total could not be exceeded and all hours were to be paid at a flat rate.

Management could, within reason, vary hours per day, or per week, to suit prevailing work levels. The system called for detailed record keeping for each employee. Such schemes worked in other industries where work loads varied across the year, with employees having a longer working week at some times of the year and a compensating shorter week at others. Monthly salary was however fixed and unaffected by differences in hours worked. It is, of course, one thing to come up with a scheme, it is another to introduce it into a unionised environment. Especially when the union involved was SOGAT, one of the more aggressive unions by reputation, that had 100% of Spicers warehouse employees in membership.

The Society of Graphical and Allied Trades union was the 1992 result of numerous mergers of print, papermaking and publishing unions that had grown up in the twentieth century. Its reach permeated many industries but it was perhaps most famous, or infamous, for its control of Fleet Street and UK national newspaper publishing. Employers there had for years acquiesced to union practices which were at best restrictive and at worst fraudulent. Their priority had been to get the papers out and they paid a high price for the cooperation of their fully unionised workforce. This modus operandi had been challenged by regional publisher Eddie Shah in 1983 but was to face a much greater challenge in 1986 from Australian born publisher Rupert Murdoch, with his titles; *The Sun, News of the World, The Times* and *Sunday Times*. He planned on breaking the union stranglehold by moving production from Fleet Street to Wapping and he was to be heavily supported by Prime Minister Margaret Thatcher. Following a bitter dispute, mass sackings and violent picketing, Murdoch won the battle. SOGAT was chastened by the experience, having lost a large number of members and at one point having had the union's assets sequestered. That was the recent historical backdrop when Spicers formally opened negotiations with SOGAT in 1992 with the intention of reducing its inflated wage payroll. I was to lead those negotiations together with a small team of senior managers. The SOGAT team was headed by Ted Chard, a national officer of the union.

Negotiations took place over many months and a good relationship was established with the union side, based on mutual respect and a preparedness to compromise on both sides. One negotiating session took place in Blackpool, to coincide with the annual TUC conference there, and involved a memorable night out with our two teams in a local Yates's Wine Lodge. Later Ted was to introduce me to Cockney cuisine in a 'pie and eel' shop in London as our negotiations drew to a close. SOGAT had learned from its Fleet Street battle and Spicers' management knew that any dispute that impacted customer service would be disastrous for the business. The outcome was that an annual hours contract was introduced, new employees were recruited onto it and existing employees were invited to transfer onto the new contract, with a lump sum payment equivalent to 18 months loss of earnings.

Some took the lump sum and promptly resigned, leaving us to recruit replacements on the new contract, others accepted the new terms and stayed. Over a relatively short period all warehouse employees were on the annual hours contract. Productivity improved considerably. In 1990 the division had sales of around £200m and employed 1350 people, by 1995 sales, having recovered after declining in the recession, now reached £230m with just 1,100 employees.

Competitive Threats

Adding to the recessionary pressure on the Wholesaling division's sales were significant changes in the UK marketplace. The majority of Spicers' sales were to small and medium sized dealers and retailers, mainly owner-managed businesses serving their immediate locale. Those dealers bought and distributed the Spicers catalogue, over-printed with their name, into local offices, then took orders over the phone and delivered on a daily basis. This model had been enhanced by the use of catalogues covering an ever greater product range. These catalogues were generally priced, that is with a recommended retail price shown for each product listed, together with a product code to facilitate ordering. As the use of catalogues grew so did a practice amongst dealers of adopting blanket discounts across the whole catalogue range. In many larger towns competing Spicers' dealers were involved in pricing wars offering 25% off or more on the whole range. Spicers' own pricing had inadvertently facilitated this discounting model by applying blanket discounts off trade price to dealers.

Three forms of competition developed for the traditional local dealer in the late 1980s and early 1990s. All had been seen in the USA earlier and had carved out significant market shares at the expense of dealers. My visits to the US from the mid 1980s had given me an appreciation of this trend and realisation that what threatened the traditional dealer, threatened the wholesaler supplying that dealer. The new channel players were of a size that meant they largely bought directly from manufacturers and only used wholesalers for a tiny proportion of their purchases.

Large contract stationers had been around for a while. They usually focused on larger end user businesses with which they entered into annual contracts. In the late 1980s the UK began to see a consolidation of these contract stationers into significantly larger national organisations. WHSmith, of high street retail fame, was one of the first to enter the fray. They bought out a number of large contract stationers, merged their distribution facilities and developed their own private label brand *Niceday* covering key high volume products, like paper and envelopes. They also produced their own full colour catalogue. In their pursuit of growth they attacked many local dealers loyal to Spicers. The landscape for contract stationers quickly changed as the 1990s progressed, a number of foreign owned players entered the UK market. The first was a Dutch company Buhrmann-Tetterode (BT) which bought up a number of large dealers in the UK and US. Then two French companies Guilbert and Gaspard (the latter trading as Lyreco), both dominant in their own marketplace, saw opportunity in the UK. They were followed by US based Corporate Express and USOP. The 1990s saw a frenzy of dealer acquisitions, by largely foreign owned entrants, all intent on gaining share of the UK market at the expense of small and medium sized dealers, Spicers' principal customer base. The growing importance of contract stationers was only one of the threats Spicers' traditional customers faced in the early 1990s.

Mail Order had a place in stationery supply to end users in the 1980s but a relatively minor one. It operated in a different way to contract stationers and traditionally focused on mailing tens of thousands of short-range catalogues, or mailers, to a very wide customer base, taking orders over the phone and delivering by carrier from a single national warehouse. It did not operate with a field salesforce negotiating contracts, it depended on an impactful mailer generating an immediate buyer response. Neat Ideas had operated in the UK in the 1980s and had moderate success. In 1990 one of the US's most successful stationery mail order companies, Viking, arrived in the UK setting up a greenfield operation. They generated millions of mailers each year and delivered high, or as they described them 'fanatical', service levels. In three years their sales reached £100 million in the UK. Managing their mailings and mailing list was key to this success. Initial limited range mailers with very aggressive pricing hooked their customers on key products. As that customer tested their service and became more loyal so they received more comprehensive mail order catalogues with higher prices. The strategy was to gain business on price and build better margin business on service. It worked extremely well. The dealer and contract stationer were calling on the stationery buyer in a larger office, whereas Viking were often mailing individual end users in those same businesses. They were also getting at much smaller businesses that never warranted a visit from a dealer's stationery salesmen.

Also catering for that small end-user business was a new form of retail that had grown dramatically in the USA. Office Depot, OfficeMax and Staples had there developed very large specialised office product superstores, stocking everything from paperclips to desks. Stores had opened across the US and turnover growth was dramatic. Aggressive pricing and strong local advertising campaigns brought in many thousands of small businesses who were happy to collect products from their local store. Staples entered the UK market in 1993.

The development and significant growth of contract stationers, mail order and superstores had dramatically reduced the number of small to medium sized office product dealers in the USA. Dealer population there was estimated to be around 17,000 in 1986 but down to 5,800 by 1993. The number of superstores had grown from 6 to 570 during the same period. It was an ominous sign for Spicers' UK customer base and consequently for Spicers.

Responding to the Challenge

Aware of what was coming Spicers chose to address the issues head on. Some had advocated a change of business model, for example by selling directly to end users and cutting out the dealer, but instead Spicers opted to find ways to help the dealer compete with the emerging threats that they faced. A range of new services were developed from aggressively priced mailers for the dealer to mail out, to a direct delivery service to the end user on behalf of the dealer, branded *pick n' wrap*. Electronic versions of the catalogue were made available as PC (personal computer) usage began to grow at both dealer and end user level. Also end-user computer links and ordering systems that interfaced with the dealer's own system were developed. Spicers' electronic links with its customers became more sophisticated, facilitating electronic transmission of invoices. The underlying logic was to remove cost from the wholesaler/dealer distribution chain to enable it to become more competitive with new forms of competition. Pricing of key products was vital also, as these were used as bait by the new channels. Having avoided private label products in the 1980s, Spicers decided that it was now crucial to have available key products at the best buying and selling price. The *5 Star* branded range was launched with 300 products in 1993 and had increased to 750 lines two years later.

Some of that product was sourced in the Far East using the US wholesaler United Stationers' subsidiary there. Dealers were encouraged to adopt a more sophisticated pricing approach, like new market entrants. They could use aggressive pricing on *5 Star* and then cut back on blanket discounting of the 7,500 products in the general catalogue, most of which were not price sensitive. The *5 star* brand presentation was deliberately language free (consisting of five stars, four white and one red against a black square background) so that it could be used across Europe, as our business grew there.

In 1992 the UK wholesaling division acquired *SpaceAge*, an office furniture business that specialised in providing a range of services to dealers, from CAD (computer aided design) an office layout planning tool, to furniture delivery and installation. Dealers would generate leads and *SpaceAge* would follow up; designing layouts and installing on behalf of the dealer. This service was seen as complementary to the *pick n' wrap* service being developed by Spicers, whereby dealers could take an order from their customer and get Spicers to deliver it on their behalf to the end user, using third party carriers. The growth of this service culminated in Spicers opening in 1995 a dedicated dealer distribution centre (DDC) near the Birmingham hubs of numerous parcel distribution couriers. It was dedicated to end user delivery on behalf of the dealer and its proximity to courier hubs enabled it to take orders until 5pm and deliver next day nationwide, to the dealers' own customers. Orders taken at DDC were exclusively taken electronically and dispatch notes were printed with the dealer's name, not Spicers'.

Dealers themselves responded to the new competitive landscape by flocking into dealer groups. A few dealer groups had existed in the 1980s and their main focus had been on improving buying terms for their members. By 1992 that number had mushroomed to 14 different groups, some now involved in warehousing and some producing their own annual catalogues. Hundreds of Spicers' customers now belonged to groups and it was very much in our interest to cultivate those groups as well as their members.

The new services, in support of dealers, developed by Spicers' senior team helped the business differentiate itself further from its wholesaling competitors in the UK. These efforts were recognised by the wider industry with the company being given the annual BOSS Federation Excellence Award for the fourth time in 1992.

Wholesaling Competition

The UK office product wholesaling landscape changed dramatically in the 1990s, partly in response to changes in the channels of distribution and partly in response to Spicers' dominance and its plethora of new services.

John Heath had been an important regional wholesaler in the Victorian era. It had established its operation in Birmingham in 1852 and had grown to become the leading national wholesaler by the 1970s under the leadership of Charles Bessell. Heath was acquired by Dickinson Robinson Group (DRG) in 1979, a group that included John Dickinson, Spicers manufacturing business's main competitor. The dramatic growth of Spicers' wholesaling business from 1980 resulted in it taking over market leadership from Heath in the late 1980s. DRG was sold to Pembridge in 1989 and that resulted in the onward sale of the John Heath business to US company Atapco. They installed a new MD, Terry Blyth, who rejuvenated the business and then went on to acquire in 1993 the next biggest wholesaler, Neville & Gladstone. That created a more substantial competitor, albeit one still with less than half the turnover of Spicers.

A relative newcomer to wholesaling was Kingfield. It was a Sheffield based regional wholesaler established in 1969 and acquired by the Kaye family in 1976. Alan Hickman joined the business in 1983 and set about building it into a national wholesaler, partly by acquiring other regional players. His efforts were helped when Heath took over Neville & Gladstone and their combined operations rationalised, resulting in some business being lost. By 1999 Kingfield's turnover was £93m and an opportunity arose that year for the Kaye family to buy John Heath from Atapco. This resulted in the departure of Terry Blyth and gave Alan Hickman an integration problem of his own to manage. Part of the logistical strategy developed involved building a new national distribution centre in the Midlands; a kind of combined CDC, RDC and DDC. Getting the service right out of this new *Arrow* facility was key to a successful merged business. Considerable work and disruption ensued. In 2001 Kingfield-Heath achieved sales of £206m but produced an operating loss of £6.5m. Alan Hickman resigned after two very stressful years.

Managing the Message

An aggressive communication programme was developed by Spicers in the early 1990s to tell dealers of the coming threats and to launch new services designed to help them remain competitive. The *Winning Combination* roadshow visited 12 locations across the UK and Republic of Ireland in the autumn of 1992. Senior management, led by Eric Smith and myself, fronted the presentations and dealers flocked to hear what we had to say, see what new services were available and to ask questions of Spicers' senior team. The *Working Together to Win* roadshow followed a year later and the *Power to Compete* a year after that. Communication during a period of often dramatic change, both within Spicers and within the industry, was vitally important. Dealers were fearful of Spicers seeking to by-pass them and go direct, employees were fearful for their jobs as the recession bit and initially sales fell into decline.

Insight was an internal publication created for distribution to employees once a quarter. It contained updates on Spicers' business alongside profiles of individuals, departments and distribution centres. Initially it served employees group-wide but after the two divisions were established separate papers were developed for wholesaling and manufacturing. A regular publication for wholesaling customers was also created, *Spicers News*. It gave updates on the new services available to dealers, as these were developed. Clear communication of Spicers' strategy helped allay customer fears and also helped internally by focusing employee effort on developing services for customers, in support of that strategy.

I had spent much effort cultivating the trade press in the late 1980s and as new publications emerged I developed close ties with their owners. The leading industry publication *Stationery Trade Review* (STR), along with Spicers, sponsored annual *Dealer Excellence Awards* that involved myself and STR MD, Alan Wells, alongside a couple of other high profile manufacturing business leaders, visiting a shortlist of candidates around the country. Trophies were presented at the annual STR Awards Dinner held at a top hotel in London.

Spicers was a major trade press advertiser and we were also able to encourage our suppliers to advertise in support of Spicers' features appearing in STR. For example, each of the annual roadshows from 1992 were supported by lengthy advertising features in the magazine that generated revenue for the publication and extensive trade exposure for Spicers. These features were then published as separate brochures and distributed at roadshows, all at no cost to the business. In the early 1990s new trade publications emerged, some with Spicers' active help. *Dealer Support* was one such publication but more important was *Office Products International* (OPI). The latter was created by two partners who had been in business together as a Hitchen based, Spicers' loyal, dealer *Jeffries-Hilleard*.

They decided to create a monthly trade publication that would not only serve the UK but also the US office products marketplace. In that they succeeded. The turmoil in the office products market, as a result of acquisitions and changing channels of distribution, created a hunger for information about the latest developments on both sides of the Atlantic. OPI caught that wave in 1991.

People Matters

As Spicers' business changed to meet the challenges of a new, quite different, decade many opportunities for advancement arose within the business. When I had been promoted to what became general manager of the wholesaling division, I promoted in turn Anselmo Lodola to the then vacant marketing manager role. That brought him to Sawston from Park Royal, where he had originally been recruited as my field sales manager. On the sudden death of Brian Lansdown in 1989, Anselmo followed in my footsteps once more and became southern region manager. As these changes demonstrate he was a trusted and increasingly experienced colleague. In 1990 shortly after SCA's acquisition of Spicers, as part of Reedpack, Anselmo fell ill with an HIV infection that migrated into AIDS. He had earlier in life been married with a family but, at some point, chose to come out as gay. By the time he joined Spicers he was in a steady gay relationship. His sexuality while never hidden was discreet and he was respected in the business for the person he was. In 1991 he lost his fight to live, as his partner had shortly beforehand. His loss was a major blow to the business and to me personally, as we had a special bond of trust. I was an executor of his will, his estate boosted by the MBO proceeds, and ensured his wishes were carried out in relation to his children, who had not then reached the age of legal majority. The Lodola Trophy became an annual award for the best central department, as voted for, across a range of criteria, by Spicers' distribution centres.

In my replacement of Anselmo, as southern region manager, I made a serious appointment mistake. The wholesaling division management team were, at that time, enthused by the insights provided by Myers Briggs' personality tests, introduced by personnel manager Bridget Tidd. Answering a small number of questions about one's preferences gave rise to a personality profile and this, for most of the team, seemed remarkably accurate. My profile characteristics came out, in the jargon of Myers Briggs, an INTJ; Introspective, Intuitive, Thinking and Judgemental. Given a dearth of internal candidates for the important southern region management role the job was advertised outside the business. In making a final appointment I was influenced by Myers Briggs, with its insight on team dynamics, and consciously chose someone who I thought would be a good 'fit' given the team's existing profile. The motive may have been laudable but the outcome was a bad mistake. The individual concerned was full of apparent confidence and did a good job as one of the presenters in our roadshow tour that year. Unfortunately he was also a bully when it came to managing his team. The flip side of his confidence was an almost pathetic need to mentally unburden himself onto his long suffering secretary, I was to learn later, occasions sometimes accompanied by his tears.

The final straw was when Chris Avery, Bristol RDC manager, handed in his resignation.

Chris, a much trusted colleague who had been with me in London and had been promoted several times, resigned citing his relationship with his boss. It was the time of *Statindex*, the industry exhibition in Birmingham's NEC (National Exhibition Centre), when I asked to meet the individual concerned in Spicers'

Birmingham RDC, pulling him off our exhibition stand. Sacking people is never easy or pleasant but sometimes it is necessary for the health of the business. Better to acknowledge a bad decision and correct it rather than live in hope and denial, to the cost of colleagues as well as the business.

David Baldrey was Spicers' charismatic buyer, a rare survivor of the Gutteridge Sampson business, bought in 1973. He was a larger than life character much loved within the industry for his infectious sense of humour. Following the MBO conclusion and payout David decided to take early retirement. I instigated recruitment of his replacement, Stewart Barton-Taylor (SBT), from one of our customers in Aldershot, having seen him in action as 'buyer' to my 'seller'. He joined us before David's departure and this facilitated the handover of responsibilities. David was an extraverted, deeply emotional man who ultimately wanted to be liked, and that impacted his negotiating style. Stewart too was extraverted, but almost had a need for confrontation and consequently had no need of being liked. He was to prove ideal for the new era. Spicers' buying terms became crucial not only to our competitiveness but also our customers' competitiveness. Five Star private label and sourcing in the Far East would be important components of the new buying strategy he oversaw.

One of the Sawston site traditions, stretching back to Spicer family days, was the annual long service awards presided over by chief executive Eric Smith. In 1993 I had clocked up 20 years with the company and that warranted a presentation and cheque, alongside other awardees. The day of the ceremony coincided with my return from visiting the *Egan Reid* dealer business in Stockport, a major potential customer currently loyal to competitor Kingfield and one that I had been cultivating for some time. The business was owned and run by two brothers and my visit there on the preceding afternoon had been extended into the evening to meet up with the second brother for dinner. Much wine and other alcohol was consumed, before I finally got to bed very late. I had to be up early the following morning to get to Sawston by 11am for the long service awards.

The three hour car journey was not helped by a serious hangover, however I arrived on time and duly received my award. Alongside certificate and cheque Eric presented me with a wreath that the Reid brothers had thoughtfully sent that morning, via Interflora, in recognition of my wrecked state.

Sold Again

In 1993 Spicers was sold by SCA. We had been acquired by them as part of a paper and packaging group and had never fitted into SCA's long term plans. Before putting the business up for sale SCA decided to have McKinsey management consultants advise them on the business. That involved much of my and my management team's time to educate McKinsey on the role of wholesaling in the office products marketplace. The timing coincided with a UK recession and major changes in the competitive landscape as previously described, as well as substantial losses in France as we sought to establish ourselves in that market. We were not given access to McKinsey's final report, it went directly to Sweden, but we gathered it did not paint an optimistic picture of the future of wholesaling and consequently of Spicers. Spicers was subsequently sold to a British publicly owned company David S Smith plc (DSS), yet another paper and packaging group. Heading that group was Canadian Peter Williams, the same person who had led that Reedpack MBO in 1988 and who had gone to DSS on the sale of Reedpack. Peter obviously knew the Spicers business intimately and did not share McKinsey's negative prognosis. DSS paid £93m for Spicers in 1993 and that compares with a nominal value of £200m, attributed to the Spicers segment of Reedpack, when sold to SCA in 1990. At the time of the DSS acquisition, Spicers France results were very poor and provision was made for the possible closure of the business. That did not come to pass as France's fortunes were transformed by Eric Schmitt, which in turn opened the door to possible further expansion in continental Europe. Peter Williams' faith in the business, fostered in the 1980s, now returned to give management encouragement to consider further expansion in the 1990s. Peter was to be a steady positive force in the development of Spicers right through until his retirement in the early 2000s. One of his final acts of support was to authorise Spicers' entry to the Italian market.

The mid 1990s

The pace of change proved no less hectic as the decade developed. My own profile within the industry continued to grow. As well as leading the major changes taking place in Spicers' wholesaling business I had played an active part in the development of the trade federation, BOSS, since the late 1980s. First as chair of a review committee charged with making the federation more relevant and useful to its members, then as chair of the newly formed board of wholesalers, one of three new boards making up the federation, and then between 1994 and 1996 as chair of the overall federation management committee. In 1996 I received industry wide recognition with a special *Achievement Award* at the Stationery Trade Review annual awards dinner, held at the London Hilton Hotel. The citation covered my work on behalf of the trade federation as well as my role in developing Spicers. The same year I was also made a *liveryman* by the Worshipful Company of Stationers and Newspaper Makers.

The Stationers' Company

The Company was founded in 1403 when text-writers who made copies of books and limners who illuminated them petitioned the Lord Mayor of London to join together in a single trading company with a warden of each craft to oversee their affairs. They set up permanent stalls around St Paul's Cathedral, hence the term *stationer* as opposed to those operating as itinerant vendors. The invention of printing in the late fifteenth century brought great changes to the book trades. Textwriters and limners were gradually eliminated as booksellers began to realise the commercial opportunities of print. Those sellers were wary of competition from books imported from abroad and the political leadership of the day feared printing as a means of spreading seditious and heretical material. A solution to both concerns was found when London stationers petitioned the Crown for a royal charter, to give them exclusive right to print and sell books and to restrict membership of the Company then trading in the City of London.

    Queen Mary granted that charter in 1557 and two years later members were permitted to wear a distinctive livery, or uniform, in the Company's colours of blue and yellow; thus the term *liveryman*. Through the charter the government gained censorship of what could be printed and the trade gained monopoly power over print. That system of control was effective until replaced by the Copyright Act in 1710 which gave those who registered their books at *Stationers' Hall*, copyright protection. That remained in place until 1911 when copyright became automatic, without having to register at the Hall. The Company has occupied halls on three sites in the course of its history, moving to its current location in Ave Maria Lane in 1606, close to its original stall location near St Paul's Cathedral. The current Hall was rebuilt on that site in 1670 following the destruction of the former building in the Great Fire of London. The Company is governed by the Master, Wardens and Court of Assistants, all usually volunteers from within the wider industry, and they are supported by the Clerk, an employee who acts as chief executive, and a small staff. Much like the Masonic Order, over time the Guild migrated from being an organisation preoccupied with matters of its trade to more an exclusive club for men (although women were later admitted). Men generally with a strong loyalty to the ruling establishment and latterly as much concerned with ceremony as with trade related issues. However, unlike the Masons, the City Guild did retain ties with the original trade that had given it birth.

Several criteria apply today to be admitted to the Company, with a basic requirement of having a qualifying occupation in the 'trades of the Guild' and then the need for sponsorship by an existing *liveryman* member. The first stage of membership is to become a *freeman*, granting Freedom of the City of London, an historic district of greater London associated with financial institutions such as the Bank of England and London Stock Exchange. This *freedom* I acquired in 1995. Membership of the Livery is restricted by number and usually requires a level of seniority within the industry, as well as vetting by a selection committee. I was nominated for the Livery by a Spicers' customer, Jonathan Straker, who had played an active part in both the Company and the trade federation, and I was duly 'clothed' in April 1996.

Other than attending regular dinners at Stationers' Hall I played no part in the administration of the Company. My one official duty on behalf of the Stationers' Company was not to occur until 2004. Jonathan Straker had been installed as Master of the Company in 2003 and early the following year he invited me to be principal guest speaker at that year's *Charter Dinner*, a dinner commemorating the granting of the 1557 Charter. I reluctantly accepted, having tried the argument 'why spoil a perfectly good dinner' with him to no effect. Public speaking, on such occasions, had always been a challenge for me, one I had learned to meet when the subject matter was relevant to my job. I managed to craft a speech, both Company and industry related, with that element of humour required on such occasions. It also included some gentle leg pulling of the Master himself. He was happy with my Charter effort and consequently so was I. Jonathan was a towering figure within the industry, in physical stature, sense of humour and reputation. His family business had a long history in the industry and had grown strongly in the 1980s.

That growth resulted in a cash flow problem. The switch of main wholesale supplier to Spicers at the end of that decade was the result of our sympathetic support at a time of financial difficulty. He was subsequently to form a strong commercial relationship with accountant Hugh Sear. Their partnership was typical of many business success stories, a combination of complementary skills produced a much better business. Hugh, the introvert, brought detached analytical skills and Jonathan the engaging people skills necessary for success. They not only built the Straker business (later to become *OyezStraker*) into a major industry player, they also created a substantial dealer group in Office Team.

Ten years after my Charter speech, in 2014, I attended the memorial service for Jonathan held at St Bride's Church, Fleet Street. It was the spiritual home of the newspaper industry of old and of the Stationers' Company. The church was packed to the doors, an indication of the respect and affection the industry had for one of its undoubted giants.

Spicers' Anniversary Acquisition

Stationers' Hall was the venue for the social highlight of Spicers' celebration of its bicentenary in 1996. John Edward Spicer had founded the business with his Hampshire paper mill in 1796 and his main customers then were London book publishers, making The Worshipful Company's Hall an appropriate setting for an industry wide commemorative dinner. Those publishers anxiously awaited Spicers delivery of paper, their first enquiry not as to price but size, as that would determine the shape of their books for the next six months. An account in the early 1800s *Idler* magazine commented *'That ancient Spicer was an autocrat who made paper just when he jolly well pleased. If a publisher desired paper for a book, he was wise to be mighty civil to old Spicer, and even then he wasn't sure of getting the article if Spicer didn't like the cut of his jib'*. So it wasn't only the publishers who revelled in their contemporary monopoly power.

In 1857-8 John Dickinson served as Master of the Stationers' Company. He had set up a business as a stationer in the City of London in 1804 and five years later was involved in papermaking, his first mill being in Hertfordshire. He was reputed to be a man of 'iron determination and courageous vision'. He was also quick tempered and fond of swearing. One of his last utterances was reputed to be 'I'm too ill to see a doctor'. The Apsley site in Hertfordshire was to become the centre of the John Dickinson (JD) papermaking and envelope and stationery manufacturing business. An operation that was destined to become UK market leader with brands such as Basildon Bond, Queen's Velvet, Croxley and Challenge. It was also a major competitor of Spicers' manufacturing business. In 1966 John Dickinson merged with ESA Robinson to become the Dickinson Robinson Group (DRG). In the 1970s it acquired several businesses adding Sellotape to its brand portfolio and also the John Heath stationery wholesaling business. That expansion was followed by financial difficulties in the following decade and resulted in DRG being acquired by Pembridge Investments in 1989. They had no interest in developing the business and proceeded to sell off its parts; papermaking, packaging, stationery manufacturing and wholesaling. John Heath was disposed of to Atapco, an American company.

The stationery manufacturing business, now re-named John Dickinson Stationery, was acquired by Swiss group Biber Holdings which had envelope making operations in continental Europe. When Biber became insolvent in 1996, Spicers' bicentenary year, the JD business was acquired by DSSmith. Spicers' manufacturing operation and John Dickinson's were similar in size with a combined turnover of around £100m. Both businesses had for much of the 1990s been loss making. The hope was that by combining and rationalising the merged business, which was then to trade under the John Dickinson name, that a profitable business would result. That hope in the end proved forlorn. The head of Spicers' manufacturing division, in place since its split from wholesaling in 1986, struggled with the integration and left the business in 1998. His successor, an internal promotion, presided over a sales decline to £47m in the financial year 2004/5. In 2005 DSS sold JD (at a loss to balance sheet asset value) to Hamelin, a major French stationery manufacturer. It subsequently relocated the business from Sawston and dropped the John Dickinson name. It was a sad end to the JD business that had celebrated its own bicentenary in 2004, not to mention Spicers stationery manufacturing business that had been merged with it. The old Ledbury business, that I had visited as budget officer back in 1973 with production director Gerry Peters, was also closed by Hamelin at the end of 2007 with the loss of 55 jobs.

The Modular Dealer Programme

DSSmith's commitment to newly acquired Spicers had been clearly demonstrated by its purchase of JD and by a £5.3million warehousing investment in the wholesaling business. The dealer distribution centre (DDC) near Birmingham was officially opened by chief executive Peter Williams in 1995. As previously described this was an important building block in Spicers' strategy to make the wholesaler-dealer distribution channel cost competitive with new, threatening, channels of distribution. The 'modular dealer' programme, as it was called, contained many elements that dealers could opt in or out of. The DDC provided consumer delivery on behalf of the dealer, Space Age provided an office furniture planning and installation module, the Progress computer system could be bought as a stand alone hardware/software package or the dealer could access the system running on Spicers' computers.

Other systems allowed end user electronic ordering on the dealer, as well as providing digital versions of the catalogue. As the internet grew in use, Spicers provided tools to exploit that new medium. The modular programme was designed to be flexible so that dealers could choose modules appropriate to their business needs. A dealer taking up all options could effectively subcontract to Spicers much of the administration and distribution of his business and focus his efforts on selling. That meant ultimately becoming a stockless dealer, able to operate on much lower gross margins. The programme evolved through the 1990s in response to a changing marketplace and by 1999 20% of Spicers sales were to modular dealers. The modular strategy had been developed entirely within the business, nothing similar had been observed in the US or other marketplaces. Enormous communication programmes, including annual roadshows touring the UK and Ireland sold the concept to the dealer community. The 1995 *Talkback* roadshow was fronted by BBC personality Jan Leeming and actively encouraged questions from the dealer community. Many dealers took up modules and some the whole modular package to become stockless. A Spicers' trade advert running at the time showed a depiction of the extinct Dodo bird with the caption 'there are alternatives to change, ask any taxidermist'. The modular programme attracted hostility from some traditional dealers. They saw Spicers helping create new startup dealerships, with minimal capital, and even potentially enabling their sales representatives to establish separate businesses in competition with their own. I was confronted by one irate traditional customer, after completing a presentation to an Office Team dealer group gathering, with "Are you accusing me of being a dinosaur young man?" delivered in an aggressive broad Ulster accent.

The programme also excited much trade interest in the UK and abroad. That resulted in numerous trade press interviews with myself throughout the 90s, Stationery Trade Review (STR) addressed the UK market and Office Products International (OPI) addressed the UK, US and, in a more limited way, other European markets. As well as presentations to dealer group gatherings, I was a regular speaker at other UK events such as the BOSS Federation conferences held in Stratford upon Avon and Coventry. When OPI began its annual conference programme, initially hosted in the USA, I was also invited to speak there. The first such conference was in Palm Springs, California in 1995 where I presented alongside Eric Bigeard of Lyreco, a French owned contract stationer with operations throughout Europe and Canada, and Jirka Rysavy of Corporate Express, a US based contract stationer growing rapidly, mainly by acquisition, in the US, Canada, Europe and Australasia. Also on the speaker list was my old boss Peter Frost then leading the Office Smart dealer group. Two years later I was back in Phoenix, Arizona to address a much larger gathering at that year's OPI conference.

Following one conference presentation I was accosted by

Irwin Helford, founder of the US based Viking mail order business which had successfully set up a greenfield operation in the UK. Spicers had gone to some lengths to show its dealer customers how Viking's pricing technique involved winning business with very low prices on key products, then pushing up subsequent pricing and margins to the same customer as they placed regular orders. That technique was later to become commonplace across many UK businesses, from banks to energy suppliers, relying on loyal customer inertia after a short period of competitive pricing. It was part of the new post-Thatcher capitalism that saw loyalty as an opportunity to exploit, rather than reward. Spicers' UK adverts used the traditionally recognised Nordic Viking helmet, with two protruding horns, to identify the market invader. As I completed my US conference presentation, which had included a slide with a Viking helmet superimposed on Irwin Helford's head (his face picture adorned most of Viking's UK mailers), I was approached by a not very happy Irwin. After a few brief introductory words he got to his point "I don't like to see my picture with horns on my head". I suppressed a smile as I offered my hand. Sometime later, back in the UK, his local head of merchandising phoned me to threaten to sue Spicers for 'corporate libel'.

We had used an advert in Ireland that showed Viking's different prices for the same product in different mailers. I am happy to report that no such court case ensued.

In May 1996 I was invited even further afield and made a presentation to the National Office Product Association of Australia in Sydney. This was coincidental with my investigation of whether, by acquisition, Spicers could establish a wholesaling operation in that country. I had made contact with a potential candidate business that was operating in a not dissimilar way to Spicers using its own annual catalogue as principal marketing tool. That business was regional, local to Sydney, and I established a good rapport with its owner. My eventual report and presentation to DSSmith's regular Spicers review meeting was sympathetically heard. Peter Williams' decision however was clear and on reflection right; "Australia is too far away if anything should go wrong and there is a need for intervention and support". My initial disappointment was moderated by recognition that I had more than enough to do without taking on the considerable challenge of setting up a new business on the other side of the world.

Spicers Deutschland

DSS was not averse to Spicers expanding geographically after France had been turned around into profit. Our focus consequently moved to Germany, the biggest market in Europe. We had learned three lessons from a traumatic start-up in France. The first was that buying existing businesses, that bore little resemblance to Spicers' wholesaling model, added to set-up problems rather than diminished them. The second was that attempting to create from day one a national warehousing infrastructure involved too high a cost base and consequent sales break-even level. Finally we had learned that it was better to have national leadership attuned to local market niceties rather than introduce a 'knowledgeable' British national to lead the business. A lot of work was done to understand the German marketplace, in terms of how office products reached consumers and what product range and service they, in turn, received. In that we were helped by a local Cambridge based research company Maurice Palmer Associates who had specialised in studying office markets across Europe. There were no national wholesalers in Germany, however there were very large dealer groups with catalogues and warehouses. Their service levels, product range and dealer systems support were a far cry from that offered by Spicers.

Eric Smith had a number of contacts in Germany as a result of his past involvement with the European Envelope Makers' Association. His linguistic and presentation skills were a further bonus. One such contact proved a suitable candidate to head up a Spicers Deutschland operation. He was a remarkable individual, crippled by polio in childhood, his iron determination had not allowed a wheelchair to blunt either his ambition or success in an office products industry career of 30 years. DSSmith approved Spicers' plan for a £6.5 million investment to set up a greenfield wholesaling business in Germany. It was to be led by the candidate Eric had identified and the first warehouse was to be built just outside of Hanover. I nominated a UK management project team to work alongside the new German MD and the local team he began to recruit.

Planning covered all the key elements; computer systems, catalogue production, sourcing of a German specific product range, logistical support and financial planning. Regular review meetings took place as the 115,000 square foot warehouse with attached head office functions was built just outside of Hanover. The business opened in the autumn of 1998 and was able to offer a next day delivery service to dealers across Germany. The new MD's strong relationships within the German office products market quickly secured business from dealers and even some dealer groups. The largest groups, having their own warehouses, saw Spicers as a potential competitor but Buroring was one of those that saw Spicers' entry to the market as an opportunity rather than a threat. The business made a great start and in 1999 sold 300,000 catalogues to German dealers.

Early in 2000 I was enjoying a winter break with my wife and daughter when I received a phone call from Eric Smith. He had interrupted my holiday to tell me that he had just returned from Germany having sacked the MD. I was truly shocked. It transpired that Eric had received a call, from one of the German management team, to tell him that he was about to face a mass resignation of that team, owing to the severe 'bullying' they were receiving from their boss. It transpired that his drive and ambition, and maybe the stress of getting a new business up and running, had led him to be both uncompromising and heavy handed with his subordinates. Eric promptly visited Hover to listen to the team's story first hand and decided immediately to dismiss the German MD. The latter's iron will was soon to be demonstrated once again, he won local financial support to set up a rival wholesaling business to Spicers close to Hanover.

Hospitality

Corporate Express was an American owned contract stationery business founded in 1986, and floated on the US stock exchange in 1994. The business had grown dramatically by acquisition both before and after flotation and had operations in the US, Europe and Australasia. In 1996 they acquired the Chisholm Group in the UK. Chisholm was a Spicers' loyal customer, originally based in Drury Lane, London and later in Cranleigh, Surrey. The business was owned and run by Alex Findlay who I had got to know well in the early 1980s, when he and I were London based, and the relationship had continued when his business moved to Surrey and I to Sawston. He, like many UK dealers, decided to sell up as office product dealer acquirers, mainly foreign owned, roamed the land seeking to continue their own dramatic growth, often IPO (stock market flotation) inspired or funded. It was another feature of the new capitalism, a tendency in the US and UK to build a business over a relatively short period of time then sell it and realise a, sometimes substantial, capital gain. Arguably the Reedpack MBO had also been an example. Short-termism was to become a growing feature of investor led businesses as opposed to the longer term commitment of family dynasty controlled businesses of old.

Alex Findlay's deal with Corporate Express involved selling his business in two tranches, over a relatively short period of time, and Spicers, as his principal supplier, was able to help him meet a cash flow criterion, laid down in the sale agreement.

A pleasant personal surprise was to follow the sale completion when Alex invited his lawyer and myself to accompany him for a weekend 'treat'. That treat involved a train journey from London to Paris where we boarded *The Orient Express*, a train made up of luxurious carriages, including elegant dining cars. There we ate as we made our way to the south of France. In Nice we disembarked to catch a helicopter into Monte Carlo.

Here we were booked into the Hotel de Paris overlooking the circuit of the Monaco Grand Prix, the most prestigious race in the Formula One calendar. We soaked up the heady pre-race atmosphere out on track the evening before the race and then were able to watch the famous race from our hotel vantage point. Our treat was not over. The return helicopter to Nice airport connected with a special Concorde flight out over the Atlantic, to acquire the speed required to break the sound barrier, and then back to London. It was without doubt the most extravagant treat that I enjoyed during my time at Spicers and was all the more extraordinary because it was given by a grateful and very generous customer.

There were many other perks over the years. Supplier treats included the Spicers' specific trip to Venice already mentioned and other locations across Europe, some with partners others singly. Schwan Stabilo, a major supplier and writing instrument manufacturer based in Nuremberg, for a number of years ran trips for groups of UK customers to its factory in Germany. The factory visit was in many ways incidental to enjoying liberal bierkeller type hospitality. It was on one such trip that I met my future second wife.

Spicers' UK and later European merchandising director SBT was a big fan of Formula One motor car racing, as was I. Consequently he and I were regular guests of suppliers at various Grand Prix circuits across Europe; Italy, France, Hungary, Spain and England were some of the venues visited. Our enthusiasm for motor sport was often mirrored by our suppliers, who found in us a perfect excuse to indulge their own passion at their company's expense. I can honestly say that such hospitality never impacted either SBT or my commercial judgement. My philosophy on hospitality, whether received or given, was that it was always a 'thank you' rather than a 'please', a distinction explained to me, early in my commercial life with Spicers, by sales manager Ron Pulford, with whom I had carried out that 'the future of envelopes' survey back in my novice marketing department days.

A motor racing experience of a different kind was provided for SBT and myself in Atlanta, Georgia when we were the guests of SP Richards (SPR), the US's second largest office product wholesaler. At some point in the 1990s our relationship with SPR had become more cordial and productive than that with Chicago based market leader United Stationers, and we entered into a formal cooperation agreement with them. SBT and I visited SPR's headquarters in Atlanta on more than one occasion, to exchange information and further our joint buying of products, particularly in the Far East. It was on one such occasion that they invited us to experience a NASCAR race. With an oval banked circuit and cars that, externally at least, looked like production saloon cars, it was a very different experience to Formula 1. I will always remember overhearing in the stadium the words of an enthusiastic nearby fan, as a number of military Thunderbolt A10 'tank-buster' planes flew low over the track stadium prior to the race, deafening all present, his proud boast "listen y'all, that's the sound of freedom". Patriotism ran deep, as did Southern hospitality, and politics could be gauged by the description given by one senior SPR executive of CNN as the 'Communist News Network'.

Spicers' own 'thank you' to loyal customers took many forms. Groups of our customers, dressed up appropriately, were regularly welcomed to Henley in the 1980s where they were dined in a marquee by the river as competing teams of oarsmen periodically sculled past. The occasion usually coincided with Wimbledon and as much attention was given to marquee television screens as to activity on the river Thames. On one notable occasion a customer, who had had a little too much to drink, decided it would be a cooling experience on a warm sunny afternoon to swim across the river. He did not consult host Spicers but stripped to his underwear and entered the water. One problem he had to contend with were the barriers that had been set up in the river, to create lanes for the competing boats. Getting over these barriers required some effort and the customer concerned lost his underpants at the second obstacle. The other problem was that on arrival at the other bank a policeman was waiting for him. I, along with other Spicers' management present, were simply relieved that the customer concerned had not drowned in his inebriated attempt to cool off. The imagined headline in the following month's trade press was not one we wanted to contemplate.

In the 1990s a smaller group of customers were annually entertained at Royal Ascot where Spicers had a box. The box would accommodate up to a dozen people and my wife and I often acted as hosts. Regular guests were **J** and his wife; he had become head of the OyezStraker business on the retirement of partners Jonathan

Straker and Hugh Sear. The afternoon began with a champagne welcome and was followed by an excellent lunch. As that came to an end and the racing got underway so attention turned to a flutter on the horses. The box would be in use over several days and was, during Royal week, used to entertain larger customers. Like Henley it involved dressing up, but in rather different garb, including obligatory tophat and tails for men. It was a much appreciated form of hospitality and was, in my experience, devoid of any Henley-like embarrassing episodes. At the conclusion of racing by now merry customers would gather around the bandstand and indulge in that peculiarly British form of patriotism; loudly singing, not necessarily in tune, *Land of Hope & Glory* and *Jerusalem*. It was always a happy end to a day in convivial company.

Spicers Germany held a notable customer hospitality event soon after its opening that involved a train trip through the Harz Mountains. In German folklore this was home to an annual gathering of witches and devils celebrating the retreat of winter following the solstice. Our destination was a local mediaeval castle with a large dining hall. Here, between courses, customer guests were entertained by a group of opera singers, in costume, performing Mozart arias. It was a magical evening. Another castle venue, Warwick Castle in England, was the venue for an industry dinner hosted by filing manufacturer Eastlight. It was a much anticipated annual event in part because of the gathering of the industry's hierarchy and in part for the lavish entertainment laid on after the meal. Many famous names provided entertainment over the years and the dinner was one of the highlights of the UK stationery industry calendar, as had been the Eldon (a US office product supplier) dinner that pre-dated it. There was no shortage of hospitality in the ever changing industry of the 1980s and 1990s. Golfers, of which I was never one, also had no problem improving their handicap in the course of the stationery year. Spicers in turn entertained our top suppliers once a year. They were invited to Sawston and there were subject to a number of presentations setting out company plans and explaining how they could help us achieve those goals. Following the 'message' a coach was laid on to take everyone to nearby Newmarket race course for a marquee lunch followed by the opportunity to lose money on the horses.

New Millennium

As the 1990s drew to a close it was a time of reflection. I had assumed leadership of the UK wholesaling business in the mid 1980s, the priority then had been to maintain high service levels during a period of rapid sales growth and infrastructure expansion. The following decade brought both recession and major changes in the channels of distribution of office products to market. Cost reduction, productivity improvement and service innovation were the watch-words of the 1990s. Successful launch of the wholesaling model in Ireland was followed by a troubled entry to the French market which when overcome led to further expansion into Germany. In 1998 DSSmith were approached to see if they were interested in selling Spicers. The price they placed on the business, reputed to be £250m, deterred that approach. By 2000 wholesaling sales had reached £419m, double that of 1990, but continental Europe was now seen to be the principal growth opportunity. Profits stood at £23m with the UK then providing the lion's share but its profitability was beginning to be challenged by a change in sales mix towards lower margin products.

Service levels over the previous two decades had been built on good management of sophisticated computer systems. This software had been constantly modified to accommodate new countries, service changes and development of E-Commerce, a cornerstone of cost reduction for both Spicers and its customer base. By the mid 90s it had been recognised that these systems were creaking, that is becoming increasingly difficult to modify given their piecemeal development over 25 years. A decision was made to rewrite the system and put it on a better footing for future development as the business became ever more European. This project was called *Focus 2000* and it also addressed the *millennium bug* (Y2K) issue, related to the date mechanism in software, which was then a major preoccupation of many businesses.

Spicers faced another challenge with the intended departures of Eric Smith, due to retire on reaching 60 in 2001 and his boss Peter Williams, chief executive of DSSmith. In June 2000 I was promoted to become CE of Spicers' European wholesaling business, Eric became executive chairman for the remaining year or so of his employment with the group. Also reporting into him was, a now legally separated, John Dickinson stationery manufacturing business. On Eric's departure Spicers and JD would report separately to the CE of DSSmith. Planning at DSS level also sought a smooth transition. Peter Williams's successor was appointed in late 2000 with a view to taking over at the end of 2001. He was new to the business and together with the other heads of DSS divisions I was to report directly to him but was not to be made a director of DSSmith. The new DSS board was consequently largely made up of non-executive directors. Little did I suspect that the transition I was about to face would be considerably more stressful than the trauma I had faced back in 1979 when I had been appointed, with no relevant experience, sales manager at Park Royal RDC.

Chapter 4
The Final Years

Part 1 My Final Years

As chief executive of European wholesaling my priority was to maintain a healthy UK business, generating good profits and cash flow, to fund the development of business growth in continental Europe. An ambitious 5 year plan was developed in 2000 that involved doubling sales over that period.

Despite the major challenge of new channels of distribution in the 1990s the UK business had continued to grow but at a more modest rate than previously. It maintained a 50-60% share of the market but its wholesaling competition had consolidated into a single business, Kingfield-Heath, through acquisition and merger. That integration had disrupted the new competitor but it was in the process of developing a leaner distribution infrastructure to which Spicers must respond. A further issue was the changing sales mix and its impact on overall gross margin. As the use of PCs in business had grown dramatically so had the demand for IT related supplies (known in the industry as electronic office supplies or EOS) such as printer cartridges.

These were the cash cows of very large corporations, like Hewlett Packard, and they strictly controlled the price and distribution of their branded consumables. Specialised 'authorised' distributors of these consumables had emerged to become major players in the office supplies market and they generally operated from a single national warehouse and managed on gross margins of around 10%. This was considerably less than the average 25% gross margin enjoyed by wide-range office product wholesalers, with their regionally based warehousing and enhanced service model. Many of these new distributors did not limit sales to the trade and supplied both dealer and end user directly. EOS was the fastest growing product segment consumed in offices and some other, margin rich, office product segments were now in decline as the use of computers grew, for example Tippex, a correction fluid for the era of typewriters, was now in dramatic decline.

I chose my replacement to head-up the UK & Ireland business. He had a long track record with Spicers, having joined in 1984, and had held many operational roles in RDCs as well as latterly being responsible for the marketing function and then the SpaceAge furniture business. He was in place by June 2000.

Spicers France had had a very good second half of the 1990s after its difficult birth. Rather than work with dealer groups, as the UK business had done, it had developed its own dealer group branded *Calipage*. A limited number of qualifying dealers joined that programme and it proved a successful growth strategy, however it cemented the alienation of other rival independent dealer groups. By 2000 French sales had grown to €152m and the business had a 39% share of the French wholesaling market. Following this success Eric Schmitt, fluent in Spanish, had been given the go-ahead to start researching the Spanish office product market. His research showed an opportunity and he was given the go-ahead to open an RDC in Barcelona in the spring of 2002. A new Spanish MD was recruited and, to enable Eric to focus on the development of Spain, a new MD was appointed in France. Both positions reported to Eric Schmitt.

In Germany Spicers had made good progress in penetrating the market. Some dealer groups, such as Buroring, were prepared to work with us while others, like Branion, regarded Spicers as a competitor. The management issue that arose soon after start-up, resulting in the MD's dismissal in early 2000, was a distraction but a replacement was recruited and he was in place later that year to lead an otherwise stable management team. Growth in business was such that a second distribution centre, just outside Nuremberg, was under construction and scheduled to open in 2001.

Spicers' centre of gravity was moving evermore towards continental Europe. The business philosophy, born of painful experience, was that each country would be independently managed and adapt to the particular service needs of its local market. However, it was clear that certain functions needed to be managed across Europe. Major vendors we dealt with were common across all markets and to maximise buying terms a small European buying function was created and SBT promoted to head this team as European purchasing director. Computer systems were also common across countries and although local systems teams were necessary, there was also a need for greater coordination and European development oversight. I recruited R to rejoin Spicers as European finance and IT director. He had a long history with the company. His father had joined Spicers when Gutteridge Sampson was acquired in 1973 and played an important part in the business until his retirement in 1991. R had started his career with Spicers as a trainee accountant and had left when he had achieved qualification. He had returned as finance director of Spicers France in the early 1990s and had helped Eric Schmitt get the business onto a profitable footing, before leaving to work in the Netherlands. He knew Spicers business well, spoke several languages and was an ideal candidate to replace Spicers' group finance director who retired at the same time as Eric Smith. In addition to finance R assumed responsibility for coordinating European IT as the roll out of the Focus 2000 system project continued.

So, with all that preparation and planning what could possibly go wrong? In the year ended April 2001 the wholesaling business's sales reached £485m, up 16%, and profits were £24.4m. The following year saw a sales decline in the UK and a dramatic fall in profits. The new UK MD wrestled with some of the underlying issues and then chose to return to his old job running SpaceAge.

Nuremberg RDC opened successfully in mid 2001 and a limited volume of business was successfully transferred from Hanover. It had been decided to put the new RDC onto the Focus 2000 system, initially with low volumes to iron out any issues, then put the new system into Hanover. This apparently cautious approach proved not cautious enough. As soon as the full German business was placed on the new system it malfunctioned, resulting in enormous service and invoicing problems. The new German MD struggled with the resulting crisis and consequently lost the confidence of both customers and his management team. He left the business in early 2002.

Now I was effectively MD of both the UK and German businesses in addition to my wider European role. Another blow was to follow. I had gained approval from DSSmith to set up a greenfield business in Italy and had recruited Angelo Mereu from Acco Italy to head that business. He had located a site to build the first RDC, just south of Milan, began that build and to recruit his senior team when he suffered a massive heart attack and died in January 2003.

Any one of these issues would have been a serious cause for concern but coming, as they did, in quick succession it felt like the onset of a perfect storm. On top of which the once calm and understanding ears of Eric Smith and Peter Williams were now gone.

Instead I faced the more sceptical response of a new boss, less committed to Spicers' strategy and probably less secure in his own role, given its short tenure.

UK & Ireland

A review of the UK business infrastructure had taken place in the late 1990s in light of a competitive need to reduce costs and given the imminent expiry of some long term RDC leases. A new larger Glasgow RDC opened in 1999 and absorbed the business previously serviced from Newcastle RDC. In 2000 Heywood RDC in Lancashire replaced both Manchester and Leeds RDCs and Dublin RDC relocated to larger premises a year later.

The following year a new Greenwich RDC opened, replacing Bermondsey, and took over stocking all furniture for the London region.

UK sales in the year ended March 2002 declined by 3%, this partly reflected market conditions and partly service issues related to both new RDC openings and the roll out of the Focus 2000 computer system. The latter two issues also resulted in some significant additional operating costs. Profits were further impacted by deteriorating gross margins, partly because of the change in sales mix towards EOS and partly the result of increased levels of customer bad debt. The result was a marked fall in profits in the UK at the same time as significant start-up losses in both Germany and Spain. This contributed to a fall in European group profit to £9.7m in 2001/2 from the previous year's £24.4m. It wasn't only Spicers that suffered. Kingfield-Heath in 2001 produced sales of £206m and a loss of £6.5m. Their result was no consolation. Spicers development in Europe depended on a strong UK base of profitability and cash flow. The many challenges facing the UK business had proved a baptism of fire for the new MD of UK and Ireland, and early in 2002 he chose to leave that role and return to his old job heading the SpaceAge business. Consequently I had no option but to assume direct management of the UK and Irish business and to get to grips with the issues undermining profitability. A recovery plan was put in place in conjunction with the management team. That involved cost reduction measures and modifications to pricing structure that would address the fall in gross margin resulting from the changing product sales mix. A combination of rationalised RDC structure and other cost reduction measures resulted in headcount falling in the UK from 1350 in 2000 to 1050 in 2003. Following discussion with my new DSS boss, I agreed to look outside the business for a new MD for the UK & Ireland business. A new appointment was made in late 2002, his background was in distribution but in the electrical supplies marketplace with RS Components. He proved a steadying influence and successfully saw through many of the initiatives then underway. UK profits improved in 2002/3 and again in the following year but sales growth proved elusive. One of the marketing initiatives subsequently launched was an annual touring exhibition of new products and services under the *Spicers Office Solutions* (SOS) banner, this was housed in Spicers' local RDCs. It proved an effective way of launching new services to dealers.

Spicers Deutschland

The new MD appointed in late 2000 had previously been employed by Corporate Express in Germany. In its second full year of trading Spicers had achieved sales of €67m and in April 2001 a second RDC opened in Nuremberg utilising the Focus 2000 computer system. After that successful launch a decision was made to migrate the whole German business to the new system. Almost immediately problems began to arise, largely a result of the interfaces with many other subsidiary systems used in Germany. Customers were no longer receiving a reliable delivery service and that was compounded by many invoicing errors. The complaints began to mount and the new MD struggled to cope with a growing crisis. To make matters worse, at some point soon after his employment began the new MD began an intimate relationship with one of his immediate subordinates. An added complication was that that person's husband held an important role heading Spicers' stock control function. This extra-marital relationship quickly became public knowledge and began to impact senior management team morale, as well as affect the stock control function in Hanover.

    I was made aware of the relationship and initially hoped the situation could be managed. In January 2002 I visited the Frankfurt Fair, the biggest annual stationery exhibition in Europe. There I consulted with numerous German industry figures, including the head of one of our biggest customers, Buroring dealer group. It transpired that confidence in our German MD was low, his credibility damaged by promising more than he could deliver, in terms of service recovery. Soon afterwards I visited the new Nuremberg RDC and there learned directly from Spicers' management team how the behaviour of the MD, and the subordinate with whom he was involved, was undermining morale, morale already seriously impacted by the systems crisis. I reached the conclusion that I must act swiftly to recover motivation and the credibility of Spicers in the German marketplace. I arranged an urgent visit to Hanover and there held separate meetings with the MD and his subordinate, dismissing them both with immediate effect. I now had no choice but to directly lead the German management team and set up a regime of weekly visits accompanied by R my European finance and IT director. He was charged with leading the effort to regain control of the computer systems, key to service and success in Germany. It required a concerted effort on both our parts over many weeks to recover the situation but it was eventually achieved.

The hoped for sales growth trajectory set out in the 5 year plan was now impossible and plans for a third RDC were shelved. In 2003/4 German sales were €65m and a loss of €3.0m was recorded. The following year a profit of €1.1m was achieved on flat sales. The search for a new MD began in earnest as the business recovered. Having got through two MDs in the four years of Spicers Deutschland's short life it was deemed more important to get the right person than achieve a quick fix. There was no suitable internal candidate but senior sales director Eberhard Bolm was able to provide calm and mature interim management of the team. Spicers' credibility in the German market slowly recovered. That was helped by the *Spicers World* catalogue launch and exhibition which subsequently became a major annual customer and supplier event.

At the 2003 launch I delivered a short speech in German, that required considerable help given my lack of linguistic ability. My English version was not only translated but a phonetic version produced. My effort appeared much appreciated by the assembled German audience, even though I suspect they all spoke perfectly good English had I chosen to speak in my native tongue. Thomas Apelrath finally joined the business in early 2004 and provided steady and credible leadership after what had been a traumatic period for the business. Germany now had to be added to the list of difficult country 'births', as Spicers expanded across Europe.

Spicers Italia

My research of the Italian market began in 1999 with a visit to the *Big Buyer* trade fair in Florence. This was the biggest office supplies exhibition in Italy and I became an annual visitor over the next few years. I met there the head of an important Italian dealer group CCA who was also head of a separate franchise retail chain BluOffice. Marco Magherini did not speak English but had a very competent assistant who did and she enabled us to communicate. Marco was instrumental in helping me understand the Italian office product market. That was partly achieved by a road trip he and I undertook in 2001, in the north of Italy, involving visits to a number of his dealer members. My wife and I were later invited to join a Blu Office member gathering in Florence, as well as meet Marco's wife and family. He impressed on me the need to recruit a serious (credible to the market) person to head up Spicers' business in Italy. I did identify a suitable candidate in Angelo Mereu who had led Acco's business in Italy, a major office product manufacturer.

    A case was developed for our entry to the Italian market. The presentation to DSSmith was powerfully reinforced by the presence of Angelo. Peter Williams, in one of his last Spicers' management meetings before his retirement from DSS, authorised Spicers to proceed with the project in 2002. A suitable site for the first 11,000 square metre distribution centre and head office was identified by Angelo at Castel San Giovanni about 60 kilometres south of Milan. Contracts were entered into and Angelo began recruiting his management team. One day in January 2003, after work, he was at home with his wife and children. Following dinner his family retired to bed and left him watching TV. When his wife returned later to look for him she found him lying dead on the sofa, having suffered a massive heart attack. There was no history of heart problems and it was an enormous shock and tragedy for his family. He was greatly respected within the Italian office products market and his funeral was very well attended by many senior industry figures, including myself. Given the embryonic state of Spicers advance into Italy my immediate priority was to find a suitable candidate to take over leadership of the new business. A selection of candidates was identified and interviews set up at Milan airport. My new DSS boss wanted to be involved in the selection process and so accompanied me on the trip to Milan. A very able candidate emerged, Franco Villa, with experience of the market and of good industry standing, definitely 'serious' to use Marco Magherini's terminology.

The conversation with my boss on the return flight to London was one of the early pieces of a jigsaw that was to see my departure from Spicers three years later. The chat went something like this; 'Bill, how do you think the market would respond if we decided not to proceed in Italy?' 'Well, we have been preparing the market for our imminent arrival for the last three years. If we pull the plug now I think it will be many years before we could consider a return to Italy, our credibility would be seriously damaged'. 'OK, what do you think the reaction would be in Spicers if we were to pull out?' 'I think the main question people in Spicers will ask is; who is the next chief executive going to be?' 'What?' 'Well I think my own credibility will be shot given the commitment I have made to setting up in Italy and I will therefore choose to leave'.

What followed was a long silence. It was to set the pattern for our unfolding relationship. He was ever cautious, had a tendency to procrastinate, and was of a disposition where even decisions made were never quite final. He also required much more involvement in decisions, like senior appointments, usually resulting in a prolonged and, for me, tortuous decision making process. This I found trying, given the many issues I was trying to deal with and in part because of the contrast in style with his predecessor, my immediate past boss Eric Smith. It seemed as if the Gods were intent on placing as many obstacles in my path as possible in the quest to build a European wholesaling business. Determined as I was by nature I saw this, initially at least, as a test of my resolve.

Franco Villa was appointed and continued with Angelo's work in setting up Spicers Italia.

In November 2004 the new RDC was opened in Castel San Giovanni and the first catalogue containing 11,300 product lines achieved a print run of 105,000.

Spicers France

The French business had begun the new millennium with strong sales growth and good profitability. The handover of responsibility for the French business from Eric Schmitt to new MD, Y, was trouble free with Eric keeping a close watching eye as he went about setting up the new Spanish business. His appointee had joined Spicers in 1997 and on promotion to MD quickly gained the confidence of his senior management team. In 2001 Spicers France acquired ownership of the *Plein Ciel* brand and warehouse. This was an office product dealer group with 400 members and it was hoped they would transfer allegiance to Spicers France, as it took on production of their catalogue and the stocking of their 350 private label branded products. By 2003 130 of those dealers had chosen to become Spicers' customers, that compared with then 275 dealers who were members of Spicers' other dealer marketing group *Calipage*. Between them the two groups accounted for 55% of sales. A further group of 100 dealers joined a Spicers created buying group *Carip*. After sales growth of 25% in the year ended April 2001, 2002 produced a more modest 5% and in the following 4 years the business struggled to grow at all. It did however produce consistently solid profits each year. At the end of 2006 a 15,000 square metre central warehouse was opened near Chateauroux in central France. Its role, like its UK equivalent, was to service the then five RDCs in Paris, Tours, Bordeaux, Toulouse and Valence, to extend their life and improve overall stock turnover as sales growth hopefully returned. In 2004 Eric Schmitt stepped down from his operational involvement in France and Spain in order to take on a part-time roving support role across Europe. The two businesses then reported directly to me.

Spicers Espana

Eric, with his fluency in Spanish, had had sole responsibility for researching and then setting up a greenfield business in Spain. His family home was in Pau, in the Pyrenean mountain range separating France and Spain, and he chose to make Barcelona in Catalonia the location for a first RDC and the business's head office. That 7500 square metre warehouse was opened in April 2002. The new managing director of the business, had joined Spicers in 2000 from Unipapel, a leading manufacturer and distributor of office products. That background meant he had a good understanding of what was a very fragmented marketplace. The approach adopted in Spain, to penetrate the market as quickly as possible, was to cultivate existing dealer groups and retail franchise operations and this was achieved with agreements in 2004 with Sett Grup and Carlin.

Sales growth was such that by year ended 2005/6 break-even was achieved. Also that year a customer catalogue launch and exhibition, covering some of the 9700 stocked product lines, was held for the first time in the new RDC. In 2006 a second RDC was opened in Madrid to enable 24 hour delivery to the whole of mainland Spain.

Benelux – The Timmermans Acquisition

In Belgium there already existed a wholesaler not unlike Spicers. It operated with a wide range annual catalogue, stocked the range contained in that catalogue and provided a nationwide reliable delivery service from a single warehouse based in Deinze near Ghent. It had been established in 1954 by the Timmermans family and in the late 1980s business ownership had passed to family brothers Michel and Patrick Timmermans. In 2004 the business turned over €44.6m, two thirds of which was in Belgium and one third in the Netherlands, and it produced a profit of €2.6m. It too had suffered as a result of sales mix swinging towards EOS and had consciously abandoned low margin business in order to protect profitability. It stocked 17,500 product lines of which approximately half were exclusively distributed in Benelux by the business. Most of those products were ultimately destined for the office market, through dealers, but it had also built a substantial business in products destined for the school market distributed through retail shops.

I had known the Timmermans' brothers for many years, we had met at fairs and conferences in Europe and further afield. We began discussions about acquiring their business in 2004, that involved principally R, my finance & IT director, and myself but ultimately required the consent of my boss and the DSSmith board. Terms were finally agreed and the acquisition announced in the autumn of 2005. The deal was structured in such a way as to retain the services of the two brothers for a fixed period, a lump sum payment was made up front with the remainder to be paid contingent on performance over the following three years. Michel and Patrick had many passions, one of which was to visit as many three star Michelin restaurants as they could. Consequently an additional, not very serious, inducement to complete the deal was a promise that R and I would treat them to a meal at the *Fat Duck* restaurant in Bray owned by Heston Blumenthal. Sometime after the acquisition was completed a restaurant booking was made and the promise fulfilled. It was probably the most expensive meal R and I had ever enjoyed, complete with supplied ipod headphones, conveying sounds of the sea, for the fish course. The brothers insisted on paying for the meal and it was a relief not to have to justify such extravagance to my boss, who had to sign off my expenses.

Building a European Business
I had begun my reign as chief executive with established businesses in the UK, Ireland and France and an embryonic business in Germany. By 2005 we had added Spain, Italy and Benelux. The business's centre of gravity was moving ever more toward continental Europe and that needed to be reflected in how the business was managed and in how we communicated with our pan-European workforce, suppliers and, when appropriate, customer base.

A new employee newsletter *Spicers Europe* began to be published in July 2001 and came out at regular intervals thereafter. It was translated into each local language and updated the workforce on important developments across Europe. To encourage relationship building at senior team level an annual conference was organised. The company language was English and a requirement of senior country appointments was familiarity with the language. The first conference was held in the UK in 2003, a year later the venue was Ireland, then France and in 2006 Spain. It was a good opportunity for different national teams to meet, develop relationships, and share experiences. It was also an opportunity to convey common messages and to make awards recognising achievements. To keep costs down one of my early economies was to dictate the use of low cost airlines for European travel.

The days of business class travel for senior management, including myself, were over.

As far as customers were concerned each country had its own annual event; SOS in the UK, Spicers World in Germany and equivalents in France and Spain. These were all nationally organised and the focus was on the local market. One major pan-European customer publication was produced in 2004, in conjunction with the publishers of OPI trade magazine, that sought to address all customers in all markets. In order to achieve that it was adapted for each marketplace, with introductions by that country's MD and other content relevantly tailored. It was produced in each language, mailed out locally and paid for by European vendor advertising in the publication.

The European buying team had developed a programme for key vendors, important suppliers to Spicers common to all countries. Those vendors had access to a number of initiatives designed to help improve their sales, such as access to local roadshows, or help reduce their costs in dealing with Spicers. In return for that we sought terms improvements and advertising support in publications, like the OPI edition.

The Systems department structure was modified to reflect our European wide business and priorities. This was also necessitated by the protracted problems with the Focus 2000 project, rollout of which was not completed until 2004, much later than originally planned. Senior French appointees strengthened R's new IT team.

Our efforts to make the Spicers business truly European were recognised at the annual OPI awards ceremony, held in conjunction with the organisers of Europe's biggest annual office product fair, *Paperworld* held in Frankfurt Germany. In 2005 I received, on behalf of Spicers, the *European Wholesaler of the Year* award for 'efficiency, great ideas, profitability and presence across Europe'

Decision to Depart

By the summer of 2005 I had reached a tentative decision to relinquish my role and take early retirement. This was a couple of years before my normal retirement age of 60 and a consequence of several factors that came together.

In 2004 DSSmith considered selling Spicers, this entailed a major exercise using external consultants and of necessity heavily involved myself and finance director R. A possible sales value for the business was arrived at of between £175m and £215 million. In the end the DSS board decided not to proceed with a sale, however their ambivalence about ownership of Spicers had become clear.

Having been pushed down the possible sale path R and I decided in early 2005 to look at a possible MBO (management buy out), this time without the prior knowledge or agreement of DSS. In conjunction with PricewaterhouseCoopers (PwC) a detailed plan for raising finance was completed by June 2005 and discussions with 3i got as far as constructing a management team equity breakdown, as well as a meeting with a possible future chairman of an independent Spicers. I was keen to spread that equity as low down the organisation as possible, as had been achieved in the Reedpack MBO of 1988. A major stumbling block then arose related to the future of the Spicers part of the DSS UK pension fund.

Post second world war many companies provided pension schemes for their workforce to supplement the relatively meagre state pension. Many of these schemes were defined benefit or final salary schemes, in that they paid a pension equivalent to a percentage of the final salary earned, immediately before retirement. That percentage would vary according to the scheme rules and number of years service with the company. Pension schemes were financed by a combination of employer and employee contributions. Those contributions were held in a fund separated from the company's finances and managed by a board of trustees, separated legally from company management. Those trustees invested the accumulated funds in order to finance future pension liabilities. Such schemes were common up until the 1990s.

Booming stock markets in that decade meant that the value of pension funds rose strongly. Companies had the right, some claimed obligation, to take pension contribution 'holidays' on the basis that fund valuations were high and more than sufficient to meet future liabilities. That meant many companies suspended employer contributions to the fund, sometimes for many years, as was the case with DSS. Employee contributions invariably were not subject to any 'holiday' and continued to be deducted from salaries paid. By the early 2000s stock markets had fallen and with them the size of pension funds, also pension fund income became subject to taxation not previously applicable. Those changes created two unwelcome problems for companies, the need to return to pension fund contributions and the problem of gross funds no longer being adequate to meet future pension liabilities, that shortfall being then the company's responsibility.

Having enjoyed their 'holiday' many companies were now intent on closing down schemes they regarded as potential future financial black holes. Very few final salary schemes are now available in the private sector. Pension provision still applies in many companies but these are mostly defined contribution schemes, where employee and employer contribute to a pension fund but the size of the resulting pension no longer relates to final salary. It instead depends on the returns generated by the invested contributions. Liability for any pension shortfall, resulting from poor returns, had been successfully passed from the company to the individual. Defined benefit schemes still exist if you are a public sector employee, however in that case there is no pension fund, the taxpayer picks up the bill for pensions paid, a growing state liability in an era of endless money printing.

A requirement of any private equity funded purchase of Spicers, it transpired, would be closure of the UK defined benefit pension scheme and its replacement with a defined contribution scheme. That for me was a bridge too far. I knew that the pension scheme enjoyed by most UK employees was generous and a substantial, if often unrecognised, future benefit for the average employee. Its removal from them on the back of potential significant financial gains for a relatively small number of Spicers' managers was not something with which I wanted to permanently burden my conscience. Consequently I terminated our discussions with PwC and 3i in June 2005.

Another couple of pension related issues arose in 2005 impacting me personally. A change in law was announced to apply the following tax year whereby a lifetime allowance was being introduced capping one's personal pension fund for tax relief purposes. For final salary schemes, like mine with DSS, a notional fund value was deduced based on multiples of likely pension size. Should one continue to accrue pension beyond that cap a penal tax rate would apply to the excess accumulated. I was well paid, had many years of service and the new cap rules directly impacted the tax I would pay on my retirement pension, should I continue to accrue pension beyond introduction of the lifetime allowance cap in 2006. This same cap issue was to be the cause of many doctors prematurely leaving their NHS employment in the years that followed.

A second pension issue arose with DSS attempts to cover off the threatened black hole in their pension scheme. That involved reducing employee's future pension accrual rate, effectively reducing their future pension size. I understood the logic of what the company was seeking to do but had personal written undertakings from DSS's company secretary, dated 1993 when DSS acquired Spicers, that my accrual rate would not change in the future. That did not stop my boss's attempt to impose the new ruling on me based on advice he had sought from a company appointed barrister. I declined to accept that view and insisted that the accrual rate not change. My insistence prevailed but contributed to a further deterioration in the prickly relationship I had with my boss.

A final factor drew me to the conclusion that it was now time to step down. Since becoming chief executive in 2000 I had managed a number of significant crises in the business. Those had taken their toll on me. Sustained stress affects different people in different ways, I suspect as a result of its impact on the immune system. How that manifests will depend on the individual's constitution and genetic make up. My health had always been excellent however a weakness manifested in the early 2000s, serious gum disease. It could have been of genetic origin given my mother had lost all her teeth by age 30. I lost most of my teeth during my period as CE, despite having faithfully visited a dentist throughout my adult life. The dentist's only solution to gum disease, it appeared, was to remove loose teeth. By 2005 most of the crises across Europe had been overcome however at the start of financial year 2005/6 another deterioration in the UK business's profitability began to show. It was not marked but I could see that the business was going to have to respond to a resurgent competitor, Kingfield-Heath (KH), now profitable and growing at Spicers' expense. That response would no doubt involve a reduction in the number of warehouses in line with the rationalised KH business now operating with a lower cost base. The task of having, once again, to get immersed in the UK business and scale back the infrastructure I had helped build in the 1980s and 1990s was not one I relished.

In the autumn of 2005 I identified a possible successor, V, and that cemented my decision to leave. That choice, left to me, would have been to appoint my right hand man R and ensure continuity of culture and direction, but I knew that he was not considered suitable for the role by my boss. V had a long track record in the European office product market. His early career had been with a UK direct distributor to the office, Office International. That business was acquired by Lyreco, a large French dealer, and V was later to become MD of Lyreco's European wide business, headquartered in Belgium. He had then joined the US owned Office Depot/Viking business, managing their European operations.

I had a meeting with him and then passed him on to my boss for consideration. His appointment was announced to a shocked industry in December 2005. He was to have an induction tour of Spicers and then take over from me at the beginning of February. I was retained on a two year part time contract to provide continuity and to complete some current projects, like integration of the recently acquired Timmermans business. At the Frankfurt Fair in January I collected, on behalf of Spicers, the *European Wholesaler of the Year Award* for the second year in succession. I also received a personal *Special Recognition Award*, to mark the end of my 34 year career with Spicers and my long involvement in the European office products industry. It seemed like a fitting conclusion to my reign. There was to be no lavish industry farewell for me, as I had arranged for Eric Smith at Stationers' Hall when he retired. Not even a more humble local Spicers' farewell. Little did I then suspect how the future would unfold for Spicers, let alone that by 2020 the company would no longer exist.

Part 2 Spicers' Final Years

As I had half expected my involvement with the business was extremely limited after V took over. He rarely consulted me and I deliberately stayed away from the business to give him the freedom to establish himself, as I would have wanted if our roles had been reversed. I had hoped to use the Spicers' European management conference, that I had set up in Spain later in the year, as an opportunity to say a farewell to colleagues, but that was denied to me at V's preference. I met with Timmermans a few times and did a little research on other European markets, in particular Hungary, otherwise I was effectively out.

The financial result for 2005/6 turned out to be considerably worse than expected. Spicers profits fell from £21.5m to £12.6m and that decline was all down to UK performance, its profits fell from £16.5m to £4.8m. What made matters worse was a failure to forecast that poor result. A deterioration in profit was anticipated but it wasn't until the final months of the year that the scale of the shortfall was appreciated by the UK team. Much of the deterioration was down to the growth in customer retrospective discounts, as business was defended from competitor Kingfield-Heath attacks. This increase in discounts had not then been reflected in the accrual system, designed to account for accumulating liabilities. On handing over to V, I was asked by my DSS boss for an analysis of the UK business and views on possible ways forward. That was the last time I was asked for my opinion. In March both the UK MD and finance director were sacked by V, presumably with his boss's knowledge if not at his instigation. My final meeting with the chief executive of DSS occurred in the aftermath of the UK result; it was in many ways a repeat performance of previous meetings. The bonus scheme for Spicers' senior management was set each year in conjunction with him. For financial year 2005/6, at his insistence, an element of that bonus was dependent on the cash flow performance of the business.

Spicers had historically a strong positive cash flow, normally dependent on profits but also on control of working capital, such as the amount of money tied up in stock. In 2005/6, despite the profit shortfall, Spicers achieved its cash flow target and thus an element of bonus payment was due to the senior European management team. I was summoned to meet my boss at DSS headquarters in London where he suggested that I had known about the scale of the UK profitability problem before I resigned. He went on to seek my agreement to the waiving of management's earned cash flow bonus, on the grounds of the poor profit result. I, honestly, said that I could not have known about something the UK management team was unaware of until towards year end, and I declined to agree to a retrospective change in the bonus scheme rules. The bonus due was subsequently paid but communication with me thereafter was via his personnel director. My relationship with him ended as it had begun, had it been different I might have stayed on at Spicers until 60, but I was glad to be out and subsequently never regretted my decision to depart.

Kingfield-Heath

Our principal UK wholesaling competitors had through merger consolidated into a single business in 1999, Kingfield-Heath. Alan Hickman who had overseen the final merger left the business in 2001 having struggled with the consolidation and rationalisation process required. His subsequent attempt to set up a new traditional stationery wholesale business *The Stationery Channel* in 2003 ultimately failed when it went into administration in 2008. The Kaye family, owners of Kingfield-Heath, appointed an internal candidate, originally part of the John Heath management team, to lead the business after Alan Hickman's departure. In 2001 sales were £206m and a loss of £6.5m was incurred as warehouses were closed and the business restructured.

By 2003 sales were little better at £212m but the business was now generating an operating profit of £10.2m before exceptional costs of £1.1m and interest costs. In 2004 KH's new MD led a management buy-out and by 2006 had increased sales to £242m, in part at Spicers expense. In June 2007 *Electra* private equity acquired both Kingfield-Heath and an EOS distributor ISA, combined sales of the two businesses was circa £500m. ISA was both a wholesaler of EOS and also sold EOS directly to the consumer. The direct business was made into a separate company *Supplies Team* and in 2008 the two wholesaling businesses were merged and rebranded *VOW*. The parent company of VOW and Supplies Team was named Vasanta. VOW results for 2008 showed sales of £307m, a gross margin of 20.6% and an operating profit of £12.4m. That profit was turned into a loss of £6.3m, before interest, by exceptional costs of £18.7m, these being a mixture of integration costs and asset impairment charges. A year later sales were down to £283m, gross margin was 19.1% and the loss was £16m after further exceptional costs. In early 2009 *Electra* wrote off its investment in Vasanta and ownership passed at virtually no cost to 'distress specialist' private equity investor *Endless*.

Management Turmoil at Spicers
Following the dismissal of his UK MD, V directly managed that business and put in place a plan to recover profitability by a combination of cost reduction and rebuilding gross margin. A new MD was appointed in February 2007. One of the early cost cutting projects was closure of Park Royal RDC in June 2007, that was the same distribution centre where I had gained my commercial education back in 1979.

In the financial year 2007/8 Spicers' European profit had

recovered to £20.1m and sales had grown to £645m. Most of the sales growth had come from continental Europe with a good contribution from the successful Timmermans acquisition. UK sales were now down to £265m but had returned to modest growth that year, a return to previous profitability however was not achieved.

A number of major management changes occurred in 2009 and 2010. First V left the business to become president of Staples European business in March 2009, a role he filled for the next three years. He was replaced as CE of Spicers by a non-executive director of DSSmith, G, who had a background in DIY retail. In November the relatively new UK MD left his post 'with immediate effect' and was succeeded by A, someone who had no previous experience in the OP industry but had a background in distribution.

Early in 2010 the chief executive of DSSmith (my old boss) stepped down to be replaced by Miles Roberts. In March that year Stewart Barton-Taylor, Spicers European buying director, unhappy with how the business was being managed decided to call it a day and take early retirement. Three months later R left his Spicers European director role to join Vasanta (Spicers' principal wholesaling rival in the UK) as chief executive. Then to add to senior management turmoil at Spicers in September 2010 G resigned as CE of Spicers to join a European private equity backed retail group. He was eventually replaced in February 2011 by a Dutch national with 20 years of experience in the European office products market, mainly with Viking and Corporate Express. His tenure as CE of Spicers was to be of even shorter duration than that of his immediate predecessor.

Consolidation in the Office Product Marketplace
At the beginning of the 1990s there were a number of acquisition driven ventures across Europe competing for a share of the office products (OP) distribution market.

One of those was **Buhrmann Tetterode** (BT) a Dutch company that had started acquiring office product dealers in the USA in 1987 with Summit and in the UK in 1989 with Copygraphic, the company to which my old boss Peter Frost had gone on leaving Spicers. The BT Office Products (BTOP) division went on to buy many dealers in the US and UK, it also grew strongly in Germany and across Europe in the 1990s. One of its biggest acquisitions came with the purchase of US listed company **Corporate Express** (CExp) in 1999, itself another prolific consolidator of the OP dealer market. This enabled BTOP to strengthen its position in many markets and spread its geographical wings even further afield. It was CExp that had bought Alex Findlay's Chisholms business back in 1996, one of many UK acquisitions. With the purchase of CExp BTOP was rebranded Corporate Express. **USOP**, another US based consolidator of the dealer segment in the US and UK, was then acquired out of insolvency by CExp in 2001. USOP had been very active in the UK in the 1990s. Its biggest investment had been in 1996, when it acquired a 49% stake in Dudley Stationers, a much respected large, family owned, dealer based in East London that had been set up by the Brient family in the 1950s. That investment set a new generation of the Brient family off on an acquisition blitz. Jarrolds and Heffers, two office product dealer subsidiaries of larger businesses in East Anglia, were followed by F.H.Brown in the north and many more. Strong sales growth followed but also integration problems including a troubled move to a large new warehouse in east London at Twelve Trees, or as a cruel industry joke had it at the time, 'eight trees and four to follow'. Sales of £189m in 1999 produced a £38.3m loss. Severe cash outflows followed resulting in the eventual liquidation of the business in 2002, a year after its USOP 'investor' had filed for creditor protection in the USA. In 2008 the much expanded Corporate Express business itself was subject to a hostile takeover bid by Staples. That bid was challenged by Lyreco, one of France's contract stationer giants, who sought a merger with CExp to fend off Staples' European expansion. That attempt failed when Corporate Express shareholders opted for the Staples' bid.

Staples business had started in the USA in 1986 with its first office product superstore.

By its 10th anniversary it had an enormous number of stores across the US and sales in excess of three billion dollars. It opened its first store in the UK in 1993 and added many more, in part through the purchase of the Office World superstore chain. In the mid 1990s it continued its expansion across Europe, and elsewhere in the world, mainly by acquisition. In 1998 it bought the second biggest US office product mail order business Quill. The hostile takeover of Corporate Express in 2008 cemented its position in the B2B (business to business) dealer supply segment of the office product market, adding to its already high profile in superstores and mail order routes to market. On acquisition it dropped the Corporate Express name in favour of the *Staples Business Advantage* brand. In March 2009 V left Spicers to become President of Staples European business, newly expanded by the CExp acquisition.

Office Depot established its first superstore in Florida in 1986, it floated on the US stock market shortly thereafter and by 1990 had 173 stores. In 1991 it merged with another retail chain, Office Club, extending its geographical reach across the USA. It then began acquiring office product dealers and to expand outside the US. In 1998 it bought the highly successful Viking business, establishing a strong foothold in the mail order office product segment both in the US and Europe. In 2003 it acquired the French based dealer business Guilbert, which alongside Lyreco, dominated the French

B2B market. Guilbert had itself grown by acquisition across Europe. Its biggest acquisition in the UK was in 1996 when it bought the WHSmith contract stationery business branded Niceday.

Niceday itself was the result of the consolidation of six acquired large UK dealers in the 1980s; Satex, Pentagon, Sandhurst, Cartwright Brice, Chapmans and Haydens.

Lyreco began life as a Gaspard family stationery shop in Valenciennes, France, close to the Belgian border, in 1926. After world war two it developed into a B2B office supply business. It grew to become, alongside Guilbert, one of two dominant French owned dealer businesses. Its international expansion began in 1989 with an acquisition in Belgium. Shortly after it acquired Office International (OI) in the UK and in doing so employed V who had joined OI in 1990. V was to become MD of Lyreco UK and then Lyreco Europe. The driving force behind Lyreco's expansion worldwide was Eric Bigeard, a fellow presenter of mine at many OP conferences. The business was to grow dramatically, largely by acquisition, across Europe, Canada and then worldwide. It formed an alliance with Staples in the USA until Staples made that hostile bid for Corporate Express and in so doing became a major competitor of Lyreco in Europe. Its attempts to prevent that takeover, by merging itself with CE, failed in 2008. The business continued to be controlled by the Gaspard family but was fronted and driven forward by Eric Bigeard until he stepped down as CE at the end of 2010. His initial successor as CEO lasted just eight months in post and over the next 6 years Lyreco sales did not grow.

Spicers Sold

In July 2011 a binding offer was received by DSSmith for the purchase of Spicers and the transaction was completed in December. Unipapel, a Spanish owned leading distributor and manufacturer of office products, was the acquirer but in a simultaneous transaction it sold the UK and Irish Spicers business to private equity investor *Better Capital*.

DSSmith received £200m for Spicers, in effect that was made up of £168m for the continental European operations and £30m, plus a deferred consideration, for the UK and Irish business.

Unipapel acquired Spicers' continental European business with a turnover of €443m and profit of €34.3m EBITDA (earnings before interest, tax, depreciation and amortisation). Sales breakdown of that business at acquisition was; France €217m, Germany €90m, Benelux €54m, Italy €50m and Spain €32m. The Unipapel business had itself been transformed in the years immediately prior to the purchase of Spicers. In 2009 it had acquired European EOS distributor *Adimpo* and in early 2011 it sold off its B2B Spanish dealer business *Ofiservice* to Lyreco. The new, post Spicers, Unipapel had sales of €1.3billion and described itself as Europe's leading office product wholesaler. Its sales mix was 66% EOS and 31% traditional office products and 3% office machines.

That was a difficult mix to manage because of the gross margin disparity between EOS and traditional office products, as Spicers and VOW had both found. By mid 2012 Unipapel announced that the Adimpo and Spicers businesses would be brought together under a single management structure and under a new business name *Adveo,* that was also to be the Spanish stock exchange share listing name. Effectively that was the end of Spicers' name in continental Europe. J, MD of Spicers France, was appointed head of the combined business and reported to the group CEO. To help reduce high debt levels a decision was made in 2014 to sell off the old Unipapel envelope manufacturing business to Swiss private equity company *Springwater*. They would in 2019 subsequently sell it on to French stationery manufacturing group Hamelin, the buyers of the John Dickinson business.

Adveo's decision to move off the Focus 2000 computer system onto a version of SAP, a leading enterprise software package widely used in Europe, proved to be very costly. In 2015 the business suffered a €65.7m loss, of which a large part was attributable to the systems transfer disruption. The group CEO lost his job. In 2016 the low margin EOS part of Adveo was then sold to Westcoast, a large UK privately owned wholesaler of IT products and EOS. This disposal in effect shrank Adveo back to the old Spicers' business. A second decision to trade directly with end users, as well as dealers, brought the business into conflict with some of its traditional customers. In 2016 Adveo declared a loss of €20.4m and its financial debt, despite disposals, stood at €142m. To address that debt it began to sell off warehouses it owned and lease them back, or in some cases sub-contract the logistics function to third parties. J left the business early in 2017. With reduced stock investment, logistical and systems problems, service deteriorated even further and the business found itself trapped in a debt and service death spiral. In the autumn of 2018 Adveo declared itself insolvent and its shares on the Spanish exchange were suspended, having fallen by over 80% in the previous twelve months. The German, Italian and Spanish operations were put into liquidation. The French and Benelux businesses were salvaged and bought for €10.5million by *Sandton Capital Partners* private equity in February 2019. Sandton also took on €134m of debt.

Deconsolidation in the Office Product Marketplace

Staples announced the closure of 224 stores in the US in 2014, in part due to the loss of business to online platforms that provided product delivery. The following year it sought to take over rival Office Depot. This was its second attempt to do so and even though terms were agreed the takeover was blocked, as it had been the first time, by the US competition authority the Federal Trade Commission (FTC). In 2016 Staples, while retaining a B2B presence in the UK, sold its 106 British stores for a nominal amount to *Hilco Capital* which then changed the brand to *Office Outlet*.

After an intervening, but short lived, MBO there were 94 stores left when the whole business was put into administration in 2019. No buyer was found and the business was closed resulting in 1176 job losses. The remaining parts of Staples European businesses were said to be in sales decline and only marginally profitable. In 2017 they were sold to private equity investor *Cerberus Capital Management*. The company was rebranded *Staples Solutions*. R, previously of Spicers and then Vasanta, became MD of the Staples B2B UK business in April 2017. That UK business was sold to Banner, part of the EVO group (see below), in 2020. Staples Solutions further rationalised its business in continental Europe with retail stores being sold off in the Netherlands and Germany as it sought to concentrate on B2B contract business. The US business itself was sold in 2017 to another private equity investor *Sycamore Partners*. They undertook a major restructuring to create three businesses; in the US contract stationery and retail entities and a distinct Canadian business. Within two years Sycamore recovered 80% of their equity investment in the form of a one off $1 billion dividend payout.

Office Depot in 2013 acquired US superstore rival OfficeMax and then proceeded to close 400 stores. In 2017 it sold off its European businesses to German private equity group *Aurelius* for a 'nominal consideration'. The Office Depot and Viking brands continued to be used in Europe; Depot for the B2B contract business and Viking for mail order. A sell off of parts of the business then followed, first in eastern Europe, then the Nordic north and then Spain. A decision was made to migrate the main European B2B businesses onto an enhanced version of the Viking IT platform and then drop the Office Depot brand in favour of Viking as the sole trading name in Germany, Austria, Switzerland, Benelux, Ireland and the UK. That programme was given the project name of *Viking+*. France was not part of the plan and in 2021 Office Depot France was placed in receivership.

Private Equity

Private Equity (PE) typically refers to funds, generally organised under limited liability partnerships, that buy and restructure companies. Acquisitions are either not publicly owned (do not have traded shares) or are subsequently taken private. The ultimate interest in the businesses owned is in making a capital gain on their eventual disposal. The median term for such investments is 8 years. PE is often presented as being a catalyst for business renewal, in reality it is more commonly a method of extracting wealth for the benefit of PE's owners and investors. The money trail is often obscured by complex ownership structures and sophisticated tax avoidance mechanisms, sometimes using international tax havens. Well paid lawyers and accountants facilitate and service this; part of what has become a UK based financial industry. Industry is something of a misnomer given that wealth extraction, rather than wealth creation, is at its core in a post-industrial, financialised era.

The management buyout (MBO), is a variation on this wealth extraction model. It involves the acquisition of an existing business and the incentivising of that business's senior management to maximise shareholder return in the short-term. Acquisitions invariably involve a mixture of borrowed money (debt) and a much smaller element of fixed capital investment (equity), provided by the acquiring firm and usually a small number of the acquired business's senior managers. That has two benefits; the debt, allocated as a loan to the business acquired, involves interest payments that reduce profits and consequent corporation tax, and the capital gain accruing, on disposal of the business, to the equity holders is substantially greater, often a multiple of their initial investment. This model is associated with the sale of company assets (asset stripping), to reduce debt, and the restructuring of the business, often involving redundancies or reductions in pay or benefits for employees. In addition, banks and vendors can be left with significant debts as the private equity investors walk away with their capital gains.

Key skills in execution of this model involve finding others willing to provide most of the finance or capital and in making a timely exit, that is in passing the (business) parcel to others. Perhaps 'chalice' is a better metaphor than 'parcel' for many of these exits.

After the US, the UK has been the next biggest market for private equity. In the post-Thatcher era financial manipulation and property speculation came to be seen as quicker routes to wealth accumulation, than by the long-term building of value in a customer orientated manufacturing or service business.

There have been a number of booms and busts in the private equity investment industry but the 2010s saw a resurgence and a focus by some on office products distribution businesses, some of which had grown dramatically by acquisition. Peter Frost, my old boss, had left Spicers for contract stationer Copygraphic, bought out later by Buhrmann(BT), then moved on to head Office Smart dealer group; it in turn was absorbed by a larger group, as groups themselves consolidated. He eventually became publisher of *Proficiency Post*, a digital news platform aimed at the office products market. His view on private equity's entry to the industry can be judged by his *Proficiency Post* description of such firms as 'vulture capitalists'.

VOW, Vasanta and EVO

VOW was the wholesaling division of Vasanta, direct competitor of Spicers in the UK and Ireland. It had been created in 2007 when *Electra* private equity bought both Kingfield Heath and ISA, an EOS distributor. An EOS business selling direct to end users, Supplies Team, was separated out and became part of Vasanta group. The integration of the wholesaling businesses into VOW proved problematic and Electra ended up walking away from its investment in 2009, handing control to another UK private equity investor *Endless*. They provided £30m of equity and persuaded banks to write off over £100m of debt in return for an equity stake in the business. In 2010 *Endless* appointed R, ex-Spicers, as chief executive of Vasanta. Group turnover in 2011 was £384m and profitability marginal. The VOW wholesaling division turnover was £258m and this produced, from a gross margin of 18.7%, an operating loss of £0.8m, before interest but after exceptional costs of £0.8m. In 2011 Vasanta opened a third highly mechanised warehouse at Normanton and VOW set up a new furniture division, *VOW Interiors*, mirroring Spicers *SpaceAge* service. Vasanta results improved by 2013, sales were up to £415m with VOW at £298m having made good inroads into Spicers' business as its problems multiplied. R played an active part in winning over some of those Spicers' customers, like Office Team. That same year VOW was named European Wholesaler of the Year at the Frankfurt Fair, and again the following year. In 2014 *Endless* acquired Office2Office (o2o) a business trading under the name *Banner* and known previously, prior to privatisation, as HMSO (Her Majesty's Stationery

Office). Banner had a turnover in 2013 of £215m and was a B2B contract stationer with large end user customers, including some government departments given its history as HMSO.

On acquisition the decision was made to combine Vasanta and Office2Office under a new parent, EVO Group, owned by *Endless*. R was appointed CE of EVO and given the daunting task of integrating the logistical side of the businesses while keeping separate the, potentially conflicting, trading platforms (Banner was in competition with a number of VOW's dealer customers). The integration process proved more difficult than anticipated. In 2015 EVO turnover was £608m but its operating profit of £10.7m translated into a loss, before interest, of £11m after allowing for exceptional costs, depreciation, impairment and amortisation of asset values. R left the business in April 2016 and was replaced by one of his subordinates. EVO results for 2016 showed sales of £538m and profit at break even before interest. The VOW wholesaling business had produced sales of £291m, a gross margin of 20.5% and a pre-interest operating profit of £0.9m before exceptional costs of £4.3m. Gross margin had been improved by reducing lower margin EOS sales and removing some non-core business. Work was also underway to move from six system platforms, used by the various companies making up the group, to two by 2017.

In 2019 EVO group sales were down to £440m and the net operating loss was £3.5 million before interest. The VOW wholesaling division produced sales of £235m, a gross margin of 22.5% and a pre-interest operating profit of £1.8m before exceptional costs of £3.7m. So, wholesaling sales were now below those achieved in 2011, despite all the problems of Spicers, and the improvement in gross margin, from 18.7% to 22.5%, had still not produced a viable operating profit. However in 2020 VOW was given a major growth opportunity as Spicers troubles reached their climax and that year EVO acquired the Staples UK business and planned to integrate that into their Banner B2B division.

Spicers – the beginning of the end

Spicers UK and Ireland business was acquired by *Better Capital* (BC) private equity in a simultaneous transaction with Unipapel as the latter purchased Spicers European wholesaling operations from DSSmith at the end of 2011. BC paid £29.5m in cash plus an element of deferred consideration. That investment was broken down on the Spicers balance sheet as £1m shareholding (equity) £14m in shareholder loan notes (longer term debt) and the balance in short term debt. BC acquired assets worth £54m at balance sheet book value. By April 2013 the shareholder loan had been reduced to £6.6m, that is, Spicers business had funded a large repayment of the debt raised to buy the company, within 16 months of acquisition. That shareholder loan had attracted a much higher rate of interest than third party debt and the latter remained considerable.

On being acquired by BC Spicers existing UK MD, A, was given responsibility for Ireland and his title elevated to chief executive. The restated accounts for the year ended April 2012 showed sales of £298m, a gross margin of 21% and a profit before interest of £2.8m, after exceptional costs of £1.5m. A year later the comparable numbers were; sales £240m gross margin 23.4% and profit £2.2m after exceptional costs of £3.7m. The exceptional costs related mainly to redundancies as distribution centres were closed and administrative functions rationalised. Shortly after acquisition A, under direction from the new owners, went on the offensive with suppliers and sought an improvement in buying terms and extended credit. That did not go down well with Spicers key vendors who had just suffered a large fall in volume as continental European purchases moved to Unipapel. A's management style was described by some as direct by others abrasive, a view expressed by some customers as well as vendors. That may, in part, have been a result of the considerable pressure he was placed under by BC. A major customer lost at this time was *Office Team* (see below) who switched allegiance to VOW, Spicers' biggest competitor.

Almost immediately after Spicers was acquired, BC decided to sell the Sawston headquarters site. It was seen as the jewel in the business's asset crown; a 550 acre farm with substantial warehousing and office accommodation spread around the site. In order to facilitate that sale new administrative offices were rented a few miles away and work started to extend the DDC warehouse in Smethwick from 142,000 square feet to 222,000 feet. The intention was that it could then take on the role of the central warehouse in addition to making deliveries to end users on behalf of dealers.

Vida Barr-Jones, who I had recruited into the business at Park Royal in the 1980s and had risen to become head of UK logistics, then resigned, faced with dictated changes in infrastructure that she regarded as unworkable. The process was driven by BC, with Spicers' chief executive A required to minimise any new investment necessary to enable disposal of assets that would reduce the company's level of debt. Other changes involved; furniture distribution being subcontracted to a third party, the closure of Chessington RDC, leaving only Greenwich to service the south east of England, and Belfast RDC being de-stocked. All changes were disruptive and costly but closure of the central warehouse (CDC) at Sawston was devastating in its impact on overall customer service, exacerbated by a failure to get the extended DDC operation up and running on time. The results proved so disastrous that *Better Capital* decided not to publish accounts for the year ended April 2014, extending the year to August. The 16 month result, when eventually released, showed sales of £248m, a gross margin of 19.1% and an operating loss, before interest, of £35.2m. After much mental anguish the UK and Ireland chief executive left the business in May 2014. The Sawston site was sold two months later for £13m (four years later that same site was sold on to Chinese technology giant Huawei for £37m). In July Better Capital acquired *Office Team*, the large UK dealer, and decided that its business should be merged with that of Spicers.

Office Team

The origin of Office Team can be traced back to the Straker business mentioned earlier in connection with Jonathan Straker, Master of the Stationers' Company. W. Straker Stationery was founded in 1863 and Jonathan joined the family retail business in the 1960s. In the 1970s the business developed to become principally a B2B operation under the name Straker Office Supplies. In 1987 Jonathan, together with partner Hugh Sear, got third party investors involved in the business thus enabling acquisitions and rapid growth. *Bridgepoint Capital*, private equity, bought the business in 1995 and their subsequent acquisition of the Solicitors Law Stationery business, known as *Oyez*, resulted in the businesses being merged and a change of name to Oyez Straker in 1997. Four years later Statplus was acquired, another large legal stationery dealer. In 2003 the Oyez Straker business was sold to *Hermes* private capital for £80m, Jonathan Straker retired, Hugh Sear became chairman and J, who had been with the company for 15 years, took over as chief executive. Growth by acquisition remained a key strategy.

Hermes' involvement ended in 2007 with sale of the business, now valued at £163m, to *AAC Capital Partners*. Hugh Sear stepped down from involvement in the business but the remaining management team under J retained a stake in the business. The name was changed to *Office Team* and it continued with an acquisition strategy resulting in £189m of sales in 2008. Two years later sales had fallen to £154m, in part as a result of the 2008 economic crash, and operating profit stood at £5.9m. Thereafter sales continued to fall and by 2013 were down to £138m. That produced an operating profit of £2.5m, before reorganisation costs of £3.5m and a much greater asset impairment charge. The Royal Bank of Scotland and other lenders took brief ownership of the business before it was sold again to *Better Capital* in July 2014 for £80m. Office Team sales in the year 2014 were £133m and operating profit was £0.8m after exceptional costs. *Better Capital* believed that by bringing together the two troubled businesses, Spicers and Office Team, under J's leadership, it could create a business cable of redeeming its investments in office product distribution.

SPOT Spicers End

The name given to the new group was Spicers Office Team (SPOT). J had the same problem that had faced R at VOW, combining the logistical platform of the businesses whilst maintaining the separate, potentially conflicting trading entities, one selling direct to users the other selling to dealers. He had an additional problem in that the newly extended warehouse of Spicers at Smethwick (DDC) was out of operation. The extension and new conveyor systems had still not been commissioned and the warehouse was temporarily mothballed. SPOT accounts for 2015 showed Spicers division sales of £164m and a pre-interest loss of £3.2m, Office Team sales were £132m and loss £0.7m. By 2018 Office Team sales had declined further and although Spicers had stabilised sales, this was at the expense of gross margin and resulted in an even bigger operating loss. The last published accounts of SPOT, for year ended 2018, showed total sales at £281m and an operating loss of £25.9m, with trading losses dwarfed by significant write-downs in asset values. Spicers sales then stood at £165m and the pre-interest operating loss was £6.2m. In January 2019 J left the business. His successor almost immediately announced plans to reduce the number of Spicers RDCs to two; Greenwich and Manchester. It fell to J's successor to place SPOT into administration in April 2020. That was necessary after it became known that *Better Capital* was trying to sell the business and that some suppliers had withdrawn credit. Spicers and Office Team remained separate legal entities even though they had shared warehousing facilities. The appointed legal administrators sold Office Team to Paragon Data Analytics for £1m. The assets acquired included stock, racking and the *Five Star* private label brand. Paragon changed the business name to OT Group. Spicers Ireland was later acquired out of liquidation by Paragon and renamed Spicers Office Supply (Ireland). The legal 'administration' of Spicers Limited was extended into 2023. Talk of Paragon resurrecting a *Spicers* branded wholesaling business in the UK would involve starting again from scratch and seems an unlikely prospect. So, with a modest continuation of its name in the Republic of Ireland, Spicers' 220+ year history appears to be at an end.

Part 4
Reflections

Chapter 1   Conversation with Thoth
Chapter 2   Proverbs of Perspective
Chapter 3   Conversation with Eleos
Chapter 4   Poems on Purpose
Chapter 5   Life a Pilgrimage

The final part of *A Life in Perspective* draws on much reading over many years. Since my teenage days I have been interested in religion, philosophy and the possible meaning of life. That reading has been diverse in its nature, ranging across religious, secular and scientific sources as well as philosophical works from ancient Egypt, Greece, India, China and the Middle East.

I believe we all, consciously or unconsciously, perceive or create a framework that helps us make sense of our life and the interaction that entails with others. This need for structure, or order, appears to be inherent in humans and manifests at individual and collective levels. The framework so created may or may not be coherent, conscious or intellectualised but underpins motive and mental health. The *age of reason* that underpins *science* has come to dominate culture in the West. Its effect has been to promote the rational and material and suppress, or invalidate intellectually, the spiritual aspects of human experience. Yet throughout history humans have seemingly sensed that earthly existence was but one aspect of ultimate reality. The awareness of the inevitability of mortal death may have played a part in driving such thought processes. The concept of a greater reality and the idea of God, Allah, Brahman or Tao stretches back into prehistory. Many tribes over time have believed that they have found a unique and exclusive path to God. The more I have learned the more I have had difficulty with the idea of such exclusivity and its inherent condemnation of those outside the tribe.

The simplistic idea of God as an authority figure effectively sitting in judgement on wayward humans, requiring them, if they are to be 'saved', to adhere to a theological checklist and provide regular fawning worship, has always seemed out of kilter with the idea of a God synonymous with love. The former authoritarian concept seems more probably the creation of religious hierarchies, seeking, consciously or unconsciously, to instil reverence and obtain consequent control of their flock, rather than one in tune with the underlying message of teachers who have sought to raise awareness of a spiritual reality.

I have attempted to bring my own understanding or framework together in *Reflections*. That has involved a search for common themes and consistencies across a wide range of sources. The result is five pieces; *Conversation with Thoth* an imagined conversation with the ancient God of Knowledge, *Proverbs of Perspective* lessons drawn from my own experience of life and reading, *Conversation with Eleos* an imagined conversation with the ancient Goddess of Compassion, *Poems on Purpose* a take on various aspects of life, including the idea of purpose, and finally a conclusion in *Life a Pilgrimage*.

Conversation with Thoth is a wide ranging look at the world viewed through the lens of my own life. It considers and challenges, no doubt provocatively for some, a number of contemporary assumptions. The objective is not to affront or persuade but to encourage research and reflection on inherited or inculcated beliefs; beliefs that can fuel conflict and undermine social cohesion. The other pieces making up *Reflections* transcend the noise of contemporary life and consider universal and perennial issues that face us as humans.

I think the acid test of any philosophy or framework is whether it helps an individual make sense of their life, move towards a greater Self and encourages positive interaction with others that in turn helps their growth.

I am happy for the framework outlined in *Reflections* to be judged by that test.

Chapter 1
Conversation with Thoth

...about power, political economy and social cohesion

Is humanity making progress?

Humanity in the aggregate is simply the sum of its parts and as long as the individuals making it up have weaknesses as well as strengths, that will manifest in society at large. Life is about the choices we make, faced with the situations confronting us, individually and collectively. That freedom of choice, an essential part of learning, comes with the freedom to make mistakes. If progress is defined as learning from the past then I am afraid there is little evidence that humanity in the aggregate has progressed. Eleos will talk later about learning at the individual level, I am happy to talk about humanity in the collective.

Surely you cannot deny that we have made progress in many ways.

That very much depends upon your definition of the word progress. Humanity has been undoubtedly successful in increasing its numbers. That success has been gained at the expense of countless other species and to some extent the environment that sustains life in general. Sustainability has become a fashionable word, much used and abused, but it will become increasingly important if humanity is to save itself from the effects of population growth. Nature of course will intervene if humanity fails to manage this success. We are collectively becoming aware of the issue and that is certainly a good step towards achieving a conscious solution.

Do you not think that people's lives and lot are better than in the past?

For many that is true but we must put things in perspective. Let us take mankind's propensity for violence. I use the word mankind here deliberately, for it is generally men that indulge that inclination. More people were killed in the twentieth century as a result of violence, or choice, than the sum of similar deaths in all the centuries preceding it. I am not just talking about the so-called world wars but include the millions killed in pursuit of ideological causes. Despite the untold misery that resulted, and the displacement of enormous numbers of people, much of that violence was justified in the name of the cause or the 'greater good'. Domestic ideological imperatives resulted in the deaths of millions of people in Russia and China. The Vietnam and Iraq wars pursued by the United States killed millions more. It indicates mankind's remarkable propensity for self-righteousness and delusion, just as in previous centuries when slaughter was justified in God's name, by one religious group or another.

That is not to say that religious based carnage has come to an end. After the second world war the UK began to actively dismantle its empire. Its parting gift to a newly liberated subcontinent was the atrociously organised partition that separated Pakistan from India. That hasty imperial exit, driven in part by local tribal interests, directly resulted in up to two million deaths, as Hindus and Muslims sought and fought to geographically separate. British imperial rule had served to strengthen separate religious identities as part of its *Divide and Rule* policy but the act of partition itself resulted in a deep-seated enmity that persists to this day.

The UK was also instrumental in the Jewish colonisation of Palestine, a process that began with the government's Balfour Declaration of 1917. That commitment to Lord Rothschild, supporting the Zionist goal of creating 'a national home for the Jewish people', was enabled by the British Mandate for Palestine, following the first world war defeat of the Ottoman Empire, and resulted in an organised migration. With the end of the second world war the US took over the parenting of what was to become a new Jewish state, Israel. It was a troubled, illegitimate birth. US guilt, at its pre-war refusal to take Jews seeking refuge from Nazi persecution and the overt anti-semitism prevalent there in the 1920s and 1930s, may have played a part in its subsequent sponsorship of the new state. This deliberate organised settlement of an alien religious group resulted in the displacement and persecution of the local Muslim population. It is ironic, if not tragic, that a group that had itself faced persecution throughout history, including the horrific 'final solution' holocaust perpetrated by Nazi Germany, should be responsible for creating an effective apartheid state and the ghetto that is Gaza. The new nation was surrounded by hostile Muslim countries and this only served to further the paranoia induced by recent history, but Israel was bolstered by an ongoing supply of money and weapons from the United States. It exercised significant influence over US policy in the Middle East, a case of David harnessing Goliath, and consequently had no qualms about military and other interventions in neighbouring countries deemed a potential threat.

Managing external perceptions, of its sometimes aggressive behaviour, was an important part of the new state's policy. The victim card was regularly played and helped provide a notionally virtuous shield. Politicians in the US and Europe were actively cultivated and any criticism of Israel's actions was consistently branded anti-semitic. It was an epithet liberally used, even against Jews who dared to question Israeli policy.

That campaign was successful in silencing much of Western media, politicians and the diaspora. Rarely did the tribe collectively ask of itself why it appeared to be history's perpetual victim and what it might learn from the past.

This act of deliberate colonisation, resulting in deep Muslim resentment and anger, has produced a seemingly perpetual tinderbox of violence and slaughter in the Middle East and beyond in the form of terrorism. That, of course, combined with the ongoing conflict between Sunni and Shia versions of Islam and the region's blessing and curse; oil, black gold coveted by empires of all colours.

Surely you will acknowledge that some wars are necessary to defeat evil?

Resorting to violence should be a last resort and then only to avoid a greater loss of life. History is full of conquerors who are later seen as civilizers, so fighting is not always the best answer to being attacked. Did Jesus not say 'to offer the other cheek if you are struck on one cheek'? The Prophet Muhammed taught 'do not cause harm or return harm'. That principle, transcending an 'eye for an eye' mentality, is rarely adopted between tribes or nations, or I should say, between the ruling elites that control those groups. You may argue that a regime making war with the intention of genocide on racial, religious or other grounds must be stopped.

That could be described as a fight against evil and be justified. Wars are rarely fought under such a noble banner, although that pretext is often used to justify action of more doubtful motivation. There is little evidence that mankind collectively has learned much from the past about peaceful resolution of potential conflicts.

When fighting eventually comes to an end, and it always does, there is rarely an objective analysis of the causes of the conflict. As someone once said 'it is the victors that write history, rarely the vanquished', so you will find many wars are described in retrospect as righteous when they could have been avoided had the underlying causes been addressed before the military mindset took hold. That mindset is a characteristic of men and is, of course, the stuff of wars and empires throughout history.

Have we not moved beyond the era of empires?

Empires take many forms but they are predominantly about power and wealth extraction for the benefit of the motherland, or more correctly those controlling that land. The conquerors of England appropriated land and exploited the local population. A later generation ventured abroad and extracted wealth from the empire they in turn conquered. That might have been in the form of plundered natural resources or simply exploitation of local people, often regarded as inferior beings. That elite attitude was not limited to native peoples abroad, the serfs at home were similarly regarded. Many of this country's grand country houses were funded by these forms of wealth extraction from the empire. Rarely did the general population benefit. Ironically, the public of today perhaps gain something, should they choose to visit these stately homes. The National Trust estimates that a third of the properties now in its care have direct connections to the country's colonial or slave trafficking past.

I am afraid we have not moved beyond the era of empires. The US empire replaced the British empire, as the dominant influence in world affairs, after the defeat of Nazi Germany and Japan. The victory over fascism in Europe was the result of an alliance principally between the US, UK and the Soviet Union. The latter, on the Eastern front, played the biggest part in the defeat of the German military, its citizens paid a heavy price with 20-27 million dead. That compares with the US's war dead of 420,000 and the UK's 450,000. In the Far East the dropping of atomic bombs, by the US, on two Japanese cities with large civilian populations, brought that war to a prompt end. Japan's war dead was between 2.5 and 3.1 million, dwarfed by China's 15-20 million. That latter death-toll contributed to the Chinese communist party gaining control of the country in 1949 and, eventually, in a recovery of national pride following decades of humiliation at the hands of the British and then Japanese empires.

Following the war, US ambition quickly became clear. The UK was encouraged to dismantle its empire and when it intervened militarily in Egypt in 1956, without prior US approval, it was promptly reprimanded. The UK thereafter adopted a subservient and supporting role in the US's pursuit of hegemony. The British ruling elite found post-imperial comfort in its 'special relationship' with the new empire. The relationship was more special to the UK than to the US. The huge effort and sacrifice by the Soviet Union during the second world war did not stop it being immediately demonised by its former allies, as soon as the war was concluded. New empires are more easily justified if faced with an enemy or ideological threat. Communism was that threat, manifested in an expanded Soviet Union, now incorporating eastern European countries liberated by the Red Army, and the birth of a communist China. The resulting new US empire involves hundreds of military bases around the world and a form of economic colonialism.

Leadership of the 'free world' is dressed in the clothes of democracy and free enterprise, but the iron fists of the military are hidden in its velvet gloves. Fists felt by those who do not bend their knee to the new empire. Regime change is the preferred strategy, rather than blatant military conquest, particularly after the US's military defeat in Vietnam.

The collapse of the Soviet Union in around 1990 produced a period of outright US hegemony as the communist Warsaw Pact military alliance evaporated. The NATO (North Atlantic Treaty Organisation) alliance, under effective US control and principally involving North America and Europe, had been set up to counter the Warsaw Pact in 1949. It might have been deemed redundant after the Pact's dissolution but instead it chose to expand to incorporate many of the countries recently freed of the Soviet yoke. That was in contravention of American assurances given to Russia's leadership when the break-up of the Soviet Union was first mooted. NATO's avowed defensive nature was contradicted by its bombing of Bosnia, during the disintegration of Yugoslavia, and of Libya in pursuit of regime change. Perhaps its part in the war of aggression and occupation of Afghanistan best illustrated that it was really a tool of the US empire.

That war followed the 9/11 terrorist atrocity in the USA when passenger planes were flown into occupied buildings in New York and Washington DC. It resulted in a significant loss of life but was only one of many outrages in the West, involving the deaths of large numbers of innocent people, perpetrated by nominally Islamic terrorist groups. 9/11 came as a massive shock to America's leaders and seriously undermined their confidence in the nation's remote impregnability. The president characterised it as an attack on the country, in part to justify the invasion of another sovereign state.

Afghanistan had not been involved in the atrocity, executed mainly by Saudi Arabian nationals, but the declared war mission was to remove the Taliban government believed to be harbouring terrorist leaders. That was quickly achieved and a client regime installed, but that did not bring the mission to an end, nor did the death of Osama bin Laden, a Saudi Arabian born terrorist leader found in neighbouring Pakistan. After 20 years of occupation, US and NATO forces withdrew only to have their installed regime immediately replaced by a Taliban one. The invasion of Afghanistan was to end with an ignominious US departure, much as it had faced in Vietnam. NATO was not consulted on that exit but rapidly followed, its 'nation building' virtuous cover quickly abandoned.

Iraq was another victim of the knee-jerk reaction of the US to the same 9/11 terrorist attack, but now on the pretext that Iraq had 'weapons of mass destruction' (WMD). Iraq had no involvement in the terrorist atrocity nor did it have any WMD, unlike near neighbour Israel. When UN endorsement of war was not forthcoming, a 'coalition of the willing', principally the US and an acquiescent UK, embarked on regime change and the destruction of Iraq, a campaign resulting in over a million deaths. Far from reducing terrorism these Middle Eastern and Asian wars only served to strengthen the resolve of Islamic inspired groups intent on revenge.

Eventually Russia's nervousness at having NATO on its western border came to a head when Ukraine was encouraged to apply for NATO membership. It was the culmination of years of economic cultivation by the West. For Russia, with its deep historical ties to Ukraine, it was a NATO expansion tipping point. Its clearly expressed concerns were ignored, diplomatic efforts were spurned and that resulted in the Russian invasion of Ukraine. This new European war only served to feed the military mindset resulting in a new arms race and further expansion of NATO. Rather than look for a peaceful solution to the conflict the US chose to add fuel to the fire with a constant supply of weapons into Ukraine. The accompanying orchestrated economic sanctions against Russia backfired when Russia began to turn off the oil and gas energy 'taps' to Europe.

Germany found itself torn between its NATO commitment and its industries' needs. An economic crisis was the result across Europe and beyond. The US was content that the destruction of Ukraine and the sacrifice of the German economy was a price worth paying for the weakening of Russia. It declined to recognise Russia's legitimate security fears or its likely response to any territorial incursion. That response would be conditioned by its experience in world war two, and the enormous death toll suffered. A real danger resulted, that should Russia feel existentially threatened it would have no qualms in making use of its formidable nuclear weapon arsenal.

Seemingly nothing has been learned from the enormous death toll of the twentieth century. Empires need a justifying narrative and are more cohesive faced with a foe, whether nebulous, like the 'war on terror', or concrete like Russia.

Communist China was first enemy, then cultivated economically, until the US empire felt threatened by its growing success and influence. Then it too faced demonisation. Russia, when freed of its communist ideology and the Soviet empire, had sought friendship with the West. That effort was spurned, especially after Russia demonstrated an independent economic and foreign policy. The unintended consequence of alienating these two nuclear weapon powers was to unite them in opposition to US military and economic hegemony. The two countries have complementary characteristics that combined create a powerful new axis; China with its enormous population, manufacturing prowess and growing technical ingenuity, Russia, a country with the greatest landmass and enormous natural resources.

The elites in control of empires generally feel threatened when embryonic new empires arise to challenge their supremacy. Military conflict is often the result. Humans are unique, no other species has ever been so intent on killing its own kind. The pinnacle has now been reached with weapons that enable the whole of humanity to be exterminated. I am sure you will agree that that is a very perverse kind of progress.

Hopefully man's rational potential, if not conscience, will come to the fore and the realisation will dawn that no-one wins a nuclear war.

Are not the United Nations and the International Criminal Court mechanisms to prevent unjustified warfare and ensure ultimate justice?

I wish that were so, but I am afraid neither is fit for purpose. The founding principle of the UN was avoidance of conflict. Its structure, giving the power of veto to the US, Russia, China and others, like the UK, means it rarely speaks with a united voice. Likewise the flawed International Criminal Court. It is not recognised by the same three major powers and others, like Israel, who would rather not be held to account for their actions. The credo of the powerful is, and always has been, *might is right* although it is usually presented in more virtuous terms. The illegal war on Iraq demonstrates the impotence of both international bodies.

I accept that we are on a potentially dangerous path but I hope you will acknowledge that we have made progress in the material well being of our generation, relative to that of our parents and grandparents.

You are right if we choose to look at progress in that context. You will acknowledge I hope that that is a picture limited in time and location, but it is an understandable view given the perspective of our limited lifespan and field of view. The lot of the average person here in the UK is much improved in a material sense. That is the result of a political system that recognised, in the aftermath of two devastating wars, that the voice of the average person must be heard and their needs met. That move toward a more egalitarian society improved both the wellbeing and opportunities for many in the UK and elsewhere. I think it important to point out that there is nothing inevitable about its continuation. Ruling elites rarely relinquish power willingly and are ever resourceful in finding ways to re-acquire power when it has been temporarily ceded. Even in so-called democracies powerful elites exist and with power comes the potential for corruption.

That may be subtler in some societies than others but it is rarely, if ever, absent or extinguished. Once present it has a tendency to grow, unless constantly rooted out. That rooting out depends first on awareness of the need, then the will to do so.

Surely there is no going back once you have an educated and enfranchised population in a democratic country?

I think you will find that there are many examples of once democratised countries reverting to authoritarian control. Control that is then often enthusiastically supported by the educated. A common ploy in bringing that about is the use of fear or threat to justify the need for unquestioned authority. Most commonly that is used in conjunction with an enemy that poses an apparent existential threat, so you will generally see democracy and freedom of expression suspended when war breaks out, or is thought to be imminent. Other types of threat can lead to the same result, such as that resulting from the prospect of disease or other perceived danger. The recent Covid 19 pandemic was a case in point. It illustrated both the world-wide contagious power of groupthink and a typically authoritarian response, whatever the form of government involved.

Science here was the authority used to justify draconian powers, massively restricting freedom. There is strong evidence to suggest that the country that 'locked down' the least, Sweden, had one of the lowest excess mortality rates – the real indicator of covid related death toll. That is not to deny the impact of covid, particularly on the elderly, but is to recognise that a more nuanced response would probably have been more effective than blanket authoritarian restrictions. Global warming is another threat being hyped with the cure suggested being potentially worse, in impact, than the perceived problem, but perhaps we can return to that issue later.

These threats may be real, imagined or fabricated, their common theme is fear and the exploitation of that fear. As someone once said 'the first casualty of war is truth'.

Managing what is perceived to be true by the majority has become ever more sophisticated and extends well beyond the exploitation of fear alone. Controlling the narrative is now seen to be an essential part of managing consent, not only under authoritarian governments but also under those described as democratic. You raise a good point about education but I fear it offers little protection against the increasingly sophisticated manipulations practised by those seeking or exercising power.

Why not? Surely an educated person can see through blatant propaganda.

I am afraid that not all propaganda we are subjected to is blatant, in fact the evidence is that it is becoming increasingly subtle. I would also say that most formal education, rather than inculcating the questioning of information being imparted, teaches the infallibility of that information. We are told to respect the specialists or experts, they know best. The *age of reason* begat science and that science has become the prevalent secular authority of the modern age. One might almost say it is the religion of our day. People are told 'not to question the science' even though 'unquestionable science' is in fact an oxymoron, likewise 'settled science'. One of the greatest scientists of all time, Albert Einstein, famously said 'unthinking respect for authority is the greatest enemy of truth'. Many areas of human endeavour are subject to authority, not just science, and with that authority almost inevitably comes, to a greater or lesser extent, doctrine and dogma. What we used to associate with religion is just as applicable to other authorities in our secular age. Accepting dogma is often a required ticket of entry into the club that grants membership and with membership, peer respect. To return to your point, I do not believe there is any evidence to show that formal education inoculates against propaganda, whether in the realm of politics, religion or elsewhere. Certainly encouraging more critical thinking in the education process would be a healthy development. Equally important would be the encouragement of, and respect for, voices which question mainstream beliefs, doctrines or narratives. I fear that there is no evidence for those trends, in fact the reverse tendency appears to be true. The demonisation of those not subscribing to prevalent narratives becomes ever more commonplace. The digital world of 'social media' has exacerbated that problem.

Why should that be the case given an increasingly educated population with access to more sources of information than ever before available?

A very good question. Paradoxically the more information available the greater the need for selectivity. It is impossible to monitor, let alone comprehend, all the information now available to the average person with access to the internet. Bear in mind that much information is not really fact so much as someone's interpretation or comment on fact, that is someone's opinion. That does not invalidate it, it simply means that it should be taken into account and ideally compared with other interpretations of the basic facts.

That seldom happens, but should be encouraged. Humans have a tendency to prefer information which confirms their interpretations or prejudices, rather than actively seek out counter arguments. Information is the basic essence of existence. All elements of life, in a sense, are processors of information, whether conscious or unconscious.

Humans are apparently unique in having the ability to take control of unconscious programming, to become the programmer rather than simply fulfil the program. The analogy is apt because of the growing power of computers to process massive amounts of information. Not only to process but to utilise it in increasingly sophisticated ways.

Giant computers are not only controlling the information disseminated to individuals but covertly gathering information from those same individuals. It is not just devices like *Alexa* that listen to every word spoken in their presence but the mobile phones that are carried by almost everyone. That listening may result in what you might regard as a co-incidental advert appearing shortly after a related conversation. It might equally be used to profile your political views and to categorise you for future targeting. There is no doubt that large amounts of information are being gathered, analysed and stored about individuals' preferences. That technique may be used to simply sell products but might also be used to reinforce preconceived points of view or manipulate opinions. All this without the individual being aware that they are being influenced. The large international companies that control information, mostly American owned at the moment, have enormous power, so far only dimly appreciated. Increasingly they are exercising that power, as de facto publishers of information, to also censor what information is made available.

As you can imagine, that is a formidable weapon for those seeking to exercise power, whether political or economic, under an authoritarian system or a democratic one. Both systems require, to greater or lesser extent, control of the narrative and that may be more or less blatant. Cooperation between information purveyors and political controllers is not new. The publishing of books in London in the 1600s was deemed a potential threat by those with political power, because it might seed dissent. Their answer was to control what was published by granting a publishing monopoly to the Stationers' Company. Today a similar effective monopoly applies with large corporations controlling and manipulating massive amounts of information. The quid pro quo for allowing continuation of these monopolies might well be an expectation of support by those exercising political power, that support in the form of the promotion of preferred political narratives and the suppression of dissenting points of view. All this in the name of managing consent. The most effective form of propaganda is that where the recipient is unaware that the information they are receiving has been consciously manipulated to influence, if not control, their response.

Are you not guilty here of concocting a conspiracy theory that does not apply in open democratic countries, even if it might under authoritarian regimes?

As I have previously explained, whatever the regime, those exercising power are human and fallible. Controlling information is a means of exercising power, it always has been and is today. The difference today is the level of sophistication, in that it can be tailored to the individual, utilising the computing power now available. That is a characteristic of the era that has begun. An era that as well as creating opportunities poses great potential threats to concepts of choice and freewill. One thing is sure, that when such power becomes available it will be used. Those utilising it will often believe that they use it for good ends. That may be an honourable motivation or a delusion. *The best disinfectant is sunlight* is an apt metaphor, meaning that transparency, rather than devious manipulation, is a better route to what is good and true. Manipulation of others for one's own ends is a perennial characteristic of human interaction. The difference today is the enormous potential for covert manipulation, resulting from computing power that was unimaginable in the middle of the twentieth century when George Orwell wrote his book *Nineteen Eighty-Four*. If one is aware of an issue, and its potential for exploitation, then it becomes a problem capable of solution. If one remains blissfully unaware of the potential, then I think the danger is clear. The demonisation of dissent and dissenters with terms like 'conspiracy theory' is a means of controlling the narrative. It along with other terms are a way of dismissing points of view without considering the merits of the arguments presented. So you will see terms like; climate denier, racist, transphobic, antisemite, misogynist, homophobic, marxist, far-right, used to close down points of view deemed threatening by a vociferous lobby. That is similar to the need to silence heretics of old and is not healthy. Understanding human nature and weighing evidence from a number of sources helps us determine what is most likely to be true.

Truth should be our perennial goal, not adherence to dogma or loyalty to the tribe.

Given the wide sources of information available today surely manipulation is ultimately doomed to fail?

I do believe that good ultimately prevails, that darkness gives way to light and that we are victims only if we accept that status. However I also believe that good is only achieved, individually or collectively, by constant vigilance and effort. Again I quote wise words once said, that 'evil prevails when good is silent'. Silence may be a result of ignorance, indifference or lack of courage. It is our perennial duty to pursue, in as much as we can, truth and good. That is in our own interests as much as in the interests of others. It is not always easy and means fighting our inherent tendencies; predispositions of our biology or those inculcated in childhood or in the culture that shaped us. An aspect of being human is the ability to rise above our unconscious habits, or programming. That requires an act of will as well as effort. We learn through interaction with others and that is often easier if we have a solid base, that base is a combination of self awareness, self worth and a sense of belonging. Eleos will talk about the process of moving from our lower to higher self but I am happy to discuss group interaction and the need for a sense of belonging.

What do you mean by belonging?

It is part of human nature to want to belong, that is to be part of something greater than oneself. It provides comfort and a sense of security; the security of knowing one is not alone. The first building block of temporal belonging is the family unit, traditionally made up of a male and female and their offspring. That usually begins with sexual attraction between potential mates and is followed by commitment, cemented by the arrival of children. The family unit provides nurture and security for its members.

Beyond the family unit there is the extended family; uncles, aunts, grandparents and so on. They can add to that sense of belonging. The family has been and still is a very important source of mental security, however, in our society, it has been weakened. That is in part because families are getting smaller, less children are being born as survival rates improve and contraception is practised. It is also in part a result of an increased incidence of relationship breakup, whether marital or otherwise, and the geographical dispersal of family members. So parental bonds are fragmenting and children are growing up with fewer siblings and relations in general. That is a major change compared with just two or three generations ago, when families were much larger and had a strong geographical connection. This has many implications for both society and individuals, impacting that psychological need to belong and how it can be satisfied.

Extended families once looked after the needs of their own members, now less personal organisations are expected to meet those needs. However well organised they are, they struggle to match the care inherent in the bonds of kinship. This, generally unconscious, weakening of some societies' foundations represents a major challenge, a challenge not yet fully appreciated.

Surely a more affluent society can find ways of compensating for this trend?

To some extent yes, particularly for the truly affluent in so-called affluent societies. Unfortunately the trend in such societies is towards greater inequality in both income and wealth, so the affluent terminology usually hides considerable numbers of less well-off citizens. That is particularly true today in some much-heralded democracies like our own, but perhaps that is something we can explore later.

Reflections

Let us take a look at the evolution of communities to try to understand what is happening and why. If family was the first building block then what lay beyond that. The Armstrong clan of old may provide a clue to one form of evolution. It was originally made up of a growing extended family and offered a sense of both belonging and security within a geographical defined boundary. Leadership of the clan may have fallen to a senior respected member of the family. They would be close enough to the group to understand their needs and were normally capable of organising others to meet the requirement for food, shelter and a safe and healthy environment. In most societies men were those leaders. Why so? Perhaps because of relative physical strength and other biologically influenced tendencies such as aggression and risk taking. Those qualities of course have both positive and negative potential. Women had strong influence but their biological role, as regular child bearers and nurturers, predisposed them to being more in touch with their feelings than men and having a more cooperative nature. Again those characteristics have both positive and negative possibilities. Complementary male and female natures were beneficial for both family and social stability.

Common interests bound the group together and leadership did not generally mean a marked difference in lifestyle from those led. As tribes got bigger differentiation in lifestyle did occur and hierarchies developed tending to separate the leaders from the led. Ultimately we see the emergence of so-called kings, and other such titles, that sought to further differentiate leaders. Their kingdoms were often initially secured and maintained by the use of violence and would involve groups of like-minded men, often ruthless in the pursuit of power. Once a kingdom was established, the threat of violence, implicit in locally built castles with resident militia, was sufficient to pacify the local population. So community acquiescence was guaranteed by a military hierarchy whose loyalty was rewarded, or bought, by the king. That often took the form of gifts of the land conquered by force, accompanied by titles based on the land granted. The effective taxation of those working the land generated income for the new lords of the manor, part of which would be returned to the king. This was feudalism and its effect could be seen in the manor of Glossopdale after the Norman Conquest. The nuclear family was still at its heart but now there was a hierarchy of families, with those at the top enjoying considerable wealth as a result of initial violence and subsequent exploitation of the local population. Ruling elite families ensured their direct descendents continued to enjoy the privileges of power, following the hereditary principle. Proximity to the 'royal' family and its head conferred status and privilege. That can still be seen today in the democratic United Kingdom. It is still described as a kingdom and large tracts of land are still owned by royalty and families that have served the interests of the various royal families over the last thousand years. That inheritance has not been blunted by more recent attempts at taxing wealth passed from generation to generation. Inheritance tax is a trap for those of more modest means. The royal family's massive wealth, largely made up of land and property, is further protected by special laws. The House of Lords, the UK's second parliamentary chamber, still contains around 100 hereditary peers as well as hundreds of life peers, with many of the latter created to reward political service or monetary contributions to political parties.

I thought the Magna Carta was a turning point and marked England's transition from royal rule to parliamentary rule.

As I said earlier, power is rarely ceded willingly and even when some power has been relinquished, often for pragmatic reasons, attempts will be made to recoup what has been lost. In 1215 King John was obliged to sign the Great Charter (Magna Carta) effectively sharing power with those land-owning leaders on whom he depended for military support and tax revenues. A rudimentary parliament was born. The king's power remained substantial and that power waxed and waned after the Charter, as one royal dynasty followed another; Plantagenets, Tudors, Stuarts etcetera. The power struggle between king and parliament reached a crisis point during the 17th century, first under the Stuart king Charles I. He believed in the *divine right of kings* and clashed with parliament over money, religion and foreign policy. That resulted in him dispensing with parliament between 1629 to 1640. It was brought back following an uprising in Scotland but Charles's attempt to assert authority over parliament eventually resulted in a series of civil wars and ultimately in his execution. Those wars between Parliamentarians and Royalists were the first in the UK to utilise printed material as propaganda. The republic that resulted, under grammar school boy Oliver Cromwell, pursued religiously puritanical policies that ultimately proved unpopular with the general population. Following Cromwell's death the army forced his son to abdicate as Lord Protector and invited Charles's son to return as King Charles II. Note that nepotism was not restricted to the aristocracy, the nuclear family dynasty dynamic was, and is, hard to resist when power is acquired. Parliament once again had to assert its authority over the monarchy in 1688 when it replaced a non-compliant Catholic king with an imported Protestant king. The non-violent so-called 'glorious revolution' resulted in a Bill of Rights that defined the limits of authority of the monarch and clarified the authority of parliament.

It is important to bear in mind that parliament represented the landowning wealthy and the established church, the Church of

England, not the general population. It was not until the Reform Act of 1832 that a wider franchise was involved in electing members of parliament. Even then only about seven per cent of the adult population were able to vote. Various reform acts in the 19th and 20th centuries gradually widened the suffrage but it took the aftermath of the first world war to win the concession of votes for all adult males and women over the age of 30. That pragmatic decision was no doubt influenced by the return home of large numbers of disillusioned men, who had witnessed senseless slaughter in the trenches, and, of course, news from Russia of the Bolshevik revolution in 1917. Women had to wait a further ten years before the suffragette goal, of votes at age 21, was secured. So you will see that the path to a parliamentary democracy has been a long and winding road. Those with power are usually reluctant to relinquish it and pragmatism is invariably required if the transition is to be peaceful.

Did you say that the church was part of the power dynamic in mediaeval times?

It not only was, but still is. Bishops of the Church of England still sit in the unelected House of Lords, the UK's second legislative chamber. You may ask how a church founded on principles espoused by Jesus ended up as part of the ruling elite. That accommodation with the rulers of kingdoms or republics is almost as old as the church. Christianity's mission of conversion received its biggest boost when the religion was adopted by the Roman empire, as its official religion, early in the fourth century. Part of that adoption involved the church accepting and advocating that the emperor's authority was derived from God. The Christian church has long been associated with force as a means of furthering its cause. The patron saint of Norway, Saint Olaf, partook in violent Viking raids on England in his youth and while there was introduced to Christianity. On his return to Norway he vowed to convert his new kingdom to that religion. The sword played as much part in that conversion as did the bible, but that did not hinder his ultimate designation as a saint. The Church has led many violent campaigns over the centuries, such as those against Islam in the Crusades or in the suppression of heretical interpretations of Christianity, such as that practised by the Cathars in Southern Europe in the 13th century. That group's eradication effectively eliminated a residual Christian belief in reincarnation.

The Holy Roman Empire, which prevailed for a millennium in Europe until the 19th century, was successor, as far as the Catholic Church was concerned, to the Roman empire of old. Its might was used to enforce church power and doctrine, doctrine decided long after the death of Jesus and often bearing little relationship to his teaching. That empire involved the Pope, as head of the church, wielding his power in conjunction with the Emperor. It is still today called the Roman Catholic Church, even if it is no longer involved in the exercise of religiously motivated military power, and Its headquarters are in Vatican City, an independent state housed in the centre of Rome.

Looking now at the English Church, it and that country's ruling elite had a long history of cooperation but the relationship underwent change after the Norman Conquest in 1066. William had secured the Pope's blessing, in advance of his invasion, by promising to reform the irregularities of the Anglo Saxon Church. He consequently imposed a reorganisation on the Church and replaced Saxon bishops with Norman. The Church benefited greatly from its proximity to, and support of, the conquering elite as its array of magnificent cathedrals attest. The gifting of the Manor of Glossopdale, by Henry II to the Abbey of Basingwerk in the 13th century, is another example. This granting of land, to supporting secular and religious elites, not only secured military power, if needed, to protect the king's temporal realm but also, it was hoped, secured his spiritual redemption in the heavenly realm to come. I am not sure what Jesus would have made of this religious transaction. Jesus, a Jew, was a noted critic of the Jewish religious hierarchy in his day, which is why that hierarchy sought and obtained the cooperation of the ruling Roman administration in his silencing.

Land that is given by a king can also be taken away. When the Pope failed to cooperate in the annulment of Tudor King Henry VIII's first marriage to Catherine of Aragon, so that he could marry Anne Boleyn, Henry broke with the Roman Catholic Church. That resulted in the founding of the Church of England with the king at its head and this required bishops and priests to switch allegiance from pope to king. Faced with the new power dynamic religious pragmatism prevailed. Henry's dissolution of the monasteries served two purposes; it effectively suppressed any religious dissent and it enhanced his own wealth. The monasteries' control over a quarter of cultivated land in the kingdom was lost. Glossopdale ownership passed from spiritual insurance to temporal when title transferred from Basingwerk Abbey to the Earl of Shrewsbury. Subsequent intermarriage amongst the aristocratic elite, a well established family wealth preservation practice, resulted in ownership passing to the Howard family, Dukes of Norfolk and, ironically, of the Catholic faith.

To return to your point, the 'established' Church of England has long been part of the state structure, or establishment, that network of interests that holds and controls effective power. That is not to deny much good work that the Church of England, and indeed the Catholic Church, has undertaken over the centuries. Nor am I dismissing the core message of most religions, including Christianity. I simply wanted to put in perspective the church's relationship over time with temporal power. Ultimately its allegiance was to Christ but that was sometimes compromised by participation in a fundamentally unequal, strictly hierarchical and often violent society. It demonstrates the weakness of humanity, and in particular men, intent on doctrine and temporal power, at the expense of spiritual principle.

Over the centuries the term Christianity has covered many groups that recognised Jesus as their inspiration and origin. They have not always agreed on what their faith entailed. The Roman Catholic version became dominant after its alliance with the Roman empire and regularly sought to extinguish alternative interpretations, sometimes using violence. Protestantism arose in the sixteenth century in protest against the perceived corruption and dogma of the Roman church. That movement ultimately fragmented and resulted in many new groups being formed, such as the Methodists and Baptists seen in the Smith and Armstrong families. Those groups often disavowed the pomp, corruption and hierarchy involved in traditional Christianity and were able to give greater succour to the disadvantaged in society by their return to the teachings of Jesus, as recorded in the bible. Religion played a significant part in most people's lives until relatively recently. The secularisation of society in the West, and shunning of overt spirituality, is another trend with major implications for both the individual and communities. An age of materialism, perhaps the ultimate by-product of the *age of reason*, is now upon us. Materialism may have been historically a distraction for the rich, with their high levels of income and wealth, now it is a distraction for many.

Surely material well-being is a good thing and is to be welcomed not criticised?

As we discussed earlier, in relatively recent times, in this country, the average person has benefited from a marked improvement in their standard of living. That, as you say, is a good thing, the majority should not be living hand to mouth. Being human involves a hierarchy of needs. Keeping the biological body alive, well and safe is a basic requirement. Beyond that lie other needs for a fulfilled life, the sense of belonging that we have discussed is another. Belonging involves giving as well as receiving, that means making a contribution to the wellbeing of others. That giving may involve more prosaic contributions in terms of one's labour or more imaginative and creative efforts. All are valuable and have a place in creating a sense of self-worth. Eleos will talk about that and the realm of spirit which lies beyond. The point I am making about materialism is simply one about individuals getting stuck in the migration of their hierarchy. When they become, consciously or unconsciously, in denial of their higher needs and pursue material goals in the hope that it will satisfy all of their needs. The role of religion, throughout the ages, has been to remind us that we are more than biological animals; that we are faced with choices, and consequent decisions, that can help us move towards a greater good. Union with that good, or God or Allah or Brahman or Tao, is possible but usually involves making a conscious choice.

The rational dynamic in humanity is a great strength. It has given rise to a greater understanding of the world we live in. That has resulted in incredible technological advances which have helped enormously in meeting the biological needs of a majority of the world's population. Its side-effect has been to increasingly deny another aspect of the human condition, that which is not rational. Many of the proponents of scientific methodology cannot cope with intuition, or belief systems that are outside the rational rules that have seemingly transformed the world we live in. In so doing they, perhaps unconsciously, create a materialistic dogma, now prevalent in our culture, that undermines the human imperative to migrate its hierarchy of needs.

Jesus said 'it is easier for a camel to pass through the eye of a needle, than for a rich man to enter the kingdom of God'. That is unlikely to have been a lesson delivered by the religious establishment to their emperor or king sponsors. Similar sentiments also appear in other religions' teachings. I do not believe that it is a condemnation of the rich per se, so much as directed at the motivation that often accompanies the pursuit of wealth at the expense of others, and the conceit that justifies wealth accumulated whether ostentatiously displayed or not. Greed, in its many forms, is ultimately self consuming.

To your point, material well-being is essential for our survival as human beings. Not having to worry about our next meal, or obtaining shelter from the elements, is a highly desirable state, one which the leaders of communities should seek to secure for all their members. With authority should come a sense of responsibility. The greatest leaders are those who bring out the best in those they lead and who believe that their leadership is in fact a form of service, rather than an opportunity to enrich or aggrandise themselves. The more hierarchical the society, the more detached leadership is from the majority, and the greater the danger of inequality and indifference to the plight of the many. The tendency of those who have a disproportionate share of wealth and income is to succumb to self-justification. Like royalty of old, they begin to believe in the myth of their special, possibly divinely ordained, status. They persuade themselves that they deserve, or have earned, their life of privilege, rather than acknowledge that their good fortune may be at the direct or indirect expense of others.

We have only partially touched on an important power block that today exercises enormous influence and which is not really subject to effective democratic control.

What is that?

Economic power is perhaps the greatest form of power, outside mankind's periodic descent into violence. Those that possess it exercise influence in many ways, overt and covert, in order to secure their interests. Those interests may sometimes coincide with the needs of the general population but the corrupting, and self-serving, effect of power is hard to avoid. As Mahatma Gandhi once observed 'the earth can provide for everyone's need, but not their greed'.

We have talked about wealth and income derived from ownership of land, often originally acquired by force. Land can be put to productive use to generate income, as did the Cistercian monks in Glossopdale through the rearing of sheep and the trade in wool. They may have been instrumental in encouraging local peasants to do that, and their monastery derived an income from the peasants' managed work. Primitive societies were largely agricultural, concerned with meeting the food, clothing and shelter needs of local communities. As the workforce involved in food production was able to meet more than its own immediate consumption needs, it allowed for specialisation of roles within the community, giving rise to weavers, cobblers, coopers, potters, blacksmiths and so on. This division of labour and honing of skills helped increase productivity further, but required a means of exchanging goods and a medium of exchange. Local markets were established and bartering eventually gave way to the use of money. A rudimentary form of economy was born, a template for the much more sophisticated economy of today.

We saw in Glossopdale the birth of weaving, using wool initially and then evolving to use cotton. The area gradually moved from an agrarian to an industrialised economy as a result of; ingenuity in the development of machines, the exploitation of sources of energy, capital investment, organising skill and the labour of many. The huge wealth that that eventually created led to the displacement of the local aristocracy's hereditary monopoly on power. The 'cottonocracy' resulting did not eradicate the aristocracy, it simply created a new form of economic power, alongside that obtained from ownership of land. The new power was derived from large-scale manufacturing. It involved the exploitation of the local population in 'satanic' mills but also the more remote exploitation of Africans, forced into slavery, and required to pick the raw cotton. Both sets of workers effectively became the servants of a new elite, the mill owners. One group was 'owned' by the plantation landowners, the other economically dependent on their factory masters. Mill owners' pursuit of economic power involved competition with other manufacturers. Faced with difficulties, they often resorted to reducing the wages of their employees. Not all were oblivious to the plight of their workers. Robert Owen showed a more compassionate approach in New Lanark. Also the, often sincere, attachment to Christian beliefs by others sometimes tempered the harsh working conditions. Just as the aristocracy's alliance with the established Church facilitated impressive cathedrals and churches, so the proximity of mill owners to their employees' community, resulted in the provision of substantial town buildings, parks and services for local inhabitants. Despite this periodic largesse, labour was a major cost of production and inevitably became the focal point for scrutiny, when that was needed to meet competitive threats, or to secure the required return for the providers of capital.

Trade unions, when eventually legalised, helped provide a counter for the power of capital and the managers of capital. As did the birth in the twentieth century of political parties whose mission was the representation of working people. That resulted in a more equitable distribution of the added value created by manufacturing, between providers of labour and providers of capital. Thus the progress you have observed in the well being of many citizens during the middle part of the twentieth century. However, the forces that brought that about weakened towards the end of the century and we now see growing inequality in income, and wealth distribution, once again.

If that is true, how can it be so, given a wide franchise and unchanged political system?

The statistical information to support my point is in the public domain and I will leave you to research it, if you are so inclined. I agree that it seems counter-intuitive, but it is another example of power, this time economic power, ceded and then recovered.

There have been many factors at play and I will touch on some of the more important. Manufacturers' search for cheaper labour, in the latter part of the twentieth century, extended abroad. In Europe the eastern part of the continent was one such source, in the USA Mexico was convenient. The export of manufacturing jobs, often unionised and consequently reasonably well paid, to developing economies was then extended to the Far East where wages were even lower. That process helped to lift living standards there, but drove down the price that labour could obtain at home. A parallel process seriously weakened the negotiating power of trade unions. The UK government in the 1980s deliberately set out to do that. They believed unions were too powerful and their campaign to weaken that power focused on breaking one of the more militant unions, that representing coal miners. Another high profile employer target, given strong government support, were the print unions then influential in the newspaper publishing centre in Fleet Street, London. The campaign was carefully planned and the privately owned, predominantly establishment supporting, media played its part in promoting the narrative necessary to win wider public support. They succeeded both in demonising union power, in the eyes of many, and in reducing its influence in the economy.

Pro-union, anti-government arguments were often effectively censored. Ken Loach, a noted pro-working class film maker of the time, produced a four part documentary series for ATV *A Question of Leadership*. This was not shown because it breached impartiality rules by attacking government policy. No such rules applied to the privately owned press's anti-union narrative.

A by-product of this assault on unions and traditional industries was the destruction of many mining and manufacturing based working class communities, particularly in the north, like that in Forth, Lanarkshire. Another factor furthered the falling income trend. As well paid manufacturing jobs shrank in number, new service jobs grew to replace them. Most of those jobs were not unionised and relatively poorly paid. If the local population were unhappy with that remuneration then immigrants from eastern Europe, or in the US from Mexico, were happy to fill the vacancies. For the immigrant it was a step onto the ladder of potential betterment. That process was furthered with the birth of the tech driven, so called, gig economy. Hard won employment rights began to be watered down, in the interests of 'a competitive economy'. Workers were now recruited as self employed, this presented as giving them flexibility but in reality depriving them of employment rights that had been hard won. As we saw with DSSmith the attack on employee benefits was not restricted to the service sector, or the gig economy. Final salary pension schemes began to disappear in the private sector, becoming 'unaffordable', this despite years of employer pension contribution holidays. It was another way in which the share of added value going to labour was reduced. Meanwhile the share of the cake going to capital, or those at the top of the employment tree, grew, sometimes dramatically.

I will not go on, you asked how it could possibly happen and I hope I have given you an insight into part of the process. The process is not the result of a co-ordinated grand plan, it is the result of point of view gradually taking hold and then becoming prevalent.

The argument, or narrative, is constructed, usually by an ideologically inclined group (or think tank), then promoted, sometimes by those with a vested interest, sometimes by those persuaded that it is for the greater good. When it reaches a certain level of acceptance then the mentality of crowds takes over, which has a lot in common with mob mentality. It involves the demonisation of alternative points of view and then the ideology becomes the accepted wisdom of the day. 'There is no alternative' (or TINA) was one catchphrase of the time that captured the prevailing economic mentality, as was 'the trickle down effect'. The latter theory was that allowing the rich to get ever richer would automatically enrich all those in society, as the wealthy spent their growing income. No such effect was seen in practice.

The remuneration of the average person has now been in decline for many years, and the pension they will receive in retirement, likewise. That is true in the USA and UK, but not necessarily in all countries. We are beginning to see in the Anglo-sphere a generation emerge who are worse off materially than their parents.

I don't see the evidence for this, people would be in revolt.

Let me again give you a few examples, but I encourage you to do your own research. The use of food banks in the UK is growing dramatically, not just by the unemployed but by those in employment and poorly paid. To make ends meet many people today work longer hours than their parents expected to work, and that is particularly true in the so-called gig economy. Whereas a generation ago, one income in a family could sustain a reasonable lifestyle, now two incomes are required. Of course expectations of what a reasonable lifestyle entails has changed. The dream of less work and more leisure is in retreat, as is the idea that each generation will be better off than their predecessor.

Young people in general are now less able to buy a house than their parents were. That is partly to do with inflated house prices and partly with an unnecessarily prolonged period in formal education that doesn't result in a better paid job but does result in significant student debt. On top of that the young face working well into their seventies because of inadequate pension schemes, schemes that place financial risk on their shoulders, rather than on those of their employer. Pricing models have been developed and widely adopted that now exploit loyalty rather than reward it. Unless you are prepared to regularly switch suppliers you will end up paying a heavy premium for many services. This is the increasingly used methodology of a capitalism less concerned with giving value, than in extracting value for its own benefit.

That is a snapshot of the brave new world now being created by an economic elite who are getting an ever greater share of income generated and the collective wealth that has been accumulated. They are also able, through a cohort of well paid accountants and lawyers, to escape their fair share of taxation. Whereas taxation policy in the mid twentieth century was progressive, that is it proportionately increased as income increased and impacted inherited wealth, now that no longer applies.

By contrast the poor and those on moderate incomes cannot escape the tax burden levied on them. They also find the services they depend on becoming more expensive, as a result of utilities and other natural monopolies being privatised, or public services, such as the NHS, deteriorating as they are starved of funding and then are quietly privatised, as dentistry already has been. That is a juicy prospect for the wealth extraction industry. Council houses, a safety net for the poorest, unable to buy housing, were deliberately sold off, so the poor now depend on renting from private landlords. A class is emerging that has been named 'the precariat' because they face a life of insecurity in terms of their employment, housing and social support.

The revolt you speak off will come. Things will become clearer to the majority as their standard of living continues to fall. As I have said there is much more to life than pursuit of purely material goals, however, expectations are to a considerable extent determined by what people are used to having, the corollary of 'what you have never had, you don't miss'. The political leadership that should represent the interests of the majority, the working class of old, has been distracted by the interests of vociferous lobby groups, other superficially virtuous causes, and in conforming with prevalent neo-liberal economic doctrine. They go to great lengths to avoid arousing the opposition of powerful establishment groups but will eventually wake up to the growing material distress of the many. Let us hope that is before pitchforks replace protest votes.

What should we learn from the demise of Spicers after 200 years in business?

It provides an example of how the UK economy has been manipulated, over the last 40 years or so, to serve the interests of a minority at the expense of the majority. *The Spicers Story* part of this book explained how latterly 'private equity' preyed upon the office product distribution industry, wreaking havoc, while extracting considerable wealth for itself. That wealth extraction was achieved by the manipulation of finance. Let us step back for a moment and look at the bigger picture.

The idea of a market, where supply and demand meet, started in the UK in those mediaeval town square marketplaces. This type of market economy became much more sophisticated over time, but proved its worth in satisfying the material needs of most people. That was clearly demonstrated when compared with 'command' or 'centrally planned' economic alternatives. These not only failed to bring out the best in people, but lacked the flexibility needed to maximise productivity and consumer choice. Adam Smith, the 18th century Scottish economist, famously talked about the 'hidden hand' mechanism, whereby beneficial social and economic outcomes can result from the self-interested actions of many individuals.

The manufacturing economy, that replaced its agrarian equivalent, required capital investment for factories, machines, the harnessing of sources of power and creation of a transport infrastructure. That investment usually came from those with existing capital to utilise. They received a return on their investment, in the form of dividend or interest payments, in exchange for foregoing other possible uses of their capital. Alternatively, as owners, they saw a growth in the value of their investment if the business created was successful. That is the basis of traditional capitalism, where demand for and supply of capital meet to create something more than the capital sum invested. It entails wealth creation, usually in pursuit of satisfying a perceived customer need and results in the creation also of employment. It was the basis of the Industrial Revolution. It is an imperfect system that can be inequitable in how it rewards the providers of capital and labour. It has inherent dangers, as in all walks of life, in the potential for power to be abused, for example if monopoly distorts the free market mechanism. Those dangers, and the need for forms of regulation, were appreciated by Adam Smith and his economist successors. They recognised that aspects of human nature, such as greed and the pursuit of power, need to be guarded against, and that some 'hidden hands' will have no qualms about tipping the market scales in their own favour.

Another form of what is sometimes described as capitalism involves no wealth creation, it entails seeking to increase one's own share of existing wealth without creating new wealth. In the jargon of economics that is called not capitalism but 'rent seeking'. It has been a growing feature of the financialised economic model that has come to the fore in the deregulated post-Thatcher era.

Financial institutions that once oiled the wheels of industry now got better returns from investing in financial assets, real estate and debt creation. Deregulation inevitably led to a growth in the manipulation of markets. That might occasionally result in fines for the perpetrators' employers but rarely were individuals held to account. Little wonder that corporate fines were increasingly seen as just a cost of doing business. The new freer 'capitalism' was further endorsed after the 2008 financial crash. 'Too big to fail' was the mantra that ensured that, in the main, the gamblers in the financial institutions who had bet and lost, walked away with their wealth intact. It was the taxpayers who picked up the bill, and the population at large that faced years of austerity. Not surprisingly the lesson learned, by the manipulators of finance, was that the government had their backs and that they could carry on much as before.

Governments, once intent on prudence and, in the medium term, balancing income with expenditure, now found that they could defy the laws of financial gravity. Government debt levels exploded and were financed by 'money printing', or in the age of computers its digital equivalent. Government debt was effectively 'bought' by the government's own bank, the Bank of England. This piece of economic chicanery was a worldwide phenomenon, designed to provide liquidity to banking systems. The resulting 'created' money never found its way into people's pockets, nor was it to be found in productive investment to create wealth and help the real economy grow. It manifested in ever greater asset prices, benefiting the already wealthy who sat on those assets.

Government debt eventually became so large that no increase in interest rates could be contemplated, as that would result in effective government bankruptcy, or perhaps more accurately, in the need for ever greater austerity. Markets and interest rates were no longer tied to supply and demand, the definition of a market in traditional economics, they now had to be manipulated to try and maintain a semblance of order in a corrupted economic system.

Tiny interest rates prevailed for many years, driving up the mortgage affordability of housing and resulted in a house price boom that could not survive any return to normal interest rates. When interest rates are below the rate of inflation they are effectively negative and that entails a transfer of wealth from savers to borrowers. In other words, a regime that disincentivizes saving and encourages debt imprudence. Those that depend on interest income, and can no longer secure it, such as pension funds, are drawn into ever riskier investments. They fall prey to the loquacious money manipulators who create or sell sophisticated derivative schemes, apparently risk free but almost all of which will eventually leave gullible investors impoverished. Unlike, of course, the scheme creators whose gains are frequently transferred to offshore tax havens.

These 'treasure islands' for the holders of considerable wealth, whether legally obtained or criminally, continue to be tolerated by democratic governments of all colours. Consequently their usage continues to grow along with sometimes complex cloaks of anonymity, facilitated by a well paid subset of the legal profession. Their prolific use of that obscure legal instrument the 'trust' is used to hide ownership and avoid tax. That can operate at both corporate and individual levels. The trust mechanism is the means by which enormous inherited wealth is passed on, tax free, by affluent families.

Inheritance tax is a burden for those of more modest means. Occasionally the truth is revealed by troves of digital information 'dumped' by whistleblowers. The *Panama Papers* revelation was a recent example and showed that the British Virgin Islands, a British Overseas Territory, was one of the most frequently used wealth shelters. The continuance of this morally indefensible practice is often justified by governments with that age-old cop-out; 'if we don't allow it, someone else will'.

What has emerged is a deformed type of financialised capitalism resulting in malinvestment, low productivity and consequent low growth in gross national product. When combined with an increased population, as a result of relatively uncontrolled and generally low-waged immigration, the result is a continuing decline in average income per head of population. That is the story of the recent UK economy, one in which the government is complicit and shows little inclination to call out or reform.

The inflation monster is now surfacing, in part driven by a growing energy crisis, and the after effects of a covid 19 response that involved even greater debt generation. The days of the money printing merry-go-round are coming to an end. Protecting the rich and those 'too big to fail' will no longer be an acceptable option when the inevitable crash comes. A major reset will be necessary and it will be painful for all, not just the rich. We have effectively been living beyond our collective means for some time, enabled by a rigged system that has favoured an economic elite.

Whereas the mill owners of the past, or the Spicer family venture, created wealth that ultimately benefited many, the wealth extractors, in the guise of private equity and the FIRE (finance, insurance and real estate) sector have been largely parasitic. The nation's wealth has not been growing, as promised under the deregulated economic regime, all that has happened is that wealth and income have effectively been transferred from the many to the few. The parasite has been so intent on extracting wealth that it is oblivious to the fact that it is slowly killing the host on which it depends. Spicers' fate is a small example of how the economic vultures came to, temporarily, rule the roost. The abuse of power by an economic elite in the UK was enabled by a political system, nominally democratic, that could be manipulated by them. In that respect it mirrored the USA.

Surely the USA's economic strength has been the result of a commitment to the principles of free market capitalism and democracy?

Few would argue with some of the principles espoused by the founding fathers of the United States, in their rebellion against

British rule. They sought to separate themselves from what they saw to be a flawed hierarchical, essentially autocratic, system of control. They were inspired by principles that promoted the freedom of the individual, encouraged personal responsibility and sought limited government. The *Declaration of Independence* stated that 'all men are created equal' and should be free to pursue their own interpretation of happiness. That rhetoric did not always match the reality, when it came to native Americans or black slaves, but some of the aspirations of the leaders of the white immigrant colonists were noble. The new nation developed strongly in the nineteenth century, often using protectionist measures against other nations to nurture their own embryonic economy. In that century the USA also laid the foundations of a nascent empire.

The Monroe doctrine of 1823 set out foreign policy guidelines that warned-off the then European powers from interference in North and South American affairs. It also created a quasi-imperialist view of the Americas that subsequently manifested in frequent US interference in the affairs of Latin and South American countries. Equality within those countries was less important than US economic interests. The treatment of Cuba is one example, there are many others over a prolonged period should you care to look.

Cuba has been subjected to US sanctions, a form of economic warfare, ever since its popular revolution in 1959. American attempts to overthrow the new government failed and a subsequent naval blockade to prevent installation of Russian missiles brought the world to the brink of nuclear war between the USSR and USA. The US retains its naval base in Cuba on a claimed perpetual lease, despite regular Cuban objections. A parallel could be drawn with Russia's retention of its Crimean naval base, following Ukraine's attempt to join NATO, although that was achieved by local plebiscite and involved the whole Crimean peninsula. Guantanamo Bay in Cuba, not being on US soil, has proved invaluable in the country's 'war on terror' as a location for the interrogation, and sometimes torture, of extradited suspects. That is perhaps preferable to an alternative US technique, developed to deal with terrorist suspects, extrajudicial death sentences carried out by remotely controlled drone strikes.

Other than the Americas, and the effective occupation of the Philippines in the first half of the twentieth century, the US contained its imperial ambitions and preferred the mantle of continental isolationism. Japan's attack on Pearl Harbour ended that isolation mentality and finally engaged the new economic giant in wars then being fought in Asia and Europe. With the end of the second world war, and much of the world in ruins, US foreign policy ambition expanded. The Marshall Plan helped rebuild a shattered European economy and also created an opportunity for the expansion of US businesses. The birth of NATO did likewise for the US armaments industry. It was a retiring US president who warned of the growing, and potentially corrupting, influence in the US of the 'military-industrial complex'. Dwight Eisenhower had been Supreme Commander of the Allied Expeditionary Force in Europe, during the latter stages of the second world war, and was US president from 1953 and 1961. His retirement speech pointed to the possibly malign political influence of an enormous industry dependent on military spending in the US and by its allies around the world. An industry less concerned with the pursuit of peace than with promulgating perpetual conflict.

US spending on defence dwarfs that of all other countries, it is greater than the aggregate of next nine highest spenders. The companies who benefit from that spending wield considerable influence over the US political process through foreign policy think tanks, lobbying and direct campaign contributions, as do other large corporations representing industries such as pharmaceuticals/health, the tech giants, and the finance and real estate business sector. The main political parties and their leaderships are often more concerned with securing political, and sometimes personal, income streams, than in pursuing the wishes of the electorate. There is little doubt that the majority of Americans would prefer to see freely available health care rather than constant growth in military spending, justified by endless conflicts in far off countries. Their voices are ignored by the political elites. So-called defence spending accounts for over 10% of all US government expenditure and exceeds three quarters of a trillion dollars per annum.

The US government's annual spending deficit, that is the excess of spending over income, is currently approaching $3 trillion. That deficit is financed by the issuance of US debt, or treasuries, some held by US institutions, some by foreign owned bodies. The US government is able to borrow trillions of dollars from world capital markets at minimal interest rates. That is as a result of the dollar being the foremost (reserve) currency for trade between nations, a decision made at the end of world war two, effectively replacing the pound sterling's role. The dollar then was backed, or interchangeable with, gold underpinning its international credibility. That important link with gold was severed in 1971. In a sense, foreign nations now finance US deficits, enabling the US to live beyond its means. This is part of the empire's economic power, wielded alongside its military power. The World Bank and the International Monetary Fund are vehicles for promoting, across the world, an economic model less concerned with local social cohesion than with directing a 'free market' dogma that ultimately serves the interests of the US empire.

Effective control of the world's monetary system allows the US to conduct economic warfare against adversaries as an adjunct, or alternative, to military intervention. The increasing use of this weapon will eventually lead to alternative monetary systems being developed, in particular by those vulnerable to sanctions, such as the powerful Sino-Russian axis. Those two countries have been steadily building their gold reserves. A gold-backed alternative to the US dollar could be increasingly attractive to other nations concerned about their dollar holdings depreciating in value, as the supply increases, or the US's weaponizing of currency control systems. Such a move would have major implications for the US economy and its management. All monetary systems, national or international, ultimately depend on the confidence of users. Confidence once lost is hard to regain. History is punctuated by the rise and fall of empires. Power brings with it the temptation of corruption and that can take many forms. A debased currency is one frequent manifestation. As abuse grows so the seeds of the empire's decline take root.

You seem to be overly critical of what you call the American empire. Compared with alternative systems it surely has much to recommend it.

You are right, my focus has been on pointing out some of the under-reported downsides of the recent past, and on providing a longer term perspective. There have been notable upsides to American influence, including growing prosperity for some and greater freedom. Perspective requires that we see the bigger picture. It also requires that we question the information we are fed by the culture we inhabit. We live in a world subject to constant change. Nothing remains the same, other than the tendencies inherent in the human condition, positive and negative.

I am not promoting a Sino-Russian alternative empire to the

Anglo-American empires of the nineteenth and twentieth centuries. Nor am I being critical of the American people who, like any other people, spend most of their lives concerned with family, friends, work and community. I could point out the excesses in the pursuit of power by the Russian and Chinese governments, but I suspect you are well versed in those given their constant denunciation in the West. The subjugation of Tibet, the denial of sovereignty for Taiwan and the interference in the governance of Asian states adjacent to Russia are examples of empire mentality. All empires are essentially about gaining or growing power and then maintaining it. That is true of democratic systems as much as authoritarian ones. They are controlled by elites, who may at times be popular, but ultimately become preoccupied with their status and retaining power. Unless we are able to reflect on the past honestly we cannot learn, we cannot progress. Reflection requires information. First we must accept that the information readily available to us is not necessarily objective or true.

In the UK we have a free press and a greatly respected institution in the BBC. Are you claiming they are not objective? The American constitution's first amendment guarantees a free press and freedom of speech.

When we think our version of reality is 'true' the corollary is that other versions, different to ours, are probably 'untrue'. Therein lies the essence of conflict. 'We are right, you are wrong'. It explains the history of religious, political and social strife.

Understanding another's point of view, and why they have that point of view, is the road to peaceful resolution of potential conflicts. First it requires a willingness to listen and then a degree of humility. The humility involved in relinquishing the need to be right and in stepping aside from both ego and emotion.

To answer your question more directly, no, the so-called free press and BBC in the UK are not objective arbiters of truth. In assessing what might be true, always consider the possible motivation of the purveyor of information. Editors decide what stories will feature in the news and often the slant that will be put on those stories. Media in the main is privately owned and will ultimately reflect the preferences or interests of that ownership. If the owner is unhappy, the editor will be replaced.

The British Broadcasting Corporation is state funded, even if it is nominally independent. Its income stream, the licence fee, is constantly threatened by governments unhappy with its, in their view, bias. That is how the BBC is controlled, along with political appointments to its Board. The organisation is also highly sensitive to certain pressure groups. That may be as a result of a belief, by those running the BBC, that the group's view is 'right', or simply a preference not to alienate a vociferous lobby. A consequence of these value judgements is that the BBC will not fairly represent the views of others, who take a different view of what is true. I could give you many examples of this often unconscious bias; pandemic response, climate change, diversity and gender identity are some recent examples.

Management of information was a crucial part of the Covid 19 response in both democracies and dictatorships. The BBC played an important part in delivering the government's preferred narrative in the UK. That involved promotion of restrictions in freedom and of doubtful advice on contagion prevention, such as the wearing of face masks. It also involved the suppression of minority view scientifically based alternative Covid responses. The restrictive regime only began to fall apart when it became known that the highest levels of government were disregarding the advice they were so assiduously disseminating. That did not end the suppression of information deemed unhelpful to the prevailing narrative, such as growing evidence of heart damage caused by mRNA vaccines that had been hurriedly rolled out.

The approach taken by the BBC is sometimes based on a belief that it has an obligation to 'educate' the population on important issues. That is a kind of arrogance shared by some of the leaders of other institutions and may be partly the result of a common educational process. A limited number of schools and universities feed the upper echelons of society, both in the UK and the US. That can result in a kind of groupthink about the nature of what is true or virtuous and in a misplaced confidence in the intellectual superiority of an educationally enlightened elite.

In the new millennium the BBC, along with other establishment organisations, became committed to 'diversity'. This resulted in a ramping up of minority racial and ethnic group representation in visible posts, as well as replacing men with women in posts historically associated with men. That, no doubt, all helped correct a previous imbalance but became a signal of virtue as far as the ruling establishment was concerned. However, the social and educational background of the new 'diverse' intake often mirrored that of the existing hierarchy. The under-representation of those from a different background, the working class of old, was not deemed worthy of focus in this re-balancing, in fact this group were the ones often seen to be in need of 'education'. It was not only factual content that became distorted by the BBC leadership's worldview. Drama too fell victim to political correctness and quality became less important than ticking the boxes that signalled conspicuous virtue.

The US media is likewise controlled by economic and political interests. It is not objective. Russia Today, a state financed alternative to western privately owned media and our own state financed BBC, was immediately closed down in the West when Russia invaded Ukraine. Russia's point of view was propaganda, whereas the uniform Ukrainian perspective was 'truth'. Honest investigative journalism still exists in the West but you will find it increasingly difficult to find. *Consortium News, The Grayzone* and *Mint Press* are US internet based consolidation sites for dissenting views, *Brave New Europe* is a European equivalent, and *Spiked* and *The Daily Sceptic* are UK versions. Numerous attempts have been made to hamper dissenters' reach. Consortium News and The Daily Sceptic both were subject to donation bans via Paypal. Social media platforms, US controlled in the main, are today for many people the main source of information. Such platforms regularly censor information deemed to be 'hate-speech' or 'disinformation'. So you see there is little doubt that free speech is under constant attack, even in the land of the free.

The silence of the mainstream media on the fate of Julian Assange tells you all that you need to know about how controlled much of journalism is in our era. Assange was guilty of no more than publishing what whistleblowers had revealed to him about the war crimes of the US empire. His prosecution and persecution by the US, aided and abetted by a compliant UK political and judicial system, is proof, if it were needed, of the inadequacy of the mainstream media's commitment to freedom of speech and pursuit of truth.

Many, if not most, journalists, in the West as well as the East, are less concerned with speaking 'truth to power' than in serving the interests of that power. That may be a conscious or unconscious process. The problem for most people is in having the time to search out alternative narratives to those that they are being fed. For the majority their information diet is understandably restricted to that which supports those in power, and tends to fuel the 'we are right, you are wrong' mindset. In doing so it fails to respect alternative points of view and sows the seeds of potential conflict.

Wars and aggression do occur occasionally but how does normal life manifest a conflict mentality?

Institutions have been established, mainly by men, that avoid violence but encourage forms of confrontation resulting in victory or defeat. I am not just talking about sporting activity or games which provide an outlet for that inherent competitive, or aggressive, instinct. Let me give you some examples.

A legal system presenting two points of view about the nature of truth and then asking a jury of laypersons to decide the 'winner' is an example of the mindset. This adversarial approach is a form of civilised aggression. The winner is often the one who can destroy the credibility of witnesses or successfully sow seeds of doubt in the jury's mind. That is a process not so much about establishing the truth as about winning an argument. The more money you have, the better the advocate you can afford, and the better your chances of winning in a court of law. The considerable failure of the legal system to deal fairly with victims of sexual assault, in the main women assaulted by men, and to deal justly with perpetrators, is an indication of how the adversarial approach to establishing truth, and ensuring justice, is failing. There are many other examples of how the legal profession has impacted the criminal justice system in a way that undermines the process of law enforcement and its cost effectiveness.

Any talk of reforming the system, or the legal profession, is firmly resisted by that powerful establishment tribe, as Margaret Thatcher, herself a lawyer, found when she was in reforming zeal mode and sought to break the barrister/solicitor role demarcation the profession insisted upon. The restrictive working practices that were reprehensible when upheld by trade unions were ultimately acceptable when practised by a profession making up part of the establishment elite. Lawyers tend to see themselves as guardians of freedom and the constitution, rarely do they reflect upon the adverse impact of their tribe's practices. In fact, that same Conservative administration saw the beginning of the legal profession's descent into commerciality. Advertising for business came first in 1986 and then in 1999 'no win, no fee' arrived. These changes fuelled today's 'ambulance chasing' mentality in civil matters, greatly adding to the costs of many organisations, like the NHS. This has contributed to the risk-averse culture that is now endemic. The country's inability to control its borders, against illegal immigrants claiming 'asylum', is to some extent facilitated by lawyers funded by the state. Exploitation of legal loopholes, as well as protracted legal processes, provide the profession with a substantial income in criminal, civil and tax matters. It is a powerful establishment tribe, one skilled in deflecting responsibility away from itself. A tribe that governments are reluctant to confront.

The pernicious influence of the legal profession on US society is also considerable, with some saying that it is not so much the 'rule of law' that prevails, as the 'rule of lawyers'. That is manifest in; the make-up of Congress, a majority of senators are lawyers, the undemocratic rulings of the politically appointed Supreme Court judiciary and the pervasive 'plea deal', some might say 'blackmail', process in criminal cases. The latter, in part, explains why the US has the highest prison incarceration rate per capita in the world. Blacks account for under 14% of the general population but over 38% of the prison population. You might think that that would indicate to the authorities that something is very amiss and needs attention. Finally, in the US a pecuniary motivation drives much civil litigation, with 'no win, no fee' inducement an open invitation to resort to the courts for usually exaggerated financial recompense, invariably portrayed virtuously as 'justice'.

Sorry, I have drifted away from your question about how a conflict mentality manifests in times of peace. The glorification of wars past is an indication of a society steeped in the virtue of conflict. Often presented as paying respect to the war dead, it is used in covert praise of the military. Remembering the war dead is important, as is gratitude for their lives and contribution. Remembrance Day originally commemorated the Armistice agreement that ended the first world war, that is it celebrated peace after a war resulting in 20 million deaths. A war that started with jingoistic propaganda and then wiped out a generation of young men, slaughtered in the trenches of northern Europe.

Following the second world war Remembrance Day morphed into a day commemorating the military war dead and was accompanied by military bands, marching medal-bearing veterans and sombre leaders laying wreaths in strict order of establishment perceived hierarchy. Perhaps it might have been more appropriate to have commemorated all war dead. One of the consequences of a transition to the use of aerial warfare is the toll it takes on innocent civilians. Whereas civilians accounted for 50% of the first world war's death toll, they accounted for 90% of deaths in world war two.

The white poppy, as opposed to the establishment required and now ubiquitous red poppy, celebrates peace, recognises all war dead and signals opposition to the glorification of war. It was developed by women and has been in use since the 1930s but you will find that the white poppy is regarded as 'offensive' by those representing the military mindset. Peace should be cherished, not war. Wars should be remembered for their devastation and pain.

Using the war dead to glorify the military, and justify past wars, is a way of manipulating the emotions of the many by the few.

A parliamentary system that has government and opposition facing each other in confrontation and that revels in gladiatorial theatre like 'Prime Minister's Questions', is not one seeking consensus so much as conflict. There are alternative systems of debate and decision-making, within the United Kingdom and elsewhere, that do not involve such overt, albeit verbal, aggression. The most successful economy in Europe, since the second world war, is that of Germany. It has almost always been governed by coalitions of different parties, using an electoral system that is based on a form of proportional representation. That has provided stability and long term continuity of direction.

Germany did not give up on its manufacturing based economy, as did the UK in the late part of the 20th century, nor was it drawn into a financialised economic construct, with wealth extraction at its heart. Its standard of living per capita is 25% higher than the UK and it does not have the polarised distribution of income that is seen in the UK and US. So you see there always was an alternative to TINA.

You talk about political power and corruption being almost synonymous but there is little evidence of that in democracies like the UK.

Corruption takes many forms and I grant you that it is subtler in the UK and USA than in some other countries, but it is still present. When political parties are privately funded then the old saying inevitably comes into play 'he who pays the piper calls the tune'.

That is true whether funding is sought from the oligarchs and corporations that increasingly dominate economic life or trade unions with their own, albeit more democratically determined, agendas. Pursuit of influence over government policy is as perennial as the state and its management. When that influence is covert, not open to public scrutiny, then corruption of motivation is more likely to result. That can take many forms, from the less consequential, such as bestowing 'gongs' and titles in return for party funds, to the more inimical such as 'revolving doors' between influential political positions of power and economically rewarding positions in business. Also note, that although MPs are paid around three times the median UK salary, plus other very valuable perks such as pensions, that is not deemed sufficient. House of Commons rules allow them to treat their parliamentary role as effectively part-time employment.

Supplementary income streams are often facilitated by their MP status and consequent association with potential political influence.

The power of money also manifests in what governments encourage and discourage. Smoking cigarettes was endemic in much of the adult population in the first half of the twentieth century. Its impact on health gradually became unavoidable. The response of the government was to continually increase taxes on tobacco consumption. That proved a double-edged sword, on the one hand, the government grew increasingly dependent on the tax generated, on the other hand it was committed to discouraging an unhealthy habit. It took almost 50 years from the beginning of restrictions on advertising in 1964 to a total ban on all forms of tobacco marketing. As curtailment began on the promotion of one form of addiction, so relaxation began on another form. Gambling contracts had been unenforceable for over 100 years when, in the 1960s, it was decided that betting should be legalised. Its promotion to the public gradually gathered pace as tobacco advertising fell into decline. Today the marketing of gambling is ubiquitous, both in the virtual and real worlds, and consequently there is a growing problem of addiction in society. You should not doubt that money generated from encouraging this addictive behaviour finds its way into political parties and some politicians pockets.

The UK parliamentary system, of an elected assembly based on 'first past the post' voting in geographically defined constituencies, has merit in tying representation to places and people. It has the disadvantage of favouring the established political party structures and under-representing minority, but potentially growing, points of view. It provides a form of stability but does not readily facilitate compromise or the evolution that is sometimes necessary for democratic health.

When a political party is elected and a government is formed it controls a vast economic resource, with state expenditure around 40% of the country's annual economic output or gross domestic product (GDP). The ministers appointed usually have little if any experience of management or of the specialised area of government they now lead.

Their average tenancy in office is usually measured in months, not years. They depend on a civil service bureaucracy with deep establishment roots. This method of managing a large proportion of the country's resources has many weaknesses. Corruption of motive is one, an example of which showed up in the placing of Covid PPE contracts to 'friends'.

Another impact, less about corruption than competence, is a tendency towards short-term thinking and avoidance of accountability. Managing perceptions then matters more than what might be in the long-term interests of the country. It is a governance weakness when compared with countries like China that have continuity of leadership and tend to develop and pursue long-term strategies.

Politicians are often, initially at least, driven by ideological motives that they believe will benefit a majority of their fellow citizens. Many factors will influence their beliefs; upbringing, conscience, education process, financial interests, tribal loyalty. The educational background of many MPs is not representative of the electorate, as one might hope for in a democratically elected government responsible for general education policy. Pursuit of power is rarely confessed as a key goal, although it undoubtedly underpins the motivation of many politicians. The desire to obtain power is often driven by the need to prevent those with alternative policies, perceived to be threatening to the tribe's interests, from gaining power. Tribal loyalty almost always surpasses objective appraisal of what is in the best interests of the majority of citizens, even in a democracy.

Is tribalism in society inevitable?
The answer to that is yes. Tribalism is a perennial tendency in humans that has manifested throughout history. It is connected with the need to belong and can be seen at family level, clan and nation state. Individuals will usually belong to a hierarchy of tribes. The bigger the grouping the more likely sub-tribes will emerge, in part to cater for differing needs, or perceptions, and partly to obtain proximity between leaders and led. Employment provides a natural tribe for many. Professions, trades and guilds usually create degrees of exclusivity to protect the tribe's interests. These can be powerful and against the interests of the community at large, giving rise to a need for political intervention. A need not always addressed.

I could give you many examples of that in addition to the legal profession's practices already mentioned, but will choose one other to illustrate the point. The NHS was founded in the aftermath of the second world war. You will find that many socially desirable initiatives follow wars, like extension of the voting franchise at the conclusion of the first world war. Winning the senior medical profession over to a 'free' national health service involved 'stuffing their mouths with gold' in the words of Aneurin Bevan, the Labour minister responsible for setting up the NHS. What he meant was allowing them to treat their NHS jobs as part-time and to supplement their remuneration with private patient income. The NHS is now no longer able to function effectively. That is for many reasons, some connected with funding. An ageing population is another important factor, especially when combined with the prevalent inclination of the medical profession to prescribe drugs on an industrial scale. That, no doubt, affected by the pervasive influence of the pharmaceutical industry. Delaying death has enormous costs not always in the best interests of the patient. Assisted dying, available in some more enlightened countries, is anathema to much of the medical establishment. I digress, the NHS is reaching a major crisis point for a number of reasons. Politicians are loath to look at how other countries operate and pay lip service to the sanctity of the British institution, at the same time as allowing creeping privatisation of many services just as they have already done in dentistry. That trend will accelerate as service available to the wider population deteriorates. The NHS requires structural reform. Part of that reform, if a free service is to continue, will involve taking on vested interests. The medical profession is one of the most hierarchical and protective of its own interests. That is not always about just protecting its income but protecting its power. Any effective organisation needs to delegate power to the lowest level competent to make decisions, and not require that prerogative to be held by a tiny minority. The NHS is the biggest organisation in Europe. Aneurin Bevin avoided confrontation with the medical profession to get the NHS underway, if the NHS is to survive then a new generation of politicians, with the best interest of the public at heart, will need to be prepared to fight. That battle will need to take on the wealth extraction industry, the pernicious influence of the pharmaceutical industry and the vested interest of a hierarchical, power protecting, senior medical profession.

To return to the question you raised about tribes in general, they can also form around; politics, religion, geography, leisure pursuits, the arts and many more things.

The twenty-first century has seen the emergence of so-called culture wars with related tribes, in part facilitated by new digital communication channels or social media.

These tribes are often founded on 'beliefs', much as were religious groups of old, however the sanctity of science has replaced supernatural agency. An example is the belief that the earth's climate is warming and that this is the result of humanity's creation of carbon dioxide. Now no one can deny that humans create carbon dioxide, they breathe it out, just as they breathe in oxygen. Nor should anyone deny that plants 'breathe in' carbon dioxide and 'breathe out' oxygen. However the belief system that emerged related to the idea that the burning of fossil fuels by humanity, releasing carbon dioxide, had tipped climate equilibrium and was the underlying cause of detected global warming. A trend that if left unchecked, it was believed, would lead to catastrophic consequences and that therefore needed to be urgently addressed. The solution required not a reduction in the number of humans but a dramatic reduction in the use of the biggest source of energy utilised by humans; carbon based coal, oil and gas. The same energy sources that had enabled humanity to technologically develop and more efficiently feed and shelter itself, in turn resulting in a dramatic growth in world population.

Global warming is a testable fact given there is honesty and consistency by those taking measurements. Explaining any warming found is however in the realm of theory with many factors possibly contributing. The belief system that emerged in the late twentieth century would accept no alternative theory to the anthropomorphically generated growth in a 'greenhouse gas', carbon dioxide, being the primary cause of global warming. The tribe that resulted required the silencing of alternative views and a constant stream of propaganda supporting their narrative. An argument was presented that 'the science was settled', ironically denying the very nature of scientific endeavour. The impracticability of immediately replacing fossil fuels with intermittent 'green' energy sources was dismissed. The recognition that change required global agreement and commitment to have any effect was paid lip service to, then ignored. Many governments expended enormous resources in 'reducing carbon emissions' despite other, often less developed, nations increasing their 'carbon footprint' as they sought to emulate wealthier nations. The energy crises of the 2020s saw the rise of tribal conflict between those believing that 'the end of the world was nigh' and pragmatists concerned with the more immediate needs and well-being of local populations. Those pragmatists recognised that fossil fuels would eventually be depleted but argued for a sensible transition to new forms of energy.

The earth's cycles of cooling and warming are written into the geological and ice-core record. The last Ice Age ended 11,500 years ago, one of many that has faced the earth and not believed to have been caused by the world's ecosystem, but certainly impacting it. The climate is subject to cycles beyond our control. We are ultimately at their mercy, as we are at the mercy of the trajectory of asteroids, or large volcanic eruptions. Carbon dioxide is not pollution, it is the catalyst that nourishes plants. Pollution is real and is caused by humans, it can be controlled by humans. It is ethically wrong to confuse the two in pursuit of a cause, however well meaning. Humans cannot control the earth's climate, that is an inconvenient truth. As American theologian Reinhold Niebuhr astutely asked; 'God, grant me the serenity to accept the things I cannot change, the courage to change the things I can, and wisdom to know the difference'.

Virtue 'signalling' (that is appearing virtuous for public consumption, what used to be known as political correctness) became increasingly fashionable in the early part of the twenty-first century amongst many of liberal outlook. Race and gender were two chosen battlegrounds. Victimhood was encouraged. Tiny minorities were adopted to the greater cause. Universal truths were denied in pursuit of 'not causing offence'. Sexual identity was no longer a matter of birth fact but 'a matter of choice'. A modern vigilante form of Orwell's *Ministry of Truth* emerged, the Twitter mob. Intent on silencing anyone that might venture to cause offence by proclaiming gender to be a fact, not choice. In that they were supported by the giant social media platforms. 'Hate crimes' appeared in law and police forces, despite an apparent lack of resources, played their part in enforcing the new illiberal liberal consensus – it should be said at the same time as failing to investigate or prosecute the vast majority of real crimes; less than 6% of reported crimes resulted in anyone being charged. The new mentality meant that women's rights to their own space were transcended by transsexuals rights (biological men identifying as women) a tiny percentage of the population. That occurred in relation to toilets, sports and even prisons. A kind of collective madness took hold. A small vociferous lobby group or tribe was able to persuade many organisations that in the interest of protecting a minority's 'rights' the majority needed to relinquish their long-held beliefs and accept deviant sexual preferences as 'normal'. Children were then indoctrinated in schools to recognise the new gender paradigm, no doubt creating untold future mental health issues.

Opinion is malleable and easier to manipulate if fear is deployed or notions of what is virtuous. It is instructive to see how the process works, how heretics are silenced, or sanctioned, and how ostensible liberals become patently illiberal in support of perceived victims. How a relatively small group with an initially covert agenda can transform, over a short period, into a very large tribe with the help of key digital media platforms. Having gained critical mass the crusade becomes overt, badges of virtue are developed and self-censorship is unconsciously practised. I think you will find many examples of this basic process throughout history, what has changed is the speed with which it can now develop.

Are there examples of covert strategies remaining covert?

Covert strategies, or even covert membership of a tribe, is one way of avoiding conflict, for example in democratic societies with significant disparities in wealth and power but which are nominally committed to equal opportunity and an equitable distribution of income, if not wealth. Social class markers used to be more blatant but today are subtler to avoid arousing majority opposition, nevertheless tribal markers still exist for those willing to look for them. These can be subtle displays of perceived social status in the form of mannerisms, clothing, tastes or pursuits, often with attendant snobberies. More importantly they can be found in some long-standing institutions. An example is the 'private education' regime that perpetuates a wealthy minority's hold on the levers of power. It is still the gateway to leadership positions in the ruling elite, especially when combined with the 'Oxbridge' badge. Cambridge and Oxford Universities have been at the heart of establishment succession for many centuries, explaining in part the enormous wealth they possess. Their historical student intake has been dominated by individuals who have been privately educated, even though that group only accounts for a small proportion of the total student population. This bias has been slightly lessened as a general awareness of the disparity has grown, however the imbalance continues. One of the characteristics of a private education is the confidence instilled in students, that confidence may or may not be deeply rooted but it nevertheless plays an important part in furthering career progression, particularly in roles involving the power of rhetoric. The Oxbridge badge combined with that power opens many doors, doors guarded by those of similar background, and helps to explain why membership of this establishment tribe has tended to be self-perpetuating.

The Sutton Trust regularly profiles the educational background of the ruling elite. A recent survey showed that around 7% of the population are privately educated, yet that group accounts for 65% of senior judges, 59% of top civil servants, 57% of members of the House of Lords and 41% of conservative MPs. The upper echelons of the City of London financial institutions are also dominated by the privately educated. Oxbridge graduates account for less than 1% of the population but account for 71% of senior judges, 57% of the cabinet, 56% of top civil servants and 38% of members of the House of Lords. Of course the tribe justify their positions of power by claiming, or assuming, that it is their superior intelligence, or knowledge, that is the foundation of their success rather than privileged background. The under-representation of those of humbler origin, those with regional accents or with lower rhetorical ability, is sometimes acknowledged and lip service paid to the need for greater inclusivity. Any talk of a blatant class-divide in operation is dismissed as inflammatory or bigoted by the controlling elite.

What a society values is indicative of its collective progress. A society that regards a person's heritage, or even intellect, as the noblest attribute, rather than the values that underpin social cohesion, will reap what it sows. The higher levels of academia, secure in their sinecures, have always enjoyed a cloistered existence, protected by unearned wealth and an establishment that has grown increasingly to revere reason over virtue.

Wealth retention and extraction, rather than its creation and equitable distribution, has also tended to be their priority. Ruling elites are, consciously or otherwise, perennially concerned with protecting their privileges and power.

That must be a challenge in a democracy.

Let us consider societal evolution, from the acquisition of land and wealth through violence and feudalism to the mythology created around royalty and the assumed importance of proximity to that 'special' family. The Industrial Revolution, born in the North and Midlands, changed the power dynamic but within two generations the Wood family of Glossop, having created considerable wealth through trade (a then derogatory term for those who had earned rather than inherited money) were acquiring titles and educating their offspring at Eton. Migration to the London-centric home of power followed. Aspiration transmuted from creating wealth to preserving it and to joining a tribe perceived to be superior in terms of social status. Absorbing a powerful new group, and potential rival tribe, into one's own tribe has long been a technique for retaining power and ensuring continuity of the existing establishment.

Loyalty to the tribe is usually a requirement of membership. It is often a natural, or unconscious, inclination. The difficulty comes when there is a conflict between concepts of truth and loyalty. Then it is not unusual to see loyalty prevailing, sometimes spontaneously, sometimes by coercion, subtle or otherwise. Truth of course is often a matter of perception but dissonance between what one might believe to be true, and what one is required to observe, is not only a source of personal conflict but may become a source of societal conflict.

Controlling the majority to maintain a minority group's privileges is best achieved by persuasion, usually through control of information and narrative. Other lines of defence follow but final insurance lies in control of the military, that is the arm of state trained to perpetrate violence. Ostensibly this function is for defence against external enemies but ultimately it can be used against internal threats, as we saw at Peterloo in Manchester when workers peacefully gathering in numbers were set upon by the militia. The situation is no different today. The miners' strike was in part defeated by an increasingly militarised police force. Violence by the state will almost invariably be used against any group that seriously threatens the status quo and those holding the levers of power.

Consequently great efforts are made to cultivate military loyalty by the ruling elite. In feudal times this was done by granting land and titles, today the higher echelons of the Army, the force ultimately depended upon, are invariably privately educated and regiments are nominally led or connected with royalty. The funeral of Queen Elizabeth II displayed this enduring bond between royalty, the establishment and the armed forces. An extravagant display of military pomp was organised in reverence to an institution many would rationally regard as an anachronism. Peacock military uniforms were *de rigueur* for royal family members, along with rows of medals, more decoration than deserved. No branch of the armed forces was neglected, rarely have so many uniforms been gathered together in one place. I think you will find that even in this democracy military loyalty is sworn to the Crown, not to the people.

As we observed earlier those with power are usually reluctant to relinquish it. Their preference is for majority acquiescence but if necessary they will resort to violence to maintain power. However, an organised majority will always have the ability to overthrow a controlling minority. The problem is how to prevent a new elite emerging whose own interests ultimately take precedence over the majority's interests, what we might call the 'Bolshevik' or 'Lord Protector' syndrome. Democracy was meant to be the answer to this problem but as we have seen the tendency of power to corrupt did not disappear with free elections and an ever wider franchise. When corruption is not systematically rooted out it will tend to grow and ultimately its effect will be felt by the majority. The danger then is that disaffection will grow and faith in democracy will be undermined.

Are you saying we are doomed to perpetual conflict, to rule by those corrupted by power and that there is no hope for humanity?

That would be a message of despair indeed. My message is; what we are aware of we can change. If we are not aware, or worse, don't care, then we become victims of circumstance and are obliged to abandon hope of progress. I use the word progress here in the sense of learning from our individual and collective mistakes. Bad prevails when good is silent or acquiescent.

No system of government is ever likely to be perfect. The

system is better if it is not only aware of human fallibility, but has mechanisms to counter manifestation of those weaknesses. Leadership involves power. We need leaders. The proximity of leaders to led is important in two respects; it keeps leaders better attuned to the needs and views of those led and it counters the 'king' or ego tendency. The more hierarchical the governance the greater the likelihood of disparity in economic share or other manifestations of power. That is an argument for devolving power to the lowest level competent to deal with issues of importance to people. The tendency of all organisations is to progressively centralise more and more power. In doing so the risk of corruption and inequality grow. As Lord Acton reflected; 'power corrupts, absolute power corrupts absolutely'.

Respect for others is vitally important for social cohesion. That is true at the individual level and the collective level. It helps to get us away from the 'I am right, therefore you are wrong' mentality, of which we spoke. What fosters respect; honesty, reliability, consideration, humility and a willingness to forgive. That ability to forgive is usually born of recognition of our own fallibility. Seeing our own weaknesses, whether as an individual or at society level, helps us put things in perspective and that opens the possibility of progress. That is why I have spent so much time pointing out the weaknesses inherent in our own culture, in order that we gain perspective, reflect on those weaknesses and resolve to do our best to overcome them. Honesty and reflection should also enable us to become more tolerant of others.

I cannot set out for you a perfect way of organising society to achieve social cohesion. I can point out areas that might be worth looking at, if there is a genuine desire to achieve that goal. First, of course, would be the need to agree that cohesion is a desirable goal.

That might start with trying to define the term; a society that shares common core values, that seeks to bring out the best in people, that encourages a sense of responsibility for oneself and for others, that values cooperation over competition, that accepts the requirement for all within it to have their basic needs for sustenance, shelter, health and safety met. Reaching consensus requires listening as well as advocacy, it also requires acceptance of the will of the majority. That does not mean the suppression of those taking a different view, or their vilification. Respecting differences is an important key to cohesion as is encouraging cooperation rather than conflict.

You said that some other areas were worth looking at in order to aid social cohesion and avoid conflict.

I said at the beginning of our discussion that it is largely men that indulge in violence and I hope I have given you evidence that there is little sign of that changing for the better.

Why do we behave as we do? There are important biological drivers of human behaviour. We are, at one level, animals. Hormones impact emotions and behaviour, sometimes positively, sometimes negatively. That is true of women as well as men. Biological imperatives propel women to embellish their appearance to attract a mate, consciously or otherwise. Similar urges drive men to seek to inseminate the object of their desire. These are powerful forces deeply seated in our animal nature. Several marriages in the Armstrong and Smith family trees began with an unplanned pregnancy. Unexpected impregnation is less prevalent today but the basic biological drivers have not changed. Rivalry between men, as we have seen, can end in physical conflict. This too is often fuelled by hormones released when a threat is sensed or there is a misunderstanding about the motives of others. These biological responses are not inevitable. The key to change is in recognition of a behavioural reaction, rising above that response and then engaging the will to transform or transmute it. That is an ability we all have, as conscious beings, and is born of my belief, no knowledge, that we can exit the program and become the programmer of our life, if we so choose. It is worth considering how we might encourage the channelling of biologically driven traits into more socially cohesive behaviour. If men, generally more than women, are programmed to aggressively compete, then how can that tendency be channelled to create positive outcomes rather than negative? Women, now freed of their long term role as baby makers, are beginning to play a more influential role in the organisation of society. What I would suggest should be avoided is them becoming more like men, in order to fill roles often historically associated with male characteristics. Women's nature, in general, is more cooperative in its approach to problem solving. If social cohesion is a goal then that might be a trait which needs to come to the fore.

Just as some of men's inherent traits need to be guarded against, so with women. A potential for emotional response is one example, suggestibility is another. I am not claiming that all men or women are the same, patently they are not. There are however tendencies, born of real biological causes, which affect an individual's response to stimuli. Understanding what those tendencies are, rather than denying them as is currently fashionable, should be part of the education for life we all need. As should an understanding of the positive and complementary characteristics that gender bestows. Social cohesion involves getting the best out of people and avoiding, if possible, the potentially negative outcomes of inherent traits. Traits we all have.

How else can the education process help social cohesion?

Education is a life-long process and it is best to constantly remind ourselves of that fact. One of the greatest influences on an individual's approach to life is the family environment into which they are born. Mothers have a vital role in the care for and nurturing of their child. Fathers may bring complementary traits to bear, potentially valuable in determining a child's outlook on the unfolding world. A fortunate child will have important values inculcated in them by the family to which they belong. Strong family units provide the best foundation for a cohesive society. That principle should be recognised and encouraged, however formal education can help reinforce community structure.

A cohesive society is more easily formed if there is agreement on core values and what constitutes virtue. We talked earlier about respect and the elements that make up that concept. If we accept that respect is a quality we wish to encourage, then it might be wise to teach children why it is important and what it entails. For some that will reinforce what they have learned from family life, for others it may give a new perspective on relationship building. A disciplined environment in school, with mutual respect at its heart, will ultimately inculcate self-discipline and respect for others.

Corporal punishment has become unfashionable but the right environment can be achieved without that, as long as there are clear rules and repercussions for breaches of discipline. What may appear harsh is in fact in the interests of children and staff, if teachers are to be freed to teach and children to learn.

That environment should also incorporate an important principle; what is sought will determine what is forthcoming. Seeking the best from pupils will drive better outcomes, both at individual and collective levels, than lowering standards and expectations.

Each pupil is different but all will respond to an environment that expects them to do their best, that avoids an 'excuse' mentality and which recognises resulting effort and progress. That principle will be found to be true throughout life. Seeing, seeking and encouraging good will bring out good. Denying responsibility, or cultivating fear and suspicion, will bring forth correspondingly negative traits.

We have talked about the importance of understanding ourselves, our strengths and our weaknesses. Some are more extroverted by nature, that is they find it easier to relate to others and need contact with others to feel energised. Others are more introverted, that is they are more self contained, reflective and require the company of others less. Both types have inherent strengths and weaknesses which can be described and therefore taught. Understanding where you are on the introvert/extrovert spectrum can help you relate better to others. It can give an insight into other personality types, helping you appreciate why you behave as you do and why others may behave differently. Such knowledge is an important building block of a cohesive society.

The organising and encouragement of sport in schools is valuable both as a way of expending energy and of channelling aggressive tendencies into harmless pursuits. Teaching how to win and lose with humility, rather than hubris or despair, also prepares children for life to come. Equally important is for schools to organise co-operative ventures which teach about the different and complementary roles that underpin successful team effort. Understanding how cooperation can transcend competition in effectiveness is a valuable lesson.

Preparing children for the choices they will face in life should be part of the education process. Teaching how to care for both body and mind is vitally important. Bad habits are less likely to be established if there is an understanding of health fundamentals.

Imparting that knowledge and emphasising the need for self discipline and the acceptance of responsibility will give them a better chance of a healthy life.

Encouraging a questioning approach to life, rather than an unconscious acceptance of groupthink, received wisdom or authority, is likely to result in an inquiring mind capable of lifelong learning. That principle is espoused in *The Emperor's New Clothes*, the folktale by Hans Christian Anderson, and illustrates the need to resist group mentality.

Teaching the importance of learning from mistakes and the need for honesty to enable that, is an important life skill. As is learning the dangers of addictive behaviour that can manifest in many ways but which is commonly associated with the use of drugs, alcohol, nicotine, gambling, sexual gratification and, increasingly, the seductive world of social media. The latter with its potential for narcissism, anonymous abusive behaviour and a narrower information diet open to overt or covert manipulation.

I have concentrated on dangers, values and personality types because of their importance and sometimes their neglect in the education process. The teaching of basic technical skills is vitally important; reading, writing and arithmetic are all essential skills when growing up in the modern world. Giving children an appreciation of a wider world, not necessarily experienced through family life, that might whet their appetite for music, art or literature is also of value.

I do not think it is necessarily wise to prolong the formal education process for all children, particularly in academic subjects which may play an insignificant part in their lives. Assessing individual aptitudes, sometimes based on personality type, and sharing those, can help them make wiser career choices. Work is important in providing an income, but also in fulfilling a useful role in society. It can be, and should be, a major source of ongoing self-worth. Finding what you are good at and love doing is the best route to a fulfilling career. Most work training is best achieved on the job, but when accumulated technical expertise plays an important part in meeting the requirements of a job then provision of a technical education is best effected in conjunction with relevant employers.

There has been a tendency over recent decades in the UK to regard vocational and technical education as inferior to so-called academic education. By academic I mean education not of immediate practical use, however interesting the subject matter might be. That has not been the case in other countries, such as Germany. Many technical colleges and polytechnics here transmuted into universities, perceived to be more prestigious. The result of that academic prejudice has been protracted periods in formal education for students, involving substantial amounts of personal debt, followed by disappointment. The disappointment of finding that, on course completion, they must start on the bottom rungs of the employment ladder, rungs they could have climbed many years earlier, without debt.

Other education initiatives such as school result league tables have not produced the higher educational standards sought. League tables generally seek to improve overall performance and initially may succeed in that goal. Then, almost inevitably, they become subject to manipulation by those being measured. Examination grade inflation has been the perverse consequence of the table system, serving to hide a deterioration in actual standards of achievement. Also, we have begun to see a change in how some universities operate as they emulate businesses seeking growth and consequently feel impelled to compete for a growing number of student customers.

The UK is loath to look at how other countries manage important services like health care and education. Much could be learned from Finland, its education system is ranked in the top 3 worldwide for outcomes. There is no private education (schools or tuition), no student streaming, little homework and few examinations. Compulsory education ends at 16, however most then go on to further education. Of those going on 60% take a three year high school course which ends with a Finnish Matriculation examination or the International Baccalaureate. The other 40% choose vocational courses with resulting qualifications. Two thirds of high school students go on to university which is free of charge and criteria for entry is determined by each institution.

I opened by saying that education is about learning and that is potentially a life-long process. That frame of mind should be encouraged in all. Learning always involves a degree of humility, in the sense that it requires tacit acknowledgment of potential ignorance and that is often more difficult as we age. Becoming 'set in our ways' or increasingly dogmatic in our views is a natural process as we get older, however, questioning our own assumptions, as well as those dominant in the culture we inhabit, helps sustain an active and healthy mind.

What about the role of religion? You have talked about how the pursuit of power has in the past corrupted religious leaders, but can religion not also play a positive role in life?

It can. Religion is a powerful force capable of transforming the lives of individuals. There are countless examples of that throughout history. I would also say that there are many ways to access that transformative power and no one faith has an exclusive path to the spiritual realm.

The vast majority of humanity is attached to a belief system that recognises a greater reality than that which reason and science proclaim. Of the largest groupings, Hinduism is the oldest, Christianity the largest and Islam the fastest growing. Between them they have 5.2 billion adherents, from nominal to dedicated, covering two thirds of the population of the earth. None of those religions have a major foothold in China, the most populous country on earth, Confucianism, Taoism and Buddhism are the 'three teachings' that have shaped Chinese culture. In the West, and in particular in parts of Europe, the influence of religion is in steep decline.

What are the characteristics of a religion? Belief in a power greater than humanity that impacts all that exists. God, Allah, Brahman, Tao are expressions that seek to conceptualise that ultimate power. Are there common characteristics across the numerous belief systems that exist? Most belief systems have a moral foundation, they contain a set of values that relate to human interaction as well as a means of accessing an immanent spiritual force. What do religions provide for adherents? They provide a sense of belonging to a group with shared beliefs and values. They provide a bedrock of constancy, or order, in a world of perpetual change and uncertainty. Are there core values in common across belief systems? There are, but too often they are regarded as secondary in importance to the religious architecture constructed to differentiate one faith from another. That man-made architecture is often a mixture of mythology, exclusivity and a temporal hierarchy, the latter often claiming the ability to bestow access to the spiritual realm.

As I said in my opening remarks, attuning to a spiritual reality beyond mortal existence can be a transformative experience for the individual. It may be transient, it may happen without apparent conscious intent, but ultimately it is a matter of choice, or will.

Recognition of a power greater than self, that gives order both to the material world and to the reality beyond that domain, has been a characteristic of human experience throughout history. Intuitive truths are no less valid than intellectual truths at the individual self level. The Prophet Muhammed urged that we should strive always to excel in virtue and truth. Zoroaster taught; good is our goal and is achieved by; good thoughts, good words and good deeds. Most religions would say 'amen' to those insights. Of course, truths and beliefs should be judged by their results.

Which raises the question as to what is 'good'.

A very important question. Eleos will talk later about what constitutes 'good' for ourselves and our interaction with others; you will also find explicit definition of the word in the poem *Good Is* one of the *Poems on Purpose* in chapter 4 of Reflections.

I would like to sum up my thoughts on the topics we have discussed. You opened our discussion by pressing me on whether humanity is making progress. You may have found what I had to say challenging or even negative. My objective has not been to depress you but to encourage you to think. There is no perfect solution as to how best to organise society to achieve social cohesion, if that is recognised as a key goal. Different conditions prevail in different parts of the world, at different times, and those conditions will bring forth different solutions. Whatever system emerges will involve leaders and led. The outcome will be subject to the strengths, weaknesses and motivations of those leaders. The system will be more effective if leaders are virtuous, honest and have the interests of those led at heart. That principle of 'leadership as service' needs to be more than lip service. As Lao Tzu explained in *Tao Te Ching* 'the best leaders are the ones that people hardly know; when organised community goals have been achieved the people say … we did it ourselves'. Beyond meeting community bodily needs is another imperative; to allow individuals the freedom to migrate their own hierarchy of needs. The values of freedom, virtue and truth are the same as those espoused by the Borough of Glossop and its grammar school; *Virtus, Veritas and Libertas.*

Beliefs and values provide good foundations that help us deal with life's vicissitudes. A perennial human response to uncertainty is to try to mitigate it by seeking control. That can manifest in many ways from pursuing isolation to trying to control those around us. The motivation that drives the pursuit of power over others, will determine its outcome. As we have seen, with power comes the danger of corruption, corruption of motive.

Societies that recognise that danger and guard against it will be more effective in its control than those that, consciously or unconsciously, ignore it. Leadership should not be avoided when it is placed in our path, but it is better regarded as an opportunity to serve the interests of others, rather than an opportunity to serve our own interests. In serving others we make progress towards our higher Self. If our motive becomes corrupted we move away from that Self.

Our thinking is conditioned by the environment into which we are born. That is natural but can lead to an absence of perspective and honest reflection. Learning, and the idea of progress, requires us to engage those capabilities. It is easy to see faults in others, whether individuals, tribes or nations, it is less easy to see our own faults, whether individual or group. Jesus said 'let he who is without sin cast the first stone'. Rising above loyalty to the tribe, with its narrow perspective, is a vital step if humanity is to make progress. Social cohesion and avoidance of mankind's perennial descent into conflict begins with understanding others' points of view and then respecting those views. That requires a degree of humility and a willingness to listen, also a preparedness to forgive when, inevitably, mistakes are made.

Life is full of change and uncertainty. That can at times be disturbing, if not frightening.

However, with those characteristics also comes opportunity. The opportunity to learn. At the heart of a greater reality is *Law* or *Tao* involving cause and effect. That order is not a cold mechanistic regime but one designed to help us migrate our own spiritual hierarchy. We cannot escape *Law* but we can choose to both understand it and work in harmony with it. Such harmony not only serves our own good but the greater good.

Moving towards that *good*, individually and collectively, defines progress.

Chapter 2
Proverbs of Perspective

...alphabet of life lessons

A
Life is about learning, potentially a lifelong process
Learning's primary ingredient is listening, questioning is its yeast
The test of learning is whether we change
Self discipline is the cement of change

B
We cannot learn for others, only for our self
Deflecting responsibility only delays honest reflection
When the student is ready the teacher will appear
All we encounter are potentially our teachers, as we are theirs

C
Love is as much a motive as an emotion
Empathy, respect and kindness are its foundation stones
Encouragement, patience and prudence are its eternal pillars
Families are the perennial testbed of love

Reflections

D
Habit is our home and then our jail
Making the unconscious conscious is the first step to change
Reflection is best viewed through the mirror of honesty
Pretension's mask cannot hide us from our self

E
Encouragement promotes growth
Criticism poisons positivity
Recrimination is salt in life's wounds
Forgiveness frees not only the forgiven, but also the forgiver

F
All forms of greed are ultimately self consuming
Gratitude serves self better than greed
That which is unappreciated is sooner or later lost
To earn respect we must first learn to give it

G
Better to give what is needed than to give what we want
The road to hell is paved with bad motivations
Conscience's prick eventually penetrates conceit's comfort
Humility is the only effective antidote to conceit

H
Help is always at hand for the humble
Accepting responsibility is the gateway to growth
Discipline and disciple share a root
Emotional reaction is best observed, then transcended

A Life in Perspective

I
Aggression may bring pacification, never peace
Vanquish fear to live in peace
Victimhood is ultimately a matter of choice
Reconciliation is the fruit of forgiveness

J
Seek and you will find; take care what you seek, for you will find it
Unquestioning faith creates false gods and corrupt intermediaries
Power will corrupt, serving others will save
Fight a lack of confidence conquered becoming conceit

K
From binary building blocks is all complexity created
Science is as pure as the motive that drives it
Beyond what and how lies why,
    therein does cause and purpose lie
Mind not only perceives order, it is also its source

L
Life is the ultimate complex system
Intervening in a complex system is subject to a perennial law
The law of unintended consequences
Purity of motive determines purity of outcome

M
Mental pain is a prompt for change
Pain is the price we pay for Spiritual growth
The pain is a matter of law, the growth a matter of choice
What is rigid eventually breaks, what adapts grows stronger

N
Understanding others starts with understanding self
It is easier to forgive fallibility in others, having acknowledged our own
Labelling others usually prevents us hearing them
Detachment enables perspective, perspective sees beyond self

O
Look beyond the shell of surface to find the kernel of truth
Following the money too often finds the motive
Purity of motive, absent expectation, is its own reward
Sharing our struggles encourages others to share theirs

P
Good fortune favours the brave
Bravery is fearing the outcome but still doing the right thing
Courage eventually conquers adversity
Swimming against the tide is a struggle, until the tide turns

Q
Manipulating the emotions of others usually ends in tears for both
Neither a guilt thrower, nor catcher, be
Picking the scab off wounds rarely helps the healing process
Hurt, hate and fear imprison us, forgiveness frees and heals

R
Detachment aids reflection, reflection encourages responsibility
Everything happens for a reason, only honest reflection will reveal that reason
Learn the lessons of victory and defeat wearing the hat of humility
Always accept the inevitable with good grace

A Life in Perspective

S
Those that know they have enough are truly wealthy
Those that think they have nothing to learn, learn nothing
Judgement defines intelligence, not knowledge
There can be no harmony without humility

T
Mistaking confidence for competence can be very costly
Kindness is more precious than gold, yet costs nothing
Virtue is what virtue does, not displays
Willpower may be cowed or dormant but never destroyed

U
Expectation is the mother of disappointment
Many small steps in the right direction lead to the right destination
Authority is best bestowed when it has been earned
Competition is ultimately conquered by co-operation

V
Critical thinking, not conformity, is learning's prelude
Learn from the past but live its lessons in the present
We may not choose the hand we are dealt but do choose how we play that hand
The truth is always waiting, when we are ready to accept it

W
We cannot avoid the consequences of the choices we make
Learning from those consequences is life's purpose
Find the motive, find the truth
In harmony lies peace, the peace that passeth thinking

X
Respect that others have their own path to tread
Seek neither to judge nor to control them
Listening is one of the greatest gifts
As is encouraging reflection and responsibility

Y
Faith in good furthers good
Good example fosters good in others
Good motive is the golden key to good outcome
Union of the Good within and the Good without is our goal

Z
Perennial purpose is found in love
As the Sun sustains life so Spirit sustains love
I feel, I think, I learn ... beyond feeling and thinking ... I AM
I AM a node in the divine network that is Spirit ... I AM ONE

Chapter 3
Conversation With Eleos

... about life, its purpose and the nature of love

What is the purpose of life?
To learn.

To learn what?
That depends upon the person.

    We are each born into different circumstances and our lives therefore face different challenges. No two lives are alike, but all face challenges and choices, correspondingly life's lessons differ for each person. What is learned by all, collectively, certainly contains common threads and it is possible to extract principles from that collective experience. Learning is often associated with the acquisition of impersonal knowledge. That is a form of learning certainly, one that primarily engages the intellect. We must look beyond the intellect if we are to progress as individual beings.

How do we learn?
We learn through experience. Having an insight into others' lives may help but we only truly learn through personal experience, through our interaction with others.

Is this a rational process?
As I have said, this process lies beyond intellect alone. Emotion plays a major part in life, perhaps the biggest part. Understanding how we react to and behave towards others requires a perspective beyond emotion and even intellect. Reflection, the key to conscious learning requires detachment. With detached understanding comes the possibility of change.

Why do we need to change?
Change is a prevailing principle of the reality we perceive. Everything changes, phenomenon timescales may vary but all is ultimately in a state of flux, with the exception of the laws that govern this reality. A Chinese philosophical work, the *I Ching* or *Book of Changes*, dating from around 3000 years ago, describes this enduring principle alongside the other cosmic characteristics of continuity and wholeness. From the moment we are born to the moment we die we face bodily and mental transition in an ever changing environment. With that comes uncertainty, challenge and choice. We intuitively understand that at some level there is a constant. Being at one with that constant enables us to gain perspective and define purpose. Purpose implies progress and that results from learning, achieved first by comprehension and then by choosing to change. If nothing changes we have not learned. So the need for change is as perceived by the perceiver at one with the constant and purpose implies change.

Who is the perceiver?
This perceiver is our greater Self. It, and what it is part of, have been given many names throughout human history. As the names have been created so tribes have formed and attendant worldviews created. These have as often led to rivalry and conflict as peace and harmony. That is the result of our inherent human nature, predispositions and fallibility, our lower selves as opposed to our higher selves. So labels do not necessarily help. Let us say that a 'greater Self' beyond mortal existence is an intuitive truth that has manifested throughout human history. That greater Self is part of an even greater reality that some have called Good or personified as God.

Where does intuition come from?
Intuition lies apart from intellect or emotion. It implies a source of information beyond our mortal experience that occasionally makes itself known to us. There are many examples of the reality of intuition for those willing to look. It can occur with personal issues or intractable issues of logic or scientific enquiry. Sometimes when we are struggling with a problem it is best to stop thinking about it consciously. If one can avoid expectation sometimes inspiration arises, inspiration outside the parameters of our previous thought process. The word itself provides an answer to your question of sorts; in-tuition, tuition from within. That within a reference to our greater Self. Humility and lack of expectation often determine the intervention of intuition.

Is there any proof of existence beyond the mortal realm we perceive?
Proof is an interesting choice of word. Most of the things we believe are not the result of proof, in the sense I think you mean it.

Reflections

We live in an *age of reason* that has resulted in a dominant role for science with its definition of the word proof. Science is in fact a methodology for investigating the observed world around us. It generates theories which explain relationships between those observations. These theories stand until new observations arise that do not fit the theory, then new theories are required. The scientific method has delivered great insights into the nature of the physical world we inhabit as mortals. The establishment created to 'do' science is made up of mortals and inevitably those mortals are fallible. That results in dogmas and corruption of motive, as in all walks of human life. One such dogma, now widely accepted, is the idea that the only reality is that which is subject to scientific proof in the physical realm. Any other perception of reality is not provable and therefore does not merit credibility. That despite a majority of the world's population over time having believed intuitively in a greater reality than that physically perceived. Even science as it has delved into the world of subatomic matter has had to concede that its previous certainties are in reality probabilities and that the observer, or perceiver, may impact what is observed.

'Proof' is ultimately a subjective test but there is strong evidence of existence beyond this mortal realm, if one chooses to look for it. There are the accounts given by those who have had a 'near-death experience' or of those who have 'died' and returned to life. Another source arises in the accounts of people who can recall former lives, whether spontaneously, usually children, or those recalled under hypnotic regression. Some more open minded scientists have explored that kind of evidence, even if such investigation is anathema to the 'rational' scientific establishment.

One thing is certain however, following our mortal death we will *know* the truth, either in experiencing a continuation of consciousness, albeit housed in a different form, or in a negative sense in the oblivion of current scientific dogma.

Are you saying scientific method is not a route to truth?

As Jesus once said about another hierarchy 'render unto Caesar the things that are Caesar's and unto God the things that are God's'. The scientific method has an important part to play in understanding the nature of perceived reality. It has given rise to much knowledge and technological development. It has also given rise to materialism and conceit. The conceit of believing that a limited worldview is the only possible valid world view. The concrete world of science has foundations of sand. It proclaims that the matter and energy it perceives are ultimately built from subatomic particles whose existence cannot be seen but can be deduced. The behaviour of those particles is, according to science, affected by the observer. That principle, if true, has enormous implications that are yet to be fully understood and explored. Science is a valid tool of inquiry if it dons the hat of humility and avoids dogma. If it seeks to understand how the laws it perceives came into being, and the role of mind in creating order from chaos, then it will continue to help our understanding of the realm we inhabit.

Surely science has helped create the modern world ?

That is definitely so, for good outcomes and not so good. Much of physical science or physics is preoccupied with matter and mechanisms. In a sense it has created a mechanistic model of reality. It can answer many questions about the physical environment we inhabit. It cannot answer many other questions; such as how something can emerge from nothing or how animate life can emerge from inanimate matter. Science itself acknowledges that its own models indicate that around 90% of the substance making up the universe is beyond its grasp, or methods of detection, so-called dark matter. That is where humility is required. A methodology that is constantly seeking the ultimate particles of matter may be akin to those ancient theologians who argued, maybe apocryphally, about how many angels could dance on the head of a pin. Perhaps the answers to ultimate questions do not lie in the constant subdivision of matter. How matter morphs into energy and how energy morphs into mind might prove an avenue of enquiry worth exploring. It would certainly be helpful if there was acceptance that other methods of inquiry, in addition to 'scientific materialism', may be valid in establishing ultimate truths.

You seem to be rather dismissive of a vitally important discipline.

Far from it, I am simply countering a way of thinking that dominates much of humanity's current mindset or worldview. Why? Not to be obtuse but simply to put science in perspective. It is a valid tool of learning about the physical realm but when it comes to human experience it is of limited value. What gives humans a sense of purpose or fulfilment lies beyond the techniques of science. It may help feed and shelter people but humans need more than that to give their lives meaning.

Isn't that the realm of psychology another branch of science?

That discipline has its role to play but hardly qualifies as science in the classical sense. Science observes phenomena and constructs theories that show connections between observations. This results in mathematical models that can predict outcomes based on theories or laws. Those theories hold until observations arise that cannot fit within the model or theory structure. Then new theories are required. The realm of research on the psyche or mind has no such universal theory/prediction regime. It may observe the behaviour of individuals and seek to segment or classify that behaviour. Its adherents certainly construct theories but these at best describe possibilities rather than mathematical certainties. In understanding the nature of mind our contemporary comprehension barely scratches the surface of its reality. That is not to dismiss efforts to learn more, in a disciplined way, but simply to ask that the hat of humility be worn by those in pursuit of knowledge. All learning requires humility. Humility implies freeing ourselves of preconceived ideas and prevailing habits or dogmas. That can be very difficult and requires courage as well as purity of motive. Heretics used to be burned at the stake today's sanction is to ostracise and banish them from the tribe. Neither treatment is commendable or respectful of the honest pursuit of knowledge.

You implied earlier that the only valid way of learning was through personal experience. If that was so surely the whole edifice of civilization would not have been possible. Do we not build upon the foundations laid by predecessors' knowledge?

We must distinguish between learning at the personal level and the collective level. The evolution of societies, or civilization as you call it, does indeed depend upon an accumulation of knowledge. We would not get far if we questioned every assumption inherited. However, advances do often result from questioning assumptions generally held. At the personal level each individual likewise enters the world and is 'educated' by the environment experienced and that environment's underlying beliefs or assumptions. Again it would not be productive or possible to question all the assumptions inculcated in us, but it should be a fundamental part of maturing as an individual to ask questions of the beliefs we hold, as to whether those beliefs are for our good or the collective good. That raises the question of course as to what is good. Is the ever growing world population a sign of evolutionary success as some might claim? Is that a kind of objective good, even though it may have been achieved at the expense of countless other species? Is the accumulation of more and more material things a sign of success and therefore good? Even though material possessions never ultimately satisfy an individual's need for meaning. What drives human needs? What satisfies them? Is satisfaction a permanent state or a temporary one? We enter the world of the individual and mind. Society provides a framework and source of interaction, it will influence the individual, it may even seek to control the individual, but ultimately the idea of need and purpose lie at the individual level. That individual is a mind housed, in this realm, in a physical body.

Are you saying that each individual is different, has different needs and therefore must find their own 'good'; that life is about us as individuals?

That is in a sense true. It may sound self-centred or selfish, in reality it is not. What we discover as we climb the ladder of life is that real contentment resides in a state of selflessness not self centeredness. That is one of the many paradoxes of this mortal coil. We all have a hierarchy of needs. We inhabit a body, the basic needs of that body must be satisfied if we are to live healthily. Beyond that we have other needs. Many of those relate to how we interact with others. These interactions will be the result of circumstances, habits of mind and past interactions. Some individuals have greater need for interaction than others, however all need interaction. 'No man is an island' as John Donne's poem proclaimed. Happiness, contentment, satisfaction and learning, at the mental level, all depend on those interactions. Isolation may allow for reflection and perspective but application of learning requires interaction with others. The circumstances we face are our opportunity to learn. Changing circumstances present us with choices, the choices we make can cement our learning. We cannot learn for others, only for ourselves. That is a fundamental truth, difficult to live. Nor should we judge the choices others make. They will face the consequences of the choices they make as we will face the consequences of our own choices. Empathy and encouragement are the most helpful responses to others' situations rather than criticism, as we know from our own experience. 'Do unto others as you would be done by' as the biblical saying has it. We are all here to learn.

Learn to what end?

To migrate our hierarchy of needs, to satisfy an inherent imperative that we cannot escape. Ultimately to obtain the 'peace that passeth understanding', or one might say, passeth 'thinking'. It is, in this life, a temporary state, nonetheless important for its transience. We have many motivations, some driven by our animal programming, these satisfy for a time. Many learn to rise above these basic drives and modify them to accommodate the needs of family, wider clan or societies we inhabit. Sometimes that is a conscious process, sometimes we are heavily influenced by the norms, determined by others, of our environment. The awakening of 'awareness' is an important step in the learning process. Awareness implies a standing aside from the day to day, to see ourself and the environment we inhabit, as an observer, rather than only occupy the more limited view of a participant. That ability, to stand aside, is sometimes vital to our progress. As we migrate our hierarchy of needs we are often faced with pain or unhappiness. What appears problematic is in fact a sign that we must take responsibility and make choices to address the source of the pain we are experiencing. It is best to view mental pain as an opportunity to learn, not as a punishment. Ultimately we are only victims if we choose to accept victimhood. No life is a tranquil pool of contentment. Indeed there would be no point to that life if it were so. All face turbulence and sometimes storms. In a sense what we learn from that turbulence is what mortal life is for. The purpose of life is to learn and from that learning grow nearer to our higher Self and union with the universal Self or Good or God.

Some people face horrible situations not of their making. What are they to learn from that? That life is basically unfair? That evil prevails?

That would be an unfortunate conclusion. Unfortunate for the individual. It would say in effect; 'I am a victim of circumstance, my fate is outside my control'. That would be a lesson of despair. Many people do conclude just that at some stage in their life. They feel overwhelmed by events. They need encouragement from others when they are in this place of despondency. We are not alone. We all need a helping hand at times. One person's despair is another person's opportunity to intervene. Out of bad can come good. That good intervention should not seek to remove responsibility from the other but encourage the individual to understand that taking responsibility is the way forward. They may have been dealt a very difficult hand but that is because they have the ability and willpower to rise above its apparent hopelessness. No situation is hopeless if we face it with courage and learn what it has to teach us about ourselves in relation to others. Drawing such lessons strengthens us, for our future interactions with others.

You may say this is wishful thinking or conversely harsh. I am saying that understanding this is one of the most important lessons in life. It is about accepting responsibility, about being in control of one's life and about growing as an individual. It is a healthy mindset that results in a valuable life, valuable to the individual and valuable to those interacted with.

It appears to be a lesson focused on the self and in praise of self-centeredness.

Ultimately we are all inevitably self-centred, in that we pursue, consciously or otherwise, satisfaction of our own needs. A great paradox of life is that pursuing our own ends does not ultimately result in the real satisfaction we seek or need. A greater satisfaction arises from helping others on their own journeys. I stress not in directing or controlling another's journey but in respecting their journey is different and that they face choices we cannot make for them. We can however give encouragement as they face the choices before them and in helping others, we grow ourselves. That is a paradox but also an unavoidable truth.

Love, a much used and abused word, is better defined as a motive rather than an emotion. The motive to help others grow towards their potential. That is why a mother's love for her child, in its purest form, is the ultimate example. That may begin with protection and even control, in the interests of the child's well being, migrate through encouragement and increasing freedom but ends with the mother taking pride in her child's independence. That is real love motivated by the desire to help the child mature. I am not saying all mothers have this purity of motivation but it represents an ideal we can all learn from. Some might say it is a biological imperative and they would be right.

Taking control of the unconscious, sometimes instinctive, drivers is part of the growth of any individual. The ability to stand back from and see unconscious causes of our behaviour is part of our growth process. It can help us distinguish between positive drivers and those that are damaging to ourselves or others. That 'seeing' is the first step to making a conscious choice and in so doing, potentially growing.

What is consciousness?

The conscious choice I referred to is an act of will, a determination to make something happen. Consciousness is a wider concept and the subject of much debate and many definitions. For most it relates to 'mind', which then raises the question as to what is mind. The current mechanistic paradigm defines the mind as a by-product of the brain. In this mortal realm there is no doubt that the two are related but it does not necessarily follow that they are the same.

Many creatures with which we share the planet have brains. Those brains are the central processors of information; they receive, process and transmit information, generally at a subconscious level, that is without the organism being separately aware of the process. The workings of the human body, as we have discovered through scientific enquiry, are incredibly sophisticated and the brain plays a fundamental part in managing those processes. All without our conscious awareness. That is one aspect of the concept we describe as mind. Mind however is more than just an unconscious processor of information. It is in one sense the home of our real self. That self is not corporeal. Let me try and give an analogy. A handheld computer, usually in the guise of a smartphone, is a sophisticated processor of information and is capable of undertaking a massive array of tasks in its own right, but it is also capable of communicating with, and being part of, a vast network of information infinitely greater than the limits of its own power. 'Consciousness', in one sense, is recognition of the entity 'self', a unique being capable of intentional thought, separated from others but aware of the need for interaction with them. A self capable of 'consciously' transcending natural imperatives, through choice, and possessing the inherent potential for creativity. In other words, a being with some 'conscious' control over itself and its environment. That awareness entails mental detachment from the machine, or mechanism, and is perhaps the defining difference between humanity and the natural world inhabited.

In the parlance of Genesis, the first book of the Hebrew Bible or Old Testament, consciousness was bestowed at the point Adam and Eve ate from the Tree of Knowledge. At that point they transcended nature, became aware of their nakedness and were cast out of the Garden of Eden. That metaphor describes the process involved in the dawning of consciousness in humanity. It describes the bestowing of self-awareness, the realisation of power, the necessity for conscious choice and the resulting separation from a natural, unconscious order.

'Conscious' mind is the means by which structure or order is created and manifests at local and universal levels. Our mortal reality is regulated by that order. At the collective level laws are generated to create order and enable learning. There can be no learning if there is no order. As our consciousness develops our awareness grows of that collective entity. The journey back to the Garden is now necessarily through conscious choice. It is for the individual a mental journey involving the ascent of a hierarchy of needs. That is the pilgrimage of life. It entails the raising of awareness to first appreciate and then seek harmony with *Law* (the ancient East Asian concept of *Tao*). That *Law* underpins creation.

What is that Law?
That Law is the *Law of Love*.

When Jesus said 'I come to fulfil the Law, not to abolish it', he was not referring to the law of the land, or to the ten commandments, nor was he saying 'I am above the Law'. He was saying that he was at one with the Law and was a manifestation of it, as he also recognised were other great teachers. Saint Paul said that 'he who loves his neighbour has fulfilled the Law'. I use these examples not to promote Christianity, as the only route to a spiritual domain, but to point out a truth understood by the founders of Christianity and long proclaimed by many belief systems. A truth easily obscured by the distractions of daily life. That flame of Truth may be temporarily lost but it is never extinguished and is always waiting for those in search of the light.

It sounds remarkably simplistic.
It may sound simple, and in one sense *is* simple, but living that truth for fallible humans is the greatest challenge we face. All mortals have within them a seed of spirit that will impel them, eventually and inevitably, to seek the light of Truth. Progress does not depend on esoteric knowledge, intellect, power over others or accumulated possessions. On the contrary, those pursuits usually entail long diversions from the Path. The journey is from a lower self, preoccupied with self, to a higher Self concerned with the well being of others. As individual participants we cannot avoid the laws created that govern interaction with others. Those laws are created to help us learn. We are free to learn or not and then again, sooner or later. That is a matter of choice. Choice that consciousness has bestowed. As we learn we find there is a hierarchy

of laws to help us towards harmony and ultimate union, the latter a state some have called heaven.

Do those same laws not give rise to the concept of hell and the age-old battle between good and evil?

Age-old indeed. Endless stories have described the battle between good and evil. They tell of a truth sometimes overshadowed by the stories that are meant to illustrate that truth. Those constructs can then become the focus of theologies that take precedence over the principle illustrated. The fundamental truth is that we are responsible individuals constantly faced with choices. The choices we make bring us either nearer to good (or God) or nearer to bad or evil (the Devil). If we learn from the wrong choices we make, and everyone will make both good and bad choices, then the experience of bad has been positive and productive. The Hindu and Buddhist concept of karma captures this principle. Karma is not punishment for 'sin' it is an opportunity to learn and move on. Just as a pain in the body is telling us something is wrong and needs to be addressed, so mental pain is an indication of something needing our attention. Conscience and consciousness are inextricably connected. In as much as we address the cause, that pain has been useful. Mental pain, or the pricking of conscience, is an opportunity, not punishment. It is for us to decide whether to take that opportunity or not. It is a mistake to believe good and bad are in conflict. They work together for our growth. Being conscious of the choices we face and of our motivation can help us make wiser choices.

Is the objective of life therefore to achieve some kind of perfection or harmony? If so I fear few will achieve that 'heaven'.

As I have explained there is much more to our existence than our spell occupying a life on earth. It is best to view our mortal life as a school for learning. There is no final examination at the end of that life that determines one's fate, eternal bliss or eternal damnation. Following a life there is a period of rest and recuperation. Reflection follows at the instigation of one's higher Self. How will you judge the life that you have lived and the choices you made? Will the measure be wealth accumulated, status achieved, intellectual prowess, power gained over others? Or will it be on whether you were able to master lower-self traits and were able to give to those with whom you interacted?

After reflection some choose a return to earth to learn more. That might entail incarnating with others we have shared past experiences with, to work out past differences or be available to support them. Some further up the ladder of learning may see a new life as an opportunity to help humanity and then incarnate as spiritual teachers. That return to the classroom of life is a matter of choice not necessity. Detailed experiences of past lives are not consciously retained for that return visit but nothing previously learned is lost to our greater Self, and we always have access to that higher Self should we seek it. Normally each life involves a focus on particular issues we deem important for our growth, so the situation we incarnate into is chosen by us to help achieve that end. Whether we are more or less successful in achieving that end is something we judge during the life and following that life. We are not judged by others. Our own judgement is always far more salutary than the judgement of others. Freedom of choice is as applicable in the afterlife as it is in the mortal life we live. We are free, in a sense, to create our own heaven or hell. Which we experience is a matter of choice and motive determines choice outcomes.

Back to that word motive. Many things drive motivation, conscious and unconscious. Much of daily life is the result of habit of thought. We cannot possibly consciously choose wisely at every decision point during the day.

It is true that the mind deals with much of life's routine unconsciously. Pretty much all of the body's functions operate thus. Its protective mechanism, the immune system, sees off many potentially harmful intrusions and generally restores us to health when we have suffered damage. All this without conscious mental process or intervention from external agencies. Of course our mental state can trigger physical symptoms and illness, for example sustained stress can undermine the body's immune system. What causes stress in one person may not induce stress in another. Stress implies loss of control or fear of loss of control. It often operates at a subconscious level. Recognising the symptoms of stress in mind or body is an opportunity to address its cause. Reflection and recognition of the cause, and our response to that cause, can be the path to freeing ourselves from stress. Not the temporary fix of drugs, often targeting symptoms, but a fix born of reflection, taking responsibility and overcoming the cause of that which is inducing stress. That entails rising above an unconscious process, making it conscious, and taking control of it. So to come back to your point; no we cannot spend our day making every decision point a conscious process but when an issue arises that is of concern we are often better served by rising above habit or programming to take conscious control. My example is simply meant to illustrate that point.

Your example might be interpreted as undermining the role of the medical profession in maintaining an individual's health. In effect saying 'heal thyself'.

I can assure you that I am not trying to undermine the medical profession or wishing to pile a burden of responsibility onto overburdened individuals. There is a growing tendency to believe, both on the part of individuals and the medical profession, that there is a pill for all symptoms displayed. That is not a healthy development especially when older individuals begin each day with a cocktail of drugs, some to counter the effects of others.

Let me try and put things in perspective. Our bodies should not, and do not, require constant intervention by doctors, therapists, dentists or optometrists. The normal state should be one of health. That health depends upon right; breathing, nutrition intake, clean environment, exercise, sleeping, and proper expulsion of waste materials. These elements one might describe as health fundamentals, not always possible but certainly desirable. For most animals these things happen naturally, that is unconsciously.

Humans, at one level, are animals and have innate instincts like other animals, however over time, as a result of the unnatural habits inculcated by 'civilization', those instincts have been overridden. As habits, harmful to health, have developed so consequences have arisen, some compromising the body's natural immune system. My overarching point is a plea to address causes not symptoms. Education has many roles to play in life, one of the first should be to teach about the health fundamentals mentioned earlier, sometimes compromised by the way we now live. Those with responsibility for organising communities should encourage an environment that fosters those health fundamentals and discourages that which undermines those principles. That is not to deny the role the medical profession plays, simply to make the case for the right environment and education in relation to health fundamentals. When things go wrong, as they will, causes should be identified rather than symptoms addressed.

The mind plays an important part in the body's health. Faith in healers can be as important as that which they prescribe, as the placebo phenomenon demonstrates. In a real sense a healthy body needs healthy thoughts. The mind, or aspects of it, are the real 'us' not the body. The body is a temporary abode for one level of our consciousness.

The fundamentals of a healthy mind require education just as much as those vital to a healthy body. That education is acquired through life's experiences and the creation of a framework that helps put those experiences into perspective. Our conversation is, in the main, about that framework.

So if we maintain these healthy fundamentals for our body and mind we will have good health and live to a ripe old age?

I am afraid it is not quite as simple as that. As I have tried to explain, we are born into a life that is intended to help us learn that which our higher Self knows we need to learn. That life will inevitably present many challenges to which we must respond. Respond implies choice. Some of those decisions will be conscious, some will be the result of subconscious processes. In turn some of those subconscious processes will be determined by our past experiences. Past experience and habits of thought do not have to bind us. We can choose to take conscious control and change our response from that which might unconsciously follow. Many processes will remain unconscious. Health, whether physical or mental, is impacted by those unconscious processes. We are not always in control of what happens, however we are always, potentially, in control of our response to that which happens. If we choose to be. Responsibility implies being in control of response. That is a frame of mind to be encouraged, first in oneself, then in others. It does not mean abandoning others, a mental washing of hands. Indeed the opposite. When we are presented with another struggling with one of life's many challenges, it presents us with a choice also. A choice of whether to help or not. Then a further choice as to how to help.

Let me return to your point. There is no guarantee of a long healthy life as a result of adopting informed disciplines. That may not be what our life has in store for us. What is ultimately important is how we respond to what happens to us and what we learn from the life lived. I suggest that if we have a mental framework that enables us to make sense of the complexities of life, that will help us lead a valuable life, however long.

Are you saying we should not fear an early death?

Like all animals we have a strong instinct for self preservation. That is natural and is there for good reason. Fear of death operates at the subconscious level. It is reinforced when we experience the death of others, especially those close to us. It marks the end of a relationship, in this domain at least. That often results in sadness, reflection and sometimes regret. Death is our inevitable fate. It is made worse if we think of it as the end of our existence. In that case logic dictates that it should be delayed as long as possible. That has resulted in ever greater efforts to keep people alive, beyond what is natural. Because we can do something does not mean we should. Allowing people to die with dignity, without constant intervention, is very important to their moving on to the next stage of their existence. Of course they will die when the animating force, the life force, is withdrawn anyway. A force identified thousands of years ago by the Egyptians and Hindus as *ka* or *prana*. The 'will' plays an important part in maintaining that life force or withdrawing it. If, as I have explained, death is not the end of our existence then we should try to put death in perspective. We should consciously overcome the fear and determine to make the dying process as peaceful as we can. That requires acceptance and a conscious decision to mentally let a person go, rather than fight their departure.

Whether that fight is an emotional need of the bereaved or the medicalised fight of those that are taught to preserve life at any cost. Those fights are as much about the instigator's needs as they are about the dying person's needs.

You have stressed that motive is key to outcome. If someone genuinely loves another, is it not natural that they want them to live and is their motive not pure in seeking continuation of a relationship that they both value?

Love is a very important force, indeed ultimately the most important. I have said it is better thought of as a motive rather than an emotion. It is natural to want to maintain a powerful bond that has formed. That bond will inevitably be broken, sooner or later in this realm. I have also said, using the example of a mother's love, that letting the other party go is perhaps the hardest but truest part of love. Putting the other party's interest before your own interest. When it is time to let someone go, that you deeply care for, the greater love not only accepts the inevitable but wishes them well on the next stage of their journey.

Motive is the key determinant of outcome. Caring for others

involves respecting that they are different, have their own path to tread and their own lessons to learn. We may understand some of what they face, from our own experience, but we are in no position to judge them or the choices they make. They will face the consequence of their choices, as will we ours. Any help we offer must ideally be absent expectation if it is to be of value. Do nothing in expectation of a desired response, that is indicative of our need not theirs. We can suggest, we can encourage but ultimately we must respect that the choice they make is their responsibility. We may believe we know what is best for them but that must be determined by them, if they are to grow. Growth through learning is what we all are here to seek. We are all on our own path with our own lessons to learn. Our paths will cross with others. They are all our teachers, as we are theirs. We all have the freedom to learn or not. Wishing the best for others and encouraging their growth, towards their higher Self, will in turn result in our own growth. That underlying motive, ultimately a conscious choice, defines love.

Chapter 4
Poems on Purpose

...insight of perspective

MIND

I RECEIVE	I PERCEIVE
I STORE	I SEARCH
I APPRAISE	I ANALYSE
I INTEGRATE	I IMAGINE
I DETERMINE	I DECIDE
I CREATE	I CONVEY
I LISTEN	I LEARN

Unconscious and Knowing AM I
Dreaming and Meditating AM I
Instinctive and Intellectual AM I
Emotional and Dispassionate AM I
Partaking and Observing AM I
Incarnate and Disembodied AM I
Seeking and Willing AM I

I AM: more than mind: SPIRIT

THE SEED OF LIFE

Consider a humble seed
A speck within the macrocosm of the universe
Dead to outward appearances
Yet contained within lies potential unimaginable
Nurtured by the ancient elements
Earth, Water, Air and Fire
The potential is released, inherent life manifests
An endless cycle of life, growth, death and rebirth is born
Stretching from and to eternity
Absorbing energy, returning it transformed
Ever adapting to conditions, something impels it onward
What is that thing, that cause, that purpose
The life-form knows not
Then the dawn of consciousness
Separation of mind from vehicle
Limited senses make matter the first focus
Then movement or energy must be explored
All is found to be in motion; vibrating, pulsing, alive
The call of why joins what and how
Materialistic science no longer suffices
Nor those basic senses
The quest continues, driving ever onward
Beyond mind to the seed that is Spirit
Our origin and our destiny

SEEKING THE SUN

GOD'S GARDEN

The garden of Earth is given to find
our true nature and the laws that bind.
Eden or Hades is ours to create,
choice was given when God's fruit we ate.

The laws are set, our choice is free
to take the fruit or tend the tree.
A tree of health needs disciplined care,
tested best by the fruit it doth bear.

A long lonely sentence is life's lot
or so it seems when our eyes do drop.
The prison we inhabit is self-made,
recognise that and the pain will fade.

To gain perspective rise above,
seek the Sun, life's source of love.
Responsibility take and then discern
the lesson now that must be learned.

Discipline and disciple share a root,
their growth our nature helps transmute.
Its flower and fruit Will we find;
meditate in Union, still the mind.

GIFT NOT GAOL

ETERNAL SPRING

A path full of shadows our common plight,
but where there are shadows, also is light.
The Sun fails not but awaits our choice,
prodigal return, Spirit rejoice.

Pray karma teach our wayward soul;
reunion with God is our real goal.
Truth may be sought by many a route,
then find within, what was thought without.

Cultivate that seed and know its source,
the flower will bloom but cannot be forced.
Love is the key that unlocks our chain
and gives life immortal in God's domain.

Love is a word much misunderstood,
its secret is simple – seeking good.
Good for one's neighbour, good in oneself.
The root of that good is God and Self.

Self is of God and in each does dwell,
find first in one, then in All as well.
Doubt not, Love prevails for those that Will,
realise the Truth and their Self fulfil.

IN THE MORTAL COIL

GOOD IS

Kind not confrontational
Generous not judgmental
Humble not hubristic
Positive not pessimistic
Empathetic not emphatic
Encouraging not expectant
Exemplary not exhortatory
Sincere not cynical
Selfless not self-centred
Pure-in-motive not polluted
Poised not perturbed
Persevering not put-off
Listening not lecturing
Consoling not controlling
Reconciling not recoiling
Responsible not reckless
Accepting not avoiding
Faithful not forgetful
Respectful not resentful
Perceptive not preconceiving
Inspiring not instructing
Self-nurturing not self-torturing
Self-disciplined not self-indulgent
Diligent not delinquent
Courageous not craven
Confident not conceited
Quiet not querulous
Patient not petulant
Prudent not impulsive
Gracious not grandiose
Grateful not greedy
Forgiving not forbidding
Serving not self-serving

CHOICE NOT CHANCE

SEEING IS BELIEVING

Life an accident of the primordial soup
mind a by-product of life's electrical loop.
The priests of science boldly proclaim
the world of matter is their domain.

Their concrete world has foundations of sand
when based on particles they can't understand.
Crashing them together to find the sublime,
like smashing a timepiece to tell the time.

Beware of creeds whatever their form
test for presence by a need to conform.
Truth is sacrificed on the altar of power
knowledge advanced by refusal to cower.

The scientific view is built on sight
so cannot see where there is no light.
No eyes are needed for us to find
real in-sight arises in the mind.

Mind is a realm little understood
the tool of creation; All and Good.
There are none so blind as Will not see;
in-tuition starts with humility.

MIND OVER MATTER

LEARNING MECHANISM

Imagine a mechanical pocket watch
An intricate construct of interconnected parts
It is inert until its spring is filled with power
We may build the mechanism
First in our mind, then in matter
We fashion the parts from material
Material that is given, we cannot create it
We impart energy to animate the watch
But only from energy that we are in turn given
We apply laws inherent in matter and energy
We cannot create those laws
Any more than the energy or matter we utilise
We can seek to understand each and so create
Our mind uses law first, then energy, then matter
Matter is related to energy, as energy is to mind
Behold this domain, cosmic timepiece,
Created and given order by mind, but life by God

TIMELESS TRUTH

GUIDING LIGHT

Teachers of Spirit no doubt are sent
but power corrupts even good intent.
Appraise interpreters of God's great plan
whether in book, ritual or holy man.

Beware those who claim an exclusive path
condemning others to righteous wrath.
Chosen certainty feeds conceit and strife,
the antithesis of true Spiritual life.

Test for truth by motive and fruit
not by obedience and blind pursuit.
Discipline is needed on the road
but applied from within, not imposed.

Our concept of good is in God enshrined,
that knowledge lies within for us to find.
Knowing the Truth we are faced with choice
and in choosing good in God rejoice

God needs nothing by fear or force,
our soul seeks harmony with its source.
Refracting light pure white from above,
ALL is ONE through the prism of love.

LOOK FOR LOVE

DEATH'S DOOR

At last comes time for fond farewell,
we all must leave this mortal shell.
Common fate and daunting door
await us all, rich and poor.

Neither gold nor pride may we take,
all earthly ties we must forsake.
The only wealth our soul can bear;
God's great gift of loving care.

Scales await, we can no longer fudge,
scales removed, our own eyes do judge.
Death brings pause for reflection clear
on life's lessons learned and what is dear.

Self will call time on this sojourn,
knowing next what our soul must learn.
The soul's school beckons, planet Earth,
there to choose a new life and birth.

Pray karma teach our searching soul;
re-union with God is our true goal.
Love is the key that unlocks our chain
And gives life immortal in God's domain

AND MIRROR

BEYOND THE ARID AGE OF REASON

Clouds are gathering, they are dark and destructive
We cannot escape the storm
It is of our own making, our cultural karma
The fury that will be unleashed is the work of Law
Cultivating greed, aggression and conceit
Brings an inevitable harvest
Sow the wind, reap the whirlwind

In awe of Reason we spurned Spirit
Materialism was born and suckled by science
The child of a God-less mechanistic world
Grown vain in its clever conceptual certainty
Mammon and Mars filled intellect's vacuum
Serving only to deliver us to our fate
But the darkest hour lies just before dawn

Death is only the prelude to re-birth
The flame of Spirit is never extinguished
God's seed is planted deep in the heart of humanity
That seed Will seek out the Light
A new day, a new opportunity to learn
That head needs heart
To illuminate the Path of Purpose

SPIRIT'S ETERNAL SPRING OF HOPE

HOMEWARD BOUND

Still the mind, time stands still
The cosmic cogs quietly stop
Energy's seminal stream ceases
Mind's matrix map evaporates
Draw into the darkest depth

Eternal Now
Awake Alert
Aware **I AM**
Purest Light
Willing Union

The strand of Self awaits
Then in sympathy vibrates
The lost chord sounds
Harmony is found
In the Music of the Spheres

PEACE PROFOUND

Chapter 5
Life a Pilgrimage

What follows is an outline of the framework, philosophy or belief system that I have arrived at to make sense of my life. It is my perspective and is the product of my experience, reading and reflection. Each person's experience is different and will give rise to their own perspective. I believe that the test of any framework is the effect it has on the life being lived. Does it contribute to the person's growth and does it contribute to the growth of others? That, of course, requires a definition of the word growth. I choose to define growth in terms of progress towards a higher Self, towards good, towards the concept of God.

Someone once defined faith as 'nothing more than an irrational belief', I prefer to think of it as a respect for an intuitional truth that is inherent in human experience and perennial in nature, albeit one that manifests in different ways.

God has been perceived and presented, through much of recent human history, as an authoritative if not authoritarian person, usually male. This is particularly true of the Abrahamic traditions that make up Judaism, Christianity and Islam. This representation has made use of familiar concepts to aid comprehension of, or adherence to, belief systems resulting from intuitive, or given, insights. Such a man-made conception of God has its strengths, particularly if the resulting belief system incorporates fundamental truths about the human condition and the laws that govern relationships and motivation. However, the concept can also be an obstacle to spiritual growth, particularly if the focus is on the metaphor rather than the underlying reality, or the belief system has become corrupted by fallible humans in conscious or unconscious pursuit of power.

As horizons expand, in our era influenced by scientific investigation of perceived physical reality, new concepts are necessary to help communicate the nature of ultimate reality and the idea of God. These new concepts will still be limited by human experience and ability to comprehend that which lies outside mortal conscious experience.

God could be perceived as a collective entity, outside concepts of space, matter and time; a creative and sustaining power, source or principle pervading ultimate reality. Today we might best understand that principle as mind-like. Mind beyond that which we associate with a physical mortal entity. Mind also beyond its function in the receipt, processing and transmission of information. Mind in its creative or Spiritual role, forming and maintaining the structure and order inherent in the reality we perceive. An order that encompasses the laws we discover in the domain we inhabit. Out of order comes predictability and the possibility of learning. That applies to the perceived inanimate physical world and to animate life, of which we are part in this domain.

According to the science of our day physical matter is ultimately made up of subatomic particles, or nebulous tiny building blocks. Investigation has shown that the behaviour of those particles, as perceived, is impacted by their observer. That observer might be construed as part of the 'mind principle'. All aspects of the reality we perceive contain a mind dimension. Animate life is the ultimate complex system where the consequences of one action are difficult to predict on all derivative affectees. That does not mean that it is unpredictable, only that the limited comprehension of the local mind element is unable to grasp the complex consequences of a particular action. That is a limitation of the individualised participant mind. The ultimate mind principle that created the reality we perceive, and the laws that govern it, determines those consequences. Attuning to that greater mind and reality may enable the individual to intuitively access a more comprehensive perspective of cause and effect in operation.

That attuning to, or harmony with, the underlying principle involves a kind of union and with union comes realisation of a domain beyond the limited individual perspective. A domain that is both source and destiny of the multiplicity of aspects of mind that emanate from the ultimate creative force. That which goes forth as an individualised unaware 'mind-self' returns with experience gained as a participant in the domain of mortal reality. The order found in that reality encourages the acquisition of attributes necessary to migrate to higher domains. Encouragement and nurture may be found in the outworkings of the law of cause and effect, but beyond that in the bedrock *Law of Love*, or compassion, underpinning creation. Learning involves change and is achieved as a matter of choice and will, freedoms given to the individual mind-self but ultimately willingly relinquished as a greater consciousness develops. Ultimate harmony with ALL is found in realisation of a greater Self; that Self is part of the perennial principle of creation; Good or God.

To summarise; the Mind of God is the creator and sustainer of ALL. That Mind, beyond our concepts of time and space, is inherent within this temporal domain. A domain of individualised consciousnesses, each subject to Law. That Law, or order, is designed to enable individuals' ascent of a hierarchy of awareness. That hierarchy's purpose is ultimate union with its source and that union is achieved by the conscious choice and will power of the individualised consciousness. The nearer to union the less the impact of structural law, as the individualised mind attunes to the underlying *Law of Love*. Fulfilment of this Law is achieved by relinquishing one's own interests in favour of the interests of others. Seeking the best in, and for, others brings out the best in them and that entails consciousness of *Love* as the source and purpose inherent in ultimate reality.

That spiritual journey, from lower to higher Self, might best be described as a pilgrimage. It is a journey shared and depends on the support of, and support for, fellow pilgrims. Help is always at hand for those who are willing to ask. It is, for most, a long road that stretches beyond one mortal lifetime, and entails a gradual mastery over the lower self.

At journey's end humility and love are the golden keys that open the Gates of Good. Beyond lies a return to the ALL that is our source and destiny, the creation of and substance of God; the Alpha and Omega.

Books of Possible Interest

Sapiens: A Brief History of Humankind by Yuval Noah Harari
A Short History of Progress by Ronald Wright
The World As It Is: Dispatches on the Myth of Human Progress by Chris Hedges
The Untold History of the United States by Peter Kuznick & Oliver Stone
Zionism, The Real Enemy of the Jews by Alan Hart (trilogy)
The New Rulers of the World by John Pilger

Super Imperialism – The Economic Strategy of the American Empire by Michael Hudson
The Corruption of Capitalism by Guy Standing
False Dawn – The Delusions of Global Capitalism by John Gray
The Finance Curse by Nicholas Shaxson

Science Fictions by Stuart Ritchie
Unsettled: What Climate Science Tells Us.... by Steven Koonin
Scared to Death by Christopher Booker & Richard North
The Madness of Crowds by Douglas Murray
Manufacturing Consent by Edward Herman & Noam Chomsky

A Life in Perspective

The Nature of Man anthology introduced by Erich Fromm
Quiet: The Power of Introverts in a World That Can't Stop Talking by Susan Cain
Hierarchy of Needs: A Theory of Human Motivation by Abraham Maslow
The Conquest of Happiness by Bertrand Russell
Beyond Order – Rules for Life by Jordan Peterson
The Art of Loving by Erich Fromm

The Art of Dying by Peter & Elizabeth Fenwick
Being Mortal by Atul Gawande
Science and the Near Death Experience by Chris Carter (trilogy)
More Lives than One? by Jeffrey Iverson
As a Man Thinketh by James Allen
From Intellect to Intuition by Alice Bailey
What is Reality? by Ervin Laszlo

The Secret Teachings of All Ages by Manly Hall
The Hermetica by Timothy Freke & Peter Gandy
The Kybalion by Three Initiates
Fourteen Lessons in Yogi Philosophy by Yogi Ramacharaka (series)
The Philosophy of the I Ching by Carol Anthony
Tao Te Ching by Lao Tzu
The Return of Arthur Conan Doyle edited by Ivan Cooke (out of print)

The Thoughtful Guide to God by Howard Jones
Honest to God by John Robinson
The Mind of God by Paul Davies
Oh my God is that you? by Anthony Gibbs (out of print)
The Quiet Mind by White Eagle (series)

Acknowledgements

Like other parts of this book the acknowledgements that follow are not typical of those associated with a conventionally published book. I have chosen the path of self publishing to obtain freedom of content and format. That may result in conflict with some publishing norms and consequently limit commercial success. Success in that sense has never been an objective. Being faithful to the truth that I perceive, and making sense of the life I have lived, have been my twin goals. That is not to deny a hope that the narrative will prove of interest to others of reflective disposition.

I have endeavoured to be as accurate as possible in conveying the large number of facts contained within this book. Inevitably there will be errors despite my best efforts and I acknowledge responsibility for any that have escaped my scrutiny.

As well as facts the narrative contains a large number of opinions. I have tried to limit these in the early sections of the book but no doubt some will have found their way into the text. The final part of the book contains a great deal of opinion. I have chosen not to try and justify opinions expressed by reference to others' work and thoughts. This may be considered a weakness by those academically inclined and if so I acknowledge that perceived weakness.

A Life in Perspective

I admit that some of the views expressed are contrary to the prevailing consensus. My objective has not been to alienate, or even persuade, but to prompt further thought. We live in an era when freedom of expression is under attack by illiberal forces that seek to close down debate on, what they deem, sensitive topics. I hope this proves a temporary phenomenon but acknowledge that, in the current climate, some expressed opinions may give rise to criticism of the book, or even attempts at censorship.

A list of books of possible interest is shown at the end of the final chapter *Life a Pilgrimage*. Those books along with numerous other sources have contributed to the opinions I have reached. I make no claim as to objectivity, my intuition has led my quest and I acknowledge that the assimilation and integration of information obtained is ultimately a subjective process.

Software now largely determines what is grammatically correct. I hope that the book meets the standards of our day and more importantly conveys content in a clear and comprehensible way. Any grammatical errors, inconsistencies of treatment or failures of clarity, I acknowledge to be my own. Hopefully they will not detract from the book's essence.

Parts of the book are quite detailed accounts of particular aspects of my life experience. That detail may be too much for some readers to absorb, for example, I think of the sequence involved in the demise of the company Spicers. It was my need to understand and put that 'death' in perspective that prompted the resulting level of detail. I have endeavoured to put developments in context, sometimes repeating the same facts in different settings to help comprehension. I acknowledge that, for some, ploughing through this detail may be laborious and fully understand should they feel the need to skip narrative aspects of limited interest.

I have chosen to hide the identity of some of the individuals

Acknowledgements

mentioned in various parts of this book. Protection of privacy is increasingly difficult in this digital age and, after much thought, I have decided that it would not be fair to provide the names of individuals who might be adversely impacted by my narrative. I do not believe this affects the authenticity of the events related. I do acknowledge that the perspectives given are my own and that others' perspectives, relating to the same events, are likely to be different.

I have tried to avoid putting others in a bad light but acknowledge that I may not have always conveyed a balanced view of individuals mentioned or with whom I have interacted. I also acknowledge that we are all fallible, both as perceived by others and, perhaps more importantly, as perceived by ourselves when in honest reflective mode. The latter is a mode we may find that we cannot ultimately escape. I freely acknowledge my own shortcomings and the need to regularly work on weaker disciplines; (6 Ps) poise, positivity, perseverance, patience, prudence (in verbal response), perception (seeing beyond that which is presented), and to reinforce in relation to others; (3 Es) engagement, empathy, encouragement.

Life is an adventure. Adventure involves uncertainty, risk and occasionally pain. Family has been the constant rock from which I could set forth to explore the world. In childhood and youth my parents and wider family were a source of care and encouragement. In adulthood marriage and children provided security and a sense of responsibility that helped me develop as an individual. Family is the testbed of love. Whereas other relationships come and go the bonds of kinship encourage persistence and are often underpinned by unselfish motivation. I gratefully acknowledge the role played by my family in shaping the person I have been and am growing to become. I would also like to express sincere thanks to my wife and daughter for their help in bringing this book to final fruition.

www.ingramcontent.com/pod-product-compliance
Lightning Source LLC
Chambersburg PA
CBHW051556010526
44118CB00023B/2730